A GENERAL ECONOMY OF TRAVEL

Identity, Memory, and Death

Afshin Hafizi

University Press of America,® Inc.
Lanham · Boulder · New York · Toronto · Plymouth, UK

Copyright © 2012 by
University Press of America,® Inc.
4501 Forbes Boulevard
Suite 200
Lanham, Maryland 20706
UPA Acquisitions Department (301) 459-3366

Estover Road
Plymouth PL6 7PY
United Kingdom

All rights reserved
Printed in the United States of America
British Library Cataloging in Publication Information Available

Library of Congress Control Number: 2011930435
ISBN: 978-0-7618-5623-8 (paperback : alk. paper)
eISBN: 978-0-7618-5624-5

Quotations from Réda Bensmaïa's *The Year of Passages* copyright 1995 by the Regents of the University of Minnesota. Used with permission from the University of Minnesota Press.

∞™ The paper used in this publication meets the minimum requirements of American National Standard for Information Sciences—Permanence of Paper for Printed Library Materials, ANSI Z39.48-1992

This book is dedicated to my father, Abdolhossein Hafizi
and to my mentor John P. Leavey, Jr.

Table of Contents

Chapter 1: Introduction   1

Chapter 2: The Restricted Economy of Travel   10

Chapter 3: Toward A General Economy of Travel   64

Chapter 4: Réda Bensmaïa's *The Year of Passages*: Mourning   116
        Becomes Diaspora

Chapter 5: Conclusion   145

Bibliography   152

Chapter One

Introduction

At the sea – I would not build a house for myself, and I count it part of my good fortune that I do not own a house. But if I had to, then I should build it as some of the Romans did – right into the sea. I should not mind sharing a few secrets with this beautiful monster.　　　　　　　　　　Nietzsche's *The Gay Science*, 214

I would like to present my argument in its most abstract form as follows: *deriving* (departure from home) and *arriving*[1] (at a destination) are forever, and always already, separated from each other by the possibility of the event of a catastrophe (death, non-return, etc), which marks the true beginning of the voyage into the unknown. No one knows, therefore, what can occur in the course of a voyage. The event, chance, danger, or disaster cannot be anticipated. No true journey is conceivable without the event, which is a drift or deviation from the predictability of a trajectory and allows the other to appear or the experience of the alterity of the other to take place. The apparent closed structure of departure (from home and origin) and arrival (at a destination) in a traditional definition of travel (something that I will call a restricted economy of travel) is usually supposed to be teleological in its movement from an *oikos* as origin towards a *telos* as destination, and, more often than not, as an incarnation of knowledge and light, an unveiling of the secrets of the other. I propose to challenge this structure by arguing that behind this traditional notion of travel lies a different itinerary (what I will call a general economy of travel) that departs from a non-origin, whose trajectory is not continuous, ordered or controlled, and whose destination is, what Derrida calls, a *destinerrance*, the being-destined-to-wander. In this general economy of travel the "other," or the foreign(er), happens as an event: it is neither reducible to a body of knowledge nor predictable; it takes place without taking "place." "The event [of the experience of the foreign] that abducts the traveler's identity and allows an opening to alterity to become experience of the world in general must occur by surprise and remain incalculable" (Malabou and Derrida 2004:2). A general economy of travel emphasizes the impossibility of *oikos* to coincide with itself and reminds us that in Greek thought it is precisely the domain of the domestic home that is the site of the tragic catastrophe. A general economy of travel happens always in-between, between points, between embarkation and disembarkation, between departure and arrival; the in-between is the boundless middle of passage, the unrepresentable horizon of the sea as the force of the outside.

A voyage, in its traditional sense, implies that one leaves a familiar shore to confront the unknown and return back home. In fact the very thing one always expects of a voyage is that it will deliver "the other" –the unknown, the unexpected– in a familiar way, a translation of the unknown into the known. This notion of travel reveals the metaphysics of voyage at its core: the dialectical *Aufheburg* of facing the alterity of the world, canceling it, but at the same time preserving it for domestic consumption within the domain of the self/same. The metaphysics of voyage is also based on, as Catherine Malabou and Jacques Derrida (2004) argue, a logic of solidarity between *deriving* and *arriving* that presupposes that *"everything that arrives derives"* (2), that is, whatever arrives is supposed to have been departed from an origin.[2] I would therefore propose to critique this metaphysical notion of travel, which gives us a very limited and reductionist understanding of the foreign, and suggest alternate ways of understanding the concept, as well as the cultural practice, of travel.

The deriving/arriving structure in a traditional notion of travel finds one of its most eloquent and sophisticated manifestations in Heidegger. I would like to discuss two texts in which Heidegger analyzes the discourse of journey and the concomitant notions of home, departure, the foreign and return. The first text is Heidegger's 1942 lecture on Hölderlin's hymn "The Ister" in which he formulates the relation to the foreign within the context of a theory of translation (a going out to the different and returning to the same). Heidegger insists to retranslate the Greek text of the second choral ode of *Antigone*[3] rather than using Hölderlin's own translation. In other words, Heidegger, in his attempt to interpret the Greeks and Hölderlin (and the dialogue of Hölderlin with the Greeks) does not use Hölderlin's own translation but rather retranslates both Sophocles's Greek and Hölderlin's German[4]. By using *"Unheimlich"* rather than *"Ungeheuer"* (Hölderlin's translation of *deinon*) Heidegger opens a discourse on the essence of the river Ister (the Greek name for the Danube) by associating *Unheimlich* (uncanny) with *Unheimisch* (unhomely)[5]. If man is *unheimlich*, it is because according to Heidegger, his essence consists in "coming to be at home" (*Heimischwerden*) and this in turn means that man is not being at home (*Unheimischsein*). In order for man to come to be at home he has to go through the mediation of the experience of the foreign:

> That poetry of Hölderlin that has taken on the form of the 'hymn' has taken into its singular care this becoming homely in one's own . . . . This *coming to be* at home in one's own in itself entails that human beings are initially, and for a long time, and sometimes forever, not at home . . . . Coming to be at home is

thus a passage through the foreign. And if the becoming homely of a particular human kind sustains the historicality of its history, then the law of the encounter [*Auseinandersetzung*] between the foreign and one's own is the fundamental truth of history. (Heidegger 1996b:49)

What Heidegger does, which according to Warminski is a misreading of Hölderlin, and is exemplified by his translating Hölderlin's *ungeheuer* (monstrous) with *unheimlich*, is to argue that the hymn "The Ister" fulfills the law of historicality, i.e., the coming to be at home by going out and back from that which is foreign. The river Ister, by inviting Hercules as a guest, manifests its hospitality to the other and "acknowledges the foreigner and his foreignness, that is, to acknowledge the fire from the heavens that the Germans lack" (141). The guest, that is, the Greek figure of the heavenly fire, "is the presence of the unhomely in the homely who makes the appropriation of one's own, which is the most distant, and therefore a "return to the hearth" possible: "The historical spirit of the history of a humankind must first let what is foreign come toward that humankind in its being unholmely so as to find, in an encounter with the foreign, whatever is fitting for the return to the hearth" (125). Heidegger's understanding of journey in "The Ister" does not sound very far from a Hegelian, speculative dialectics in which consciousness sublates the negativity (of the world and its own experience) in its journey towards self-consciousness. Nor is it far from the eighteenth century German notion of *Bildung* (discussed in subsequent chapters) as a cultural process of translating the foreign into one's own.

Warminski, however, argues that Heidegger is misreading Hölderlin. Let me reconstruct, in my own way, Warminski's argument by starting from Heidegger's position. According to Heidegger:

> For the Greeks, what is their own is 'the fire from the heavens' . . . Yet in order to appropriate this as their own, the Greeks had to pass through something foreign, namely through the 'clarity of presentation' . . . Conversely, however, what is 'natural' to the Germans, that is, that with which they are endowed as their own, is the clarity of presentation . . . . What is thus 'inborn' cannot properly become what is their own for the Germans so long as this ability to grasp has not been made to confront the necessity of grasping the ungraspable . . . . What the Germans lack, what must therefore first come to be encountered by them as that which is foreign to them, is the 'fire from the heavens.' (Heidegger 1996b:135)

That is to say, what is natural and *das Eigene* for the Greeks is foreign and *das Fremde* for us. Therefore, if Germans want to go through the detour of the foreign, i.e., the Greeks, in order to arrive at their own, they (Germans) should enter into a relationship with what was foreign to the Greeks themselves, i.e., the Orient. The Orient is the other of the Greeks, which is precisely what Heidegger suppresses. Heidegger turns what is, for Hölderlin "a threefold historical scheme of the Orient, Greece and Hesperia [Germany] into a twofold scheme of Greece and Hesperia: in other words, Heidegger turns a scheme of us (Hesperians) and them (Greeks) and their them (the Orient) into a scheme of us and them, Hesperia (or 'Germany') and Greece" (Warminski 210). In "The Ister" the threefold is marked by the names of three rivers: one Oriental (the Indus), one Greek (the Alpheus), and one Hesperian (the Ister). Heidegger's rhetorical strategy of suppressing the radical difference of the nature of the Greeks, i.e., the Orient, the East, Egypt, would allow Heidegger a closure of what remains ungraspable: the Orient is the dead of the dead, the other of the other, and beyond representation: "To say 'Hesperia is the Orient' or 'We are the Orientals' is to say 'We are dead.'. . . This would be one way to read Hölderlin's determination of man's historical essence as monstrous: the monstrosity of history, history as monster" (213). Heidegger prefers to turn monsters into domesticated "pets," while Hölderlin realizes that there is, and will be, no return back to the domesticity of home (nonexistent from the very beginning). In our journey, through the mediation of the foreign, in search of our own, there is a ghost, without ontology, that does not arrive but nevertheless keeps haunting us, something that is, always already, irretrievably lost from the very beginning, turning us and our history into monsters: monstrosity as an allegory of a radical, unrepresentable disjunction of self and other that cannot be mediated by any history of ontology or hermeneutics.

Heidegger's insistence on return (or *Versammlung*, the gathering of Being) is also apparent in the discussion of the triadic structure of home, exile and return in his "*Sprache und Heimat*." Heidegger begins his 1960 lecture on "*Sprache und Heimat*" with the claim that *Heimat* is necessarily pluralistic: a single *Heimat* for everyone is unthinkable. Much the same, according to Heidegger, can be said about language. Both language and *Heimat*, in their interconnectedness, necessarily evoke the plural. Language, Heidegger argues, must be understood as the language of *Heimat*. This language is a regionally specific one, in other words, a dialect. "Language is originally [*nach ihrer Wesensherkunft*] dialect." As such, "dialect [*Mundart*] is not only the language of the mother, but the mother of language" (88). Heidegger then goes on to analyze a poem by Johann Peter Hebel written in dialect. Dialect poetry [*Mundartdichtung*] is not, says Heidegger, a reflection of *Heimat*, but that which enables *Heimat* to become present. "Language, due to its poetic nature, being most concealed and reaching farthest, is the intensely giving production of *Heimat* [*das inständig schenkende Hervorbringen der Heimat*]" (qtd in Hammermeister 2000:314). Poetry, and poetic language, as Heidegger had already argued for all art in his 1936 *The Origin of the Work of Art*, discloses that which has preceded our existence but remained concealed and secret. Only through the use of (poetic) language does *Heimat* become itself. This is why Heidegger closes the essay by rewriting its title. Instead of "Sprache *und* Heimat" [Language *and* Heimat], he now suggests to call it "Sprache *als* Heimat" [Language *as* Heimat].

Heidegger, however, goes further and makes the remembrance of the lost *Heimat* the definition of poetry. "The nature of *Heimat* only begins to shine in exile [*in der Fremde*]. Everything that the great poets say and sing is viewed from the perspective of homesickness and is summoned into language by pain [*durch diesen Schmerz ins Wort gerufen*]" (qtd in Hammermeister 2000:318). Therefore, Heidegger's notion of *Heimat* does not indicate or refer to its existence in the present; it is rather a nostalgic, melancholic remembrance of something absent and lost. Poetry, for Heidegger, mourns the loss of *Heimat* rather than celebrates its glory in the present. But the mourning for the loss of *Heimat* is only one aspect of the poet's relation to his/her *Heimat*. The other aspect is the poet's nostalgia for the future return to *Heimat*. In other words, according to Heidegger, the poet, in his/her relation to *Heimat*, bridges the melancholic and the prophetic or utopian modes. The double bind of the melancholy of loss and the prophesy of return places the poet within a Hegelian dialectics that is at work here (it also informs the process of *Bildung* as I will argue in this chapter): the task of the poet is to return home [*Heimkunft*], and thereby close the circle of peregrination and displacement, after going through a detour of exile and estrangement. This is the metaphysical core of a restricted economy of travel.[6]

The motif of the voyage and travel is among the most manifestly banal in Western letters. From Homer and Virgil, through Dante and Cervantes, Defoe and Goethe, Melville and Conrad, Proust and Céline, Nabakov and Butor, to postmodern and postcolonial writers like Salman Rushdie, V. S. Naipaul, Bharati Mukherjee, one can scarcely mention a work of literature in which the theme of the voyage does not play some role. Therefore among the imperatives of a study like this is not only to delimit the range of possible objects of study, but also to draw distinctions between different words, concepts or figures (travel, voyage, peregrination, displacement, exile, diaspora, etc.) that might otherwise be used interchangeably. As a way of narrowing down the spectrum of my object of study, I decided to put aside the question of travel within the colonial administration (which is in fact the subject matter of most of the studies of travel narratives written in the last ten years), for the simple reason that I could not possibly add anything new to them. There are numerous postcolonial writers who have studied and written on colonial travel writing from various perspectives. David Spurr's *The Rhetoric of Empire: Colonial Discourse in Journalism, Travel Writing and Imperial Administration* (1993), Mary Louise Pratt's *Imperial Eyes: Travel Writing and Transculturation* (1992), Ali Behdad's *Belated Travelers: Orientalism in the Age of Colonial Dissolution* (1994), and Stephen Greenblatt's *Marvelous Possessions: The Wonder of the New World* (1991) are arguably among the most sophisticated and comprehensive studies of colonial travel discourse. What I, however, would like to retain from these studies is the notion of colonial travel as travel with "return" (in both physical and economical senses of the word). The subject of colonial travel embarks on a journey with, more often than not, the intention of returning to his/her homeland, having incorporated/appropriated the experience of the foreign, in the form of a cultural or financial capital. This Hegelian structure is what I would propose to call a restricted economy (to borrow from Bataille) of travel, in which the triadic structure of home, abroad, return results in an *Aufhebung* (sublation) whose synthesis comes very close to what Marx called the logic of the "accumulation of capital." A restricted economy of travel, in which *deriving* and *arriving* allegedly coincide within the same topography, may also be called "mimetic" in its concern with re-presentation (*Darstellung*) and adequation.

Having excluded the colonial travel narratives (which is a movement from the center to the periphery), I focus, for the most part, instead on a rather reverse process, that is, on the travel accounts of individuals (and their experiences and writings) from the periphery to the center. I will discuss this category of travel narratives (fictional or non-fictional) under the rubric of immigrant and exile literature. While acknowledging the differences between immigrant and exilic writings (and experience), I am more interested in their similarities in order to draw a further distinction between both of these categories and what I call diasporic writing. If colonial travel narratives involve travel with return, both immigrant and exilic narratives of displacement as well as of the diasporic condition might be viewed as travel without return. However, by distinguishing immigrant/exile, on the one hand, and diasporic writing, on the other, I would like to argue that, despite the absence of a physical return in the case of the former, they seek an imaginary return, which, more often than not, is a homecoming in language. Therefore the immigrant/exile discourse of displacement in fact repeats, on an imaginary level, the logic of the colonial travel narratives: both are concerned with closing off the circle of peregrination and arriving at the safety of a home, whether physical or linguistic. This is an aspect that sharply separates immigrant/exilic discourses from what I call diasporic discourse. Diaspora, as I discuss it as a term and a condition, is a displacement without placement, a movement of the subject into the unknown and unpredicted, and a refusal of homecoming and return, that is, an acknowledgment of the impossibility of a dénouement and a tragedy of destination, i.e., a *destinerrance*. I will call the displacement under the diasporic condition a general economy of travel, which is, as I will try to show, an open-ended journey toward the unknown, which is mediated by a (non)relation to death. In a general economy of travel, *deriving* and *arriving* do not coincide; catastrophe (derangement, danger, death, etc.) is the name for this non-coincidence.

In an attempt to contrast diasporic with immigrant/exile discourse of displacement, I will focus on the faculty, and the trope, of memory and its vicissitudes: in a restricted economy of travel, memory is being put to an instrumental, reified use, while in a general economy of travel memory becomes an event that, far from being controlled by the individual, haunts the subject and places him/her outside him/herself.

In chapter two, I investigate some of the theoretical aspects of a restricted economy of travel. In order to prevent my distinction (between a restricted and a general economy of travel) from becoming a binary opposition, I will explore the presence of nonmimetic elements (or moments) in mimetic accounts of travel (moments of destabilization, and excess, as well as the possibility of death, madness and danger) within the colonial context. I then proceed to examine the logic of a restricted economy of travel within the eighteenth-century German context, and argue that in general the German understanding of culture (*Bildung*) exemplifies a restricted notion of peregrination. I continued my discussions of the restricted economy of displacement by analyzing Bharati Mukherjee's *Jasmine* (1989), Eva Hoffman's *Lost in Translation* (1990) and Richard

Rodriquez's *Hunger of Memory* (1988) (all belonging to the so-called "immigrant genre") in which I focused on a demonstration of the economic rhetoric of loss and gain at work in them. These works, like many immigrant autobiographies, are characterized by a tendency in which displacement and deterritorialization are overcome by a desire to settle down, reterritorialize and find a new home. The nostalgia for the past is balanced by a desire to capture the present; the loss of identity (through a process of displacement) is compensated by gaining a new one. In analyzing the phenomenon of displacement in these immigrant autobiographies, I will focus on a demonstration of the rhetoric of loss and gain at work in them. I will try to show that the stories of place and displacement as narrated by Richard Rodriguez, Eva Hoffman, and Bharati Mukherjee are characterized by a certain tendency to closure, a desire to build a home away from home, a re-fashioning of identity, and a settling down, an arrival, by creating an economic equilibrium between loss and gain. This is the economy of loss and gain in immigrant autobiographies: the nostalgia for the past is balanced by a desire to capture the present; the loss of identity (through a process of displacement) is compensated by gaining a new one. In immigrant autobiographies, furthermore, writing itself becomes a means par excellence for retrieving what is lost.

These immigrant autobiographies are not chosen because they realize the universal essence of the restricted economy of displacement, but because, apart from being among the most famous of immigrant autobiographies in US, they foreground the different aspects of the immigrant condition (the relationship to the past, the role of memory, the formation of new identity, etc.) in a more conscious and complex way than, for example, the more traditional immigrant writing of Mary Antin's *The Promised Land* (1912).

In the third chapter, I will explore some of the theoretical aspects of a general economy of travel. My aim here is to refute the claim that one, as an exile or a displaced subject, can ever arrive or return or can find a home in language (Heidegger, Aciman, etc.). I will argue that the circle of peregrination cannot be closed off in the wake of both the possibility of death and the hauntological forces of memory. The question of death as finitude and as excess is therefore analyzed in relation to both Dasein and language. The restricted economical aspects of the phenomenon of death (the death of the Object/Event) and the subsequent process of mourning in language (language as a topos in which death is incorporated and assimilated) are elucidated and critiqued in order to reveal the underlying general economical forces. Within the framework of a general economy of representation, death is non-sublatable. The haunting memory (memory as event, as elaborated later, or ghostly memory) of the death of the Object/Event, therefore, disrupts and disjoins the temporality of mimesis, and language (as *Oikos* of *oikēsis* (the house of death)) becomes rather a haunted house. In sum, the twin figures of death and (haunting) memory, while undermining any restricted economy of travel, opens it to the unrepresentable forces of the outside. I further explore the extent to which the general and restricted economical moments/forces are at work in Kader Abdolah's *Spijkerschrift*, and Kiarostami's *The Taste of Cherry*. Kiarostami's *The Taste of Cherry* foregrounds, within a cinematographical framework, a general economy of representation by positing death as an outside, to which one has no relation, and is therefore cannot be sublated. Kiarostami's *The Taste of Cherry*, unlike the sedentary tendencies in Kader Abdolah's *Spijkerschrift*, is quite literally a journey without return where the event of death is presented, within the narrative structure, as the unrepresentable.

I will read, in chapter four, Réda Bensmaïa's *The Year of Passages* as a diasporic novel that epitomizes a general economy of displacement. Both in its approach to the dilemma of memory, where any instrumental and restricted economical use of memory becomes untenable, as well as in its employment of the figure of spectrality (the living dead) within the context of a diasporic experience, Réda Bensmaïa's *The Year of Passages* opens itself to the outside of knowledge and representation, whereby both the subject and her experience of the foreign are reduced to ashes. In Réda Bensmaïa's *The Year of Passages* arrival is simply impossible because the disruption brought about by driftings and deviations are so overwhelming that wandering becomes rather the norm while departure and arrival are forever separated. It is for these reasons that I think Bensmaïa's novel is moving away from the traditional, immigrant/exilic autobiographical works in which homecoming whether physical or linguistic is of prime importance.

In the concluding chapter I will discuss the political economy as well as the ethics of displacement, where I try to explore some of the political/ethical consequences that the economy of traveling without return might have for creating a possibility for the emergence of a new subjectivity that is less essentialist, less nationalistic and less fascistic. A general economy of travel disrupts the process of the formation of national identity. While national identity may or may not be based on ethnicity or even language, it always contains a territorial component. The development of a sense of homeland and an emotional attachment to that homeland coincide with the development of national identity and self-consciousness. Therefore, in a general economical discourse of peregrination and displacement where home becomes increasingly impossible and national boundaries permeable, national identity in its conventional sense increasingly fades away to be replaced by, what Agamben calls, a "whatever" identity.

From an ethical perspective, the subjects of diaspora (in its double genitive meaning) form a community of those who do not have community, wherein a new understanding of ethics becomes the first philosophy. A general economy of travel and displacement by emphasizing disruption, drifting, deviation, non-return, and non-arrival, opens the possibility of an ethical relation to the other or the alterity of the world. The ethical relationship with the other, I conclude, is in fact an "immobile voyage" in which the paradoxical axiom of what I call "non-peregrinatory essence of peregrination" reveals itself at the heart of the experience of the foreign.

Notes

1. I borrow these two terms from Catherine Malabou and Jacques Derrida's *Counterpath: Traveling with Jacques Derrida* (2004), where Malabou points out to the two different and opposing meanings of these terms. *Dériver*, from the Latin *rivus* (stream) or *ripa* (bank), literally means "leaving or departing the bank or shore." *Dériver* has however two contrary senses: "In the first instance, deriving can characterize a continuous and ordered trajectory from an origin to an end" (1). In its second sense, "deriving as drifting refers to a loss of control, to deviation or skidding. A boat that is *à la derive* is drifting off course, losing its way" (1). The same semantic duality is again found in arrival. "To arrive, from the same Latin root, refers to the fact of approaching or reaching the bank, shore, or port. To arrive is first and foremost to reach a destination and attain one's goals, reach the end of one's voyage, succeed. But *arriver* is also the term for what happens, what comes to, surprises, or falls from the event in general, what is anticipated as well as what is not expected. What 'arrives' – or befalls – can thus sometimes contradict, upset, or prevent arrival in the sense of the accomplishment or completion of a process" (2). According to Malabou, the metaphysics of travel in the West has always presupposed a coincidence, a "solidarity" or even a "synonymy" between these two terms: "For a long time, deriving and arriving have been traveling together" (2).

2. This phrase plays on the two senses of the word "arrive." In the first sense "arrive" means to attain one's goal and reach a destination. This metaphysical sense assumes that whatever arrives is coming from an origin as a point of embarkation. In the second sense "arrive," as the term for what happens as an event and is unexpected, undermines the first meaning and points to what arrives as *arrivant* as an "absolutely undetermined messianic hope. . . this eschatological relation to the to-come of an event and of a singularity, of an alterity that cannot be anticipated" (Derrida 1994: 65). In this second sense, not everything that arrives derives.

3. Hölderlin's translation of the opening of the second choral ode in *Antigone*: Ungeheuer is viel. Doch nichts Ungeheuerer als der Mensch. [Much is monstrous. But nothing more monstrous than man]Heidegger's translation (52): Vielfältig das Unheimliche, nichts doch über den Menschen hinaus unheimlicher waltet. [Manifold is the uncanny, yet nothing beyond the human being prevails more uncannily]

4. For Heidegger translation, which is the same as interpretation and vice versa, is not confined to what takes place between different languages but rather is what, always already, takes place within one and the same language: "Every translation is interpretation. And all interpreting is a translating. To the extent that we have the need to interpret works of poetry and of thought in our own language, it is clear that each historical language is in and of itself in need of translation, and not merely in relation to foreign languages (65).

5. "We are hereby pointing to a connection that presumably extends beyond the merely extrinsic resonance of the words "*unheimisch*" ["unhomely"] and "*unheimlich*" ["uncanny"]" (69). Also: "We mean the uncanny in the sense of that which is not at home – not homely in that which is homely. It is only for this reason that the un-homley [*das Un-heimische*] can, as a consequence, also be "uncanny" ["*unheimlich*"] in the sense of something that has an alienating or "frightening" effect that gives rise to anxiety (71).

6. Derrida calls Heidegger the "non-traveler par excellence" (Malabou and Derrida 17).

Chapter Two

The Restricted Economy of Travel

Always at home — One day we reach our goal, and now point with pride to the long travels we undertook to reach it. In fact, we were not even aware of traveling. But we got so far because we fancied at every point that we were at home.
                                                                    Nietzsche, *The Gay Science*, 216

In this chapter I address the conventional theories of travel writing in order to raise certain theoretical and philosophical problems that the former have always tried to foreclose or preclude in their egocentric and humanistic attempts at (re)constructing a coherent discourse on the experience of the foreign. In order to bear witness to (the possibility or even probability, not to say actuality of) that which has been excluded (but has left its traces[1]) from either experiential or textual representation, I will foreground the *différend* of a mimetological peregrination and draw a distinction between a mimetic and a non-mimetic theory of travel (writing). In order to prevent this typology from forming a binary opposition, and since the mimetic elements of travel discourse are, as I will show shortly, more familiar than the non-mimetic ones, I will try to show (in order to demonstrate the mutual contamination of these apparent oppositions) the presence of certain non-mimetic moments (and their immediate taming and domestification) within a mimetic framework. I further analyze three immigrant autobiographies in order to explore some of the aspects of a restricted economy of travel and displacement as they are exemplified in the works of Mukherjee, Rodriguez, Hoffman.

In the last ten, or perhaps fifteen, years there has been a resurgence of interest in travel writing, whether general or restricted, colonial or postcolonial, exilic or touristic, unprecedented since the twenties and thirties. The revival is evident not only in the recent reprinting of classical works of travel narratives but also in the remarkable number of new travel writers and otherwise established authors who try their hand at this genre. Despite all this interest, however, criticism of modern (I mean twentieth century) travel writings, and to an even lesser extent, the theoretical and critical approaches to travel narratives, has been scanty. There have also been very few critical and theoretical efforts to analyze this burgeoning body of work within the context of the insights gained by the discourses of what one might call the postmodernity. One of the general aims of this study is to reexamine the modernist presuppositions of travel and travel writing in the light of postmodernist philosophies.

The particular challenge of travel writing — of "one civilization reporting on another," as Colin Thurbron puts it — have attracted an impressive range of writers in this century. Many may associate Lawrence Durrell, Graham Greene, George Orwell, D. H. Lawrence, or even John Steinbeck with the genre. Fewer people know that Edith Wharton, William Carlos Williams, Aldous Huxley, John Dos Passos, Saul Bellow, Wyndham Lewis, W. H. Auden, William Golding, Heinrich Böll, Nikos Kazantzakis, Le Corbusier, Antoine Saint-Exupéry, and even a film producer like Pier Paolo Pasolini have all written travel narratives.[2]

There is a long tradition of condescending to travel books as a second rate literary form. Ernest Hemingway once remembered showing a first draft of *The Sun Also Rises* to the novelist Nathan Asch, only to receive the ultimate put-down: "Hem," Asch said, "Vaht do you mean saying you wrote a novel? .... You are riding a travhel büch."

Evelyn Waugh lamented in 1946, in the wake of WWII, of the demise of the genre: "I do not expect to see many travel books in the near future." In a world of displaced persons, Waugh believes, true travel seems impossible. Writing nine years before Waugh, the Canadian writer Stephen Leacock saw the conventions of travel writing themselves as having superseded their own usefulness: "All travel writing and travel pictures in books are worn out and belong to a past age. It is no longer possible to tell anyone anything new about anywhere."[3] The problem is partly attributable to contemporary form of mass travel. As Wolfgang Shivelbusch has shown in his remarkable study of nineteenth-century railroads, *The Railway Journey* (1986), new modes of transport effect changes not only in conveyance and communication but in thought, feeling, behavior and human consciousness. Railroads, automobiles and airplanes have all placed new demands on travelers' eyes and minds. The motor car, E. M, Forster claimed in *Howards End*, was quickly turning landscape into "porridge."

Paul Theroux, a seminal figure in contemporary American travel writing, acknowledges the legitimacy of Waugh's complaints about postwar travel, but he finds in those conditions not the death of but the incentive for new forms of travel. There has been resurgence in travel writing, Theroux argues, precisely because new methods of travel have defeated the more arduous traditional ones. There are two types of travelers in his opinion, real and mock travelers. Real travelers are those who often tolerate hazardous, comfortless conditions and endure some form of alienation in foreign places. Opposed to them are mock-travelers who, like Anne Tyler's "accidental tourist," make a journey without seeming to have left home. Deeply opposed to exertion and dislocation, mock-travelers are afflicted by what Michael Kowalewski calls the "Winnebago Syndrome."[4] Like self-contained turtles or snails, these travelers take their homes with them, not just in RV's on America's backroads but abroad as well.

Mock-travelers arrange for their peregrination to be, as Theroux puts it, "familiar, unshocking, homely and even immobile."[5] But Theroux is also aware of the rather unintended cultural significance of these mock travelers:

> It is very important to understand what is happening to travel and tourism . . . because only by examining them one can see why people get on donkeys and ride across Ethiopia, or hitchhike to India, or go slowly down the Ganges, or simply disappear in Brazil. The interest in travel today, which is passionate, arises out of the fact that there is a form of travel prevalent that is now very easy — people want to find an antidote for the immobility that mass tourism has produced; people want to believe that somewhere, somehow, it is still very dangerous, bizarre, anxiety-making and exotic to travel . . . . Mock travel has produced a huge interest in clumsy, old-fashioned travel, with its disgusting food and miseries and long nights. It has also given rise to a lively interest in travel literature, and the affirmation that the world is still large and strange and, thank God, full of empty places that are nothing like home. (Theroux 1985:132)

Further indications of the revival of interest in this genre are not hard to find. William Least Heat-Moon's *Blue Highways* has sold more than 1.25 million copies since it first appeared in 1982. Major anthologies of travel writing (by publishers such as Penguin, Norton and Knopf) have helped solidify the genre's academic legitimacy and economic marketability. The biannual *New York Times* supplement, *The Sophisticated Traveler*, promotes a variety of new and established writers, all relating personal journeys and encounters with the foreign and the exotic.

Part of the reason the genre of travel writing has been insufficiently recognized until recently may have to do with its dauntingly heterogeneous character. Travel writing involves border crossing both literal and figurative. The first person nonfictional narratives that form the heart of the genre usually display what Bill Buford terms a "generic androgyny," which is not easily categorized. Travel writing borrows freely from memoir, journalism, letters, guidebooks, confessional narrative, and, most important, fiction. "Its omnivorous appetite for writing of all kinds," Jonathan Raban asserts in his "The Journey and the Book," testifies to "the resilience of the form":

> As a literary form, travel writing is notoriously raffish open house . . . . It accommodates the private diary, the essay, the short story, the prose poem, the rough note and polished table talk with indiscriminate hospitality. It freely mixes narrative and discursive writing. Much of its "factual" material, in the way of bills, menus, ticket-stubs, names and addresses, dates and destinations, is there to authenticate what is really fiction; while its wildest fictions have the status of possible facts. (253-60)

Motivated in large part by a curiosity about the habits and costumes of other people's lives and surroundings, travel writers have traditionally included vivid descriptions of flora, topography, climate, animal and insect life, foodstuffs and local sexual customs. This preponderance of factual material (which explains why the genre has traditionally attracted the attention of historians and geographers rather than literary critics) or "mere" ethnography, coexists with the autobiographical and the personal. The amalgamations of the lyrical and the pragmatic, the personal and the factual, in travel writing "serves both to sustain and to counter impulses toward personal intimacy on the one hand, and sociological abstraction on the other" (Kowalewski 1992:8).

A good travel narrative is not only an account of an exterior voyage, of descriptions of scenery, and so forth, but also of an interior, sentimental or temperamental voyage, which takes place side by side with the former one. The most successful travel narratives usually combine outward, spatial aspects of travel (social or ethnographic observation as well as evocation of alien settings and sensibilities) with the inward, temporal form of memory and recollection.

Insofar as travel writing involves cultural description (especially of non-Western cultures) it has/should become aware of the problems encountered in interpretive ethnography. European and American travelers and explorers have increasingly confronted the representational inadequacies of language in describing alien cultures. The limitations of representation have also to do with the visitor's social and perceptual biases, which determine, to a great extent, the nature of the report. James Clifford's remarks about contemporary ethnography bear pertinently upon the study of travel writing:

> Anthropology no longer speaks with automatic authority for others defined as unable to speak for themselves ("primitive," "pre-literate," "without history"). Other groups can less easily be represented as if they were not involved in the present world system that implicates ethnographers along with the peoples they study. "Cultures" do not hold still for their portraits . . . an interest in the discursive aspects of cultural representation draws attention to a specification of discourses in ethnography: who speaks? Who writes? When and where? With or to whom? Under what institutional and historical constraints? (Clifford 1986:20)

"Writing up" a country or evoking a different culture has increasingly become a more tentative and ambiguous activity, one that often replaces confident encapsulation or total representations of cultures (the so-called "the spirit" of a nation or culture) with more provisional, contingent, or partial description. Studies such as Edward Said's *Orientalism* (1978), Stephen Greenblatt's *Marvelous Possessions* (1991), Mary Louise Pratt's *Imperial Eyes: Travel-Writing and Transculturation* (1992), David Spurr's *The Rhetoric of Empire: Colonial Discourse in Journalism, Travel Writing and Imperial Administration* (1993) have all deepened our understanding of the tropes and rhetorical strategies by which Western explorers have imagined oriental, Arab, African, or Native-American cultures. These and other works have sharpened our awareness of the ideological characteristics of writing and helped show how the remains of imperialism continue to linger: less, until very recently, in the narrow sense of militant jingoism or explicit advocacy for annexing new territories than in a more ingrained and bibulous confidence in one's racial or cultural superiority towards other cultures.

Many travel narratives promise their readers a dramatic departure from the mundane and the familiar and an encounter with the exotic and the foreign. To achieve this, many travel writers, who find a lack of evidence of otherness within the foreign, invent such otherness. A great number of travel writings include complaints about the lack of alterity in individual places: the lament "It might be London," uttered by the heroine of E. M. Forster's novel *A Room with a View* (1908) on her first evening in a Florentine *pensione*, recurs, in various form, throughout the history of writing about the foreign. Travelers, as well as travel writers, therefore, impose on the foreign a demand that it should in some way proclaim itself as different from the familiar. At the same time, they define their task as one of grasping that difference. Travel writings sometimes note the response of those travelers who are irritated by the unresponsiveness to alterity of their fellow-travelers. Byron contemptuously describes a woman "fast asleep in the most anti-narcotic spot in the world" (in Switzerland, between the Château de Chillon and Clarens). This incident reminds him of another example of unresponsiveness to alterity: "I remember at Chamouni — in the very eyes of Mont Blanc — hearing another woman — English also — exclaim to her party — "did you ever see anything more rural" — as if it was Highgate, or Hampstead — or Brompton — or Hayes." He then continues: "'Rural' quotha! — Rocks — pines — torrents — Glaciers — Clouds — and Summits of eternal snow far above them — and 'rural!'" (Byron 1994, vol. V: 97).

As Percy Adams argues in his *Travel Literature and the Evolution of the Novel* (1983), travel accounts have historically formed one of the main sources for the novel. Travel writers, on the other hand, continue to utilize fictional devices such as the episodic structure, picaresque motifs, and, most importantly, the foregrounding of the narrator. As a consequence, question regarding the narrator's role remain central to the genre. The reliance upon narrative voice remains crucial simply because the whole genre is a form of personal testimony, at times elegant and inventive, and at times cranky or irritated: Who speaks in a travel narrative and why should we listen to him/her? How does the narrator gain his/her knowledge of other places and peoples? How does he/she establish a compelling authority over the subject? To what degree are a writer's journeys mediated by the observations and perceptions of those who have preceded him/her? What relationship does a traveler establish with his/her fellow travelers? Does the narrative voice represent any particular national or ethnic community with stable identities? Or he/she is forming, together with fellow-travelers, a community of those who do not have community?

One of the most interesting aspects of travelogues is the way they ambivalently conjure up their implied opposite: home. Home is seen, more often than not, as where a traveler has a history and a sense of connectedness with familiar landscapes and cultural traditions. Nevertheless, not everyone rejoices upon returning home. "I admit that my first night home I woke up in a sudden sweat of fear," writes F. O. Matthiessen after returning from a six months sojourn in Europe, "I was no longer in the favored position of an observer in a foreign country. I was back in a very uncertain battle" (Matthiessen 57). Travel usually remains meaningful precisely because its exhilarations are thrown into relief by some notion of home. Travel writings promise both adventure and return, escape and homecoming. The temptation of leaving home to find another home is expressed in the following lines from Canto IV of Byron's *Childe Harold's Pilgrimage* (1818): "and should I leave behind/ The inviolate island of the sage and free,/ And seek me out a home by a remoter sea" (Byron 1992, vol. II:127).

In the aftermath of the national liberation movements of colonized countries and an increasing awareness of Eurocentric travel accounts, there has recently emerged a need to rewrite the travel records from other perspectives. Contemporary travel writing is rooted in a colonial past: it is acquisitive, exoticizing and, to a large extent, dependent on the racial associations of the travelers who are from enabled classes. The rewriting of travel accounts as well as new experiences of travel by writers from ex-colonies, have gained a great deal of popularity within literary and cultural studies during the last thirty years.

As Michel Butor, in his "Travel and Writing," reminds us the kinds of journeys a traveler can take comprise a complicated typology of motion and motivation. The travel literature seeking primitive "undiscovered" frontiers abroad, for example, differs markedly from that about encounters within Western cultural realms (exemplified in the nineteenth century, especially with regard to Americans visiting Europe — in the theme of the Innocent or Ingenue Abroad). Travel writings can also be categorized as involving exploration, colonial expansion, ethnography, spiritual quests, or entailing migrancy, exile, or displacement. Tourism and the Grand Tour are two types of travel in which the traveler is engaged in a controlled exploration of the foreign. The concept of Tour determines the way in which travel in Europe is envisaged and undertaken from the beginning of the seventeenth century up until 1830 (Chard 1999:11). Bruce Redford, in his *Venice and the Grand Tour* (1996), identifies the general characteristics of the Grand Tour:

> . . . the Grand Tour is not the Grand Tour unless it includes the following: first, a young British male patrician (that is, a member of the aristocracy or the gentry); second, a tutor who accompanies his charge throughout the journey; third, a fixed itinerary that makes Rome its principal destination; fourth, a lengthy period of absence, averaging two or three years. (14)

John Urry, in *The Tourist Gaze* (1994), distinguishes between the Grand Tour and tourism in terms of class structure:

> But before the nineteenth century few people outside the upper classes traveled anywhere to see objects for reasons unconnected with work or business. And it is this which is the central characteristic of mass tourism in modern societies, namely that much of the population in most years will travel somewhere else to gaze upon it and stay there for reasons basically unconnected with work. (5)

Chard (1999) draws a distinction between two opposing attitudes, in the period between the beginning of seventeenth century up until 1830, toward the experience of the foreign in travel narratives, both of which still play a crucial role in determining the ways in which encounters with the foreign is imagined today. One of these approaches, which was first discernible in travel writing at the end of the eighteenth century, is the view that "travel is a form of personal adventure, holding out the promise of a discovery and realization of the self through the exploration of the other" (11). This romantic approach entails crossing symbolic as well as geographical boundaries, resulting in transgression of limits which in turn invites various forms of danger and destabilization. The second approach appears at about the same time and presents itself in more or less explicit opposition to the Romantic theory of travel. This second approach is the tourist approach, which recognizes that travel might constitute a form of personal adventure, and might entail danger and destabilization, but, as a result of this recognition, attempts to keep the more dangerous and destabilizing aspects of the experience of the foreign at bay. The problem with this distinction is that it is too general. It therefore, does not consider the difference between individual romantics and their often opposing and contradictory views on travel and the experience of the foreign. It also gives the impression that the romantic notion of travel is something that can be an alternative to a more touristic one. This, I will argue, is by no means the case. I will try to show that the Romantic movement is by no means homogenous in its approach to travel and the experience of the foreign. As a matter of fact, many aspects of the romantic theory of travel are inherently similar to those of a touristic approach. But there are also, it should be noted, certain figures within the Romantic Movement (poets like Byron) who challenge the dominant views of travel. I propose to analyze the tourist approach as well as the ideas of various figures within the Romantic Movement (figures such as Goethe) under the rubric of mimetic theories of travel. A mimetic notion of travel, I would like to argue, is what is dominant in both the touristic and the Romantic approaches to travel and participates in a restricted economy of peregrination in which the traveler-tourist wishes both to have the "truth" of the foreign and to make sure that there is revenue and profit resulting from his/her investments in the experience of the foreign, and that this profit is somehow safeguarded from possible dangers of expropriation and dissemination. But profit is only possible if there is a return back home. Therefore, in a mimetic experience of the foreign, economy (as "the law of the house") becomes intimately entangled with return/homecoming. Non-mimetic theories of travel, on the other hand, participate in a general economy of peregrination in which the traveler is exposed to the possibility (or actuality) destabilization, derangement, danger and death, with no guarantee of profit and/or return. Certain romantic figures such as Byron or Hölderlin might be associated with this view.

An example of mimetic travel writings can be seen, during much of the eighteenth century, in the rhetorical strategy of constructing binary opposition between the familiar and the foreign, in which the most common strategy was to translate (in the sense of finding an equivalent) the foreignness into familiar discourse. Assuming a power of comparison conferred by the experience of travel, the speaking subject adopts his/her own native region as a constant point of reference. Robert Gray, for example, in his *Letters during the Course of a Tour through Germany, Switzerland and Italy* (1794), declares:

> In England, thanks to the existence of religion and a respect for the true happiness of life, the value of fidelity and virtue are still felt; and they who depart from them are compelled to affect their appearance or to retreat from society: — such, alas! Is not the case at Naples. (399)

The setting up of a binary opposition between the foreign and the familiar may often obliquely lead to the opposition between North and South invoked in Montesquieu's *The Spirit of Laws* (1741) in which the distinction between these two regions is reduced to contrasts between industry and idleness and between liberty and slavery:

> In Europe there is a kind of balance between the southern and northern nations. The first have every convenience of life, and few of its wants: the last have many wants, and few conveniences. To one, nature has given much, and demands but little; to the others, she has given but little, and demands a great deal. The equilibrium is maintained by the laziness of the southern nations, and by the industry and activity which she has given to those in the north. The latter are obliged to undergo excessive labor, without which they would want everything, and degenerate into barbarians. This has naturalized slavery to the people of the south: as they can easily dispense with riches, they can more easily dispense with liberty. (22-23)

In a non-mimetic travel writing a binary opposition between the foreign and the familiar is deconstructed[6]: the familiar is shown to be estranged and the foreign is charged with familiarity. Therefore, the experience of the foreign can be described as an uncanny experience, an estranged familiarity.

Chloe Chard (1999) distinguishes between "organized" (tourist) and "disorganized" (Romantic) travel. The "organized" travelers are determined to maintain control over their travel and to carefully keep at bay the more dangerous and destabilizing elements within the foreign. In their assumption that the foreign is best enjoyed by keeping at bay the more troubling elements within it, or editing these elements out of the travelers' experience altogether, the "organized" travelers, or rather the tourists, shows us a glimpse of their approach to the alterity of the other, formed in opposition to the view of travel as transgressive and destabilizing. While the Romantic view of travel positions the traveler as the subject of urgent desires, impulses and inner needs, the touristic view affirm the position of the traveler as the subject of more modest demands, seeking out carefully regulated and controlled pleasures. The touristic attitude and the relation to the foreign remains in marked tension with destabilizing travel today; together, the two approaches, often found in impure forms, still determine the range and limits of what can be said and written about the experience of the foreign.

Destabilization and danger, in the context of tourism, are, what one might call, the non-mimetic elements within a mimetic framework. They assume a double role within the phenomenon of tourism: on the one hand, they are seen as threats to be contained; on the other hand, when kept at a proper distance, they may provide acceptable touristic gratification by allowing a pleasurable mixture of the remains of risk and a domesticated excitement. An analysis of tourism in Evelyn Waugh's *Labels* (1930) offers an astute assessment of the gratification to be derived from flirting with danger from a position of safety. The many references to banditti on the roads in early nineteenth-century accounts of travel in Italy assure the reader that the topography of the Grand Tour, however frequently traversed over the centuries, may well contain lurking dangers.[7] While incipiently dangerous fantasies may be rendered domesticated, sweet and wholly legitimate by careful management and organization which keeps the foreign at a distance, the touristic approach is contaminated by the possibility, and in fact probability, of the eruption of the unexpected. The literature of tourism is full of accounts of danger suddenly erupting amid the most sedate varieties of encounter with alterity. In E. M. Forster's *A Passage to India*, the English picnic arranged by Dr. Aziz is dramatically transformed into a disaster. Another example is again E. M. Forster's "Story of a Panic" (1902), in which a party of English picnickers in the countryside near Florence are visited by the god Pan, who takes possession of a young boy in the group.

One of the aspects of travel which makes it possible to see it as destabilizing is the affect of wonder, in which the traveler's stability is seriously threatened. In *Rome in the Nineteenth Century* (1820), Charlotte Eaton presents herself as so enraptured by the Apollo Belvedere that she teeters on the brink of derangement. As if trying to counter disbelief, she cites another traveler more unhinged than herself:

> You will think me mad — and it were vain to deny it — but I am not the first person who has gone mad about the Apollo. Another, and a far more unfortunate damsel, a native of France, it is related, at the sight of this matchless statue, lost at once her heart and her reason. Day after day, and hour after hour, the fair enthusiast gazed and wept, and sighed her soul away, till she became, like the marble, pale, but not like the marble, cold. Nor, like the lost Eloisa, nor the idol of her love, could she "forget herself to stone," till death at last closed the ll-fated passion, and the life, of the maid of France. (169-170)

Having raised the possibility of death and extreme derangement, however, Eaton immediately forecloses it: "But I have not the least intention of dying; I only congratulate myself that I have lived to see that glorious work, whose perfection will never be paralleled upon earth" (170). The experience of the sublime, in which the subject is placed outside him/herself, and the anticipation of danger is here quickly glimpsed and then promptly avoided.

The rhetoric of tourism deploys yet another strategy to sublate (i.e., to cancel and preserve) the inherent danger in the experience of the foreign. A sight is often used as a starting point for a deflection to the past, whether personal or historical. In many travel accounts of the late eighteenth century and early nineteenth century, describe places where the past, somehow unintentionally, threatens to resurge, in a way that may prove unsettling to the travelers. Tourism, in contrast, designates the sights sought out by the travelers as places where the past, however full of energy, turbulence, and danger, nonetheless maintains its distance. In the conversation between Sydney and Mr. Milton in Elizabeth Bowen's *The Hotel* (1927), Sydney's remark "Wouldn't be nice . . . if the Saracens were to appear on the skyline, land, and ravage the Hotel?" is followed by the reflection that the "dust, panic and ecstasy" of the past is all too easy to keep at bay:

> "But I wonder," she added, while a cloud of depression crept over her, "how many of us they would really care to take away?"
>
> He did not know how she wished him to answer and risked: "It would be an embarrassing choice."
>
> She sighed flatly. The dust, panic and ecstasy with which she had filled for a moment the corridors of the Hotel subsided. Once more she saw her fellow-visitors as they were to remain — undesired, secure and null. "Not many," she said, and turning away from him seemed to be gazing down some distant, barred-away perspective of feminine loveliness. (35)

The Romantic period is not just an era of great journeys — real and poetical, physical and metaphorical — but also a period in which the journey, in both its structure and nature, undergoes profound change. There is no single pattern to the romantic journey, but rather many patterns, each of them nonetheless marking a definite break with past eras. Romanticism knows travel above all as a philosophical metaphor, an odyssey or path through the world in quest of one's identity. Thus the question asked in Novalis's *Heinrich von Ofterdingen*, "Where are you going?" meets with the reply, "Homeward, always homeward." Like Odysseus of old, Novalis's hero plunges into the whirl of things to find, in the end, himself; his journey leads him to discover his own truth, which at first seems uncertain, but which on confrontation with the world, and through a mediation of the experience of the foreign, achieves a complete identity. Like Ithaca, every *Heimat*, homeland, birthplace is found, as Ernst Bloch would say, not at the start, not in childhood and the past, but rather at the end of the journey: home is a destination, not a point of departure. In that great travel novel, Hegel's *Phenomenology of Spirit*, the subject takes leave of itself, immerses in the world and thereby comes into its own, into a self quite other than it initially was, just as the Ithaca Ulysses rediscovers on his return takes on its true meaning only at that moment, much different from that of the one he left behind.[8]

A certain charge of destabilization and danger, destruction and death, uprootedness and betrayal, is always inherent in the romantic travel view of travel. The voyager not only relativizes values, he also break himself loose from his original values and so destroys them, only to re-find himself in the totality of his subsequent experiences. This Phoenix-like figure of the traveler is an idealized construct, which starts to look problematic in case of romantics like Eichendorff, Hölderlin, or Heine. Eichendorff's romantic wayfarer happily abandons himself to the joys of the open road. He does not travel in order to arrive somewhere, a fixed goal; rather, he travels to pause, to sojourn, to ramble, to stray from all pre-established routes and from all destinations, never to arrive[9]. This happy wayfarer is, however, assailed by a troubling thought, which reveals one of the aporias of travel: he would like, through his journey, to overtake and capture Life, real and essential life, though such a life seems possible only if it is stripped of all concrete historical and social particularities and determinations, and if the traveler is literally good for nothing (Eichendorff's novella literally "From the Life of a Good-for-Nothing"), unfit to do anything whatsoever, to fit, in any way, into the productive mechanism of reality.[10] The grand utopia of Wilhelm Meister crumbles. In order truly to *be*, the traveler — the individual — must be *nothing* specific or else he cannot truly be; life becomes a hindrance, an obstacle to itself.

In romanticism, the great prototype of refined travel geared toward concrete discovery of the world, as practiced and perfected in Enlightenment tradition, seems almost irreparably lost now. It was as though one no longer traveled for edification and education, but rather to lose oneself, to erase one's traces, to camouflage oneself amid the busy hum of things. From the promotional, edifying Grand Tour, travel is transformed into a line of flight and an experience of the uncertainty of one's identity.

The idea that travel might actually provide a temporary escape from identity, rather than a consolidation of it, is emphasized in a discussion of the pleasures of traveling in a prose section of Samuel Rogers's poem *Italy* (1822). According to Rogers, the travelers, in their peregrination, are offered a temporary escape from the relentless "pursuit of wealth and honor": an escape that leads them away from wearisome adult existence and back towards "the golden time of their childhood":

> Now travel, and foreign travel more particularly, restores to us in a great degree what we have lost. When the anchor is heaved, we double down the leaf; and for a while at least all effort is over .... All is new and strange .... We surrender ourselves, and feel once again as children. Like them we enjoy eagerly; like them, when we fret, we fret only for the moment. (171)

Hazlitt, in his essay "On Going a Journey" (1822), emphasizes that traveling abroad may well be in some sense instructive but in general it is too disconnected from everyday life to allow the traveler either to consolidate his own virtues and social skills or to gain permanent intellectual authority. As in Rogers's account of the pleasures of travel, the experience of the foreign does not pose any permanent threat to the traveler's identity, but it does suspend that identity:

> There is undoubtedly a sensation in traveling into foreign parts that is to be had nowhere else: but it is more pleasing at the time than lasting. It is too remote from our habitual associations to be a common topic of discourse or reference, and, like a dream or another state of existence, does not piece into our daily modes of life. It is an animated but a momentary hallucination. It demands an effort to exchange our actual for our ideal identity .... Our romantic and itinerant character is not to be domesticated. Dr. Johnson remarked how little for-

eign travel added to the facilities in conversation in those who had been abroad. In fact, the time we have spent there is both delightful, and, in some sense, instructive; but it appears to be cut out of our substantial, downright existence . . . . We are not the same, but another, and perhaps more enviable individual, all the time we are out of our own country. We are lost to ourselves, as well as to our friends. (39-40)

Danger and destabilization may also result from traversing boundaries and crossing barriers. Laurence Stern's *Sentimental Journey* (1768) concludes with a section in which Yorick is trapped in an Alpine inn because the road along which he is traveling is blocked by stones falling down from the mountains. This event traps him in an inn, where he soon finds out that he must share his bedchamber with two women, a lady and her *fille de chamber*. It soon becomes evident that the maid will sleep in a small closet, leaving Yorick and the lady with two adjoining beds. The narrative ends with the crossing of the Alps and the traversal of the lesser boundary between the beds both thrown off course by unexpected obstacles. In Book VI of Wordsworth's *Prelude*, the narrator sets out to cross the Alps, but discovers that his plans have been unexpectedly thwarted. He and his traveling companion take the wrong path when trying to traverse the crucial symbolic boundary, and then find that they have made the crossing inadvertently. After finding himself diverted from "the regular road" in the course of his traversal, the narrator declares that travel is a "theme which may seduce me else beyond/all reasonable bounds." John Whitaker's *Course of Hannibal over the Alps Ascertained* (1794) is a book thoroughly devoted to the question of which route Hannibal may have taken to cross the Alps. The book presents the Carthaginian general finding himself diverted from the "regular road." Hannibal is often introduced into travel writings, from the beginning of the Grand Tour onwards, as a figure whose story anticipates the dangers the traveler may encounter in crossing boundaries (Chard 177). The desire to cross a boundary is often motivated by the promise of a superior pleasure and, at the same time, indicates the dangers that such a desire may contain.

Freud's essay "A Disturbance of Memory on the Acropolis" (1936), which is an open letter to Roman Roland on the occasion of his seventieth birthday, is also a story of danger and the possibility of destabilization inherent in traveling. This essay tells the story of a holiday that Freud has spent in the company of his brother and is marked by two strange experiences. First, at Trieste, an acquaintance advises the brothers to travel on to Athens rather than their intended destination, Corfu. They spend the hours before they can buy their tickets in a state of gloom, foreseeing "nothing but obstacles and difficulties." Once the Lloyd offices open, however, they buy their tickets as if it were a matter of course. The second strange experience occurs once they reach Athens: "When finally . . . I stood upon Acropolis and cast my eyes around upon the landscape, a remarkable thought suddenly entered my mind: 'So all this really *does* exist, just as we learnt at school!'." Freud identifies the thought as a displaced expression of "a momentary feeling: 'what I see here is not real'" (308). He classifies this "feeling of derealization [*Entfremdungsgefühl*]" (308) as a form of defense mechanism and in which "the subject feels either that a piece of reality or that a piece of his own self is strange to him. In the latter case we speak of depersonalization . . ." (309). Derealization does not only function as a defense mechanism; it is also "dependent upon the past, upon the ego's stores of memory" (310). In other words, the experience of Freud the traveler on the Acropolis culminates in a "disturbance of memory and a falsification of the past" (310). The reason, according to Freud, for all these derangements of memory and of the past lies simply in the feeling of guilt for having gone "further than one's father":

> It must be that a sense of guilt was attached to the satisfaction in having got so far: there was something about that was wrong, that was from earliest times forbidden. It was something to do with a child's criticism of his father, with the undervaluation which took the place of the overvaluation of earlier childhood. It seems as though the essence of success were to have got further than one's father, and as though to excel one's father were still something forbidden. (311)

Travel is marked, Freud seems to intimate, by a contradictory, dialectical coexistence of desire and guilt: the desire to escape away from the father and the pressures of home and family results in the pleasure of travel that bring about feelings of not only guilt but also destabilization and danger. The guilt that Freud ascribes to himself and his brother, however, is not a manifestation of inadequacies and shortcomings with reference to the social context of a particular practice of travel, but a form of danger, to be assessed with reference to the domain of the personal. Danger is furthermore manifested in the form of a destabilization: in analyzing the despondency that the travelers evince at Trieste, Freud likens it to the experience of people "wrecked by success" (306) in which people "fall ill, or even go entirely to pieces, because an overwhelmingly powerful wish of theirs has been fulfilled" (306). His description of the "derealization" on the Acropolis emphasizes the unsettling effects of travel yet more explicitly: it causes a splitting of the subject. He notes a division between the subject of the remark "So all this really does exist," and the subject who takes cognizance of this remark, and describes both subjects as "astonished." The first behave "as though he were obliged, under the impact of an unequivocal observation, to believe in something the reality of which had hitherto seemed doubtful," and the second is "justifiably astonished, because he had been unaware that the real existence of Athens, the Acropolis, and the landscape around it had ever been objects of doubt" (304). When Freud investigates the feeling that he had seen a marvel, he does so in order to emphasize the unsettling rather than self-affirmatory aspect of his experience of the foreign. Freud's "A Disturbance of Memory" not only maps out a narrative in which a traveler crosses boundaries and undergoes destabilization, but also draws the sublime into the narrative of transgression. The experience of sublimity is accompanied by an expression of a sense of liberation from the oppressive limitations of the familiar. Mary Shelley in one of her journals dismisses her own country (an equation of rainy London with a "formless mist" of the mind) as one that offers her only "prison." She then invokes the aesthetic pleasures of sublime infinitude ("the resplendent sky," "the blue expanse of the tranquil sea," "the unclouded stars") in order to endorse her need to transcend the bounds of melancholy:[11]

> I have now been nearly four months in England and if I am to judge of the future by the past and the present, I have small delight in looking forward. I even regret those days and weeks of intense melancholy that composed my life at Genoa — Yes — solitary and unbeloved as I was there, I enjoyed a more pleasurable state of being than I do here. I was still in Italy, & my heart and imagination were both gratified by that circumstance. I arose with the light and beheld the theater of Nature from my windows — The trees spread their green beauty before me — the resplendent sky was above me — the mountains were invested with enchanting colors — I had even begun to contemplate painlessly the blue expanse of the tranquil sea . . . then my solitary walks and my reveries — they were magnificent, deep, pathetic, wild and exalted — I sounded the depths of my own nature. (vol. II, 470)

Freud's theory of travel owes a great deal to the Romantic vision of travel as an escape to a domain of freedom. The notion that the foreign offers powerful pleasure of superior freedom is conspicuously absent from eighteenth-century travel literature (Chard 1999:187). A discussion of the historical difference between discourses of travel is beyond the scope of this study. I would, however, like to examine in more details the previously-made distinction between a mimetic and a non-mimetic discourse of travel and further address some of the theoretical issues and problems that I identify to be both relevant and constitutive of these discourses on travel (experience).

In a mimetic view of travel, I would argue, the subject represents the world to itself (in acts of memory and recollection) only to recuperate the memorialized world, within a restricted economical framework, as a reified commodity. The question of representation or mimesis (*Vorstellung/Darstellung*) becomes that of correspondence, equivalence and adequation ("*homoiosis*, in terms of the justice or rectitude (*orthodes*) of a seeing or saying"[12]) and the traveler-tourist's memory of the absent object is treated as a reservoir of images (as if having performed a complete mourning), recollected in tranquility, i. e., after the fact of traveling. A mimetic (discourse on) travel is inscribed within a restricted economy in which the subject is often concerned with what (s)he gains in the experience of the foreign. The non-mimetic theory of travel, on the other hand, bears witness to the impossibility and the ruins of representation. Representation is here not adequation but allegorical figuration, which is nothing but a "fictioning" (*UmBildung*) as well as a catachrestic relationship to the event of the experience of the foreign. The subject is more concerned with loss rather than gain.

Mimesis is first of all, Lacoue-Labarthe tells us, *Darstellung*, which immediately calls up *Herstellung*,[13] that is, production, installation or restoration in the most active sense of the word, "even if it is necessary to limit or restrain the autonomy of this "activity" by conceding that what is proper to it (supposing that it has any property whatsoever), that is, fashioning or fictioning (*Umbilden, Erdichten*), is of the order of counterfeiting (*Nachmachen*) or reproduction (*Ab-*

bilden) — and thus of a certain 'passivity'" (Lacoue-Labarthe1998:77). Understood this way, it is better to say *Herstellung*, Lacoue-Labarthe advises us. The essence of mimesis is therefore not imitation but production or fabrication.[14] Mimesis as *Herstellung* is in fact closely related to *aletheia* (truth) as *Unverstelltheit* (non-dissimulation, *Unverborgenheit*), as discussed by Heidegger. "Because *aletheia* can be said to be *Unverstelltheit*, all *installation* is properly an inauguration, the unveiling of a *stele* or a *statue*. Or — what amounts to the same thing — all *installation* is an *establishing*, that is to say, a production" (80). Lacoue-Labarthe problematizes Heidegger's identification of mimesis as *Herstellung/ Darstellung* with *aletheia*. Heidegger, argues Lacoue-Labarthe, fails to see the "abyss" implied in *Darstellung*, that is, the hiatus between truth and representation, as well as the "fictioning" function of *Darstellung*:

> In fact, as soon as we consider the abyss, as soon as the suspicion arises that the abyss is always in one way or another implied in Darstellung (and inversely, that Darstellung always gives rise to a mise-en-abyme), it is still necessary to agree on the status of the Darstellung in question and, consequently, the exact nature of the abyss itself. What, for example, is happening here with this "lack of the abyss," or this inattention to the abyss? For the difficulty doubtless derives not only from the inevitable distance that opens up between the Heideggerian commentary and the text or texts that this commentary covers. It is not enough here to say that Heidegger is not concerned with the abyssal, and that he thus fails to see what is involved in the problematic of Darstellung, etc. The difficulty derives perhaps also, and especially, from the structure of the abyss "itself," inasmuch as what is reflected there (though if not by "figure," imperceptibly) is fictioning, that is to say, the fiction whereby the fictioning essence of reason or of thought must itself be (re)presented and exposed. (72)

In place of a Heideggerian notion of mimesis as *aletheia*, Lacoue-Labarthe proposes mimesis as *Wiederholung*, a repetition, always with a difference, in which one is relieved of the burden of a determinate origin:

> The *Wiederholung* represents another model, the determination of another means of identification and another relation of imitation, in reality infinitely more powerful than all the others because it is the model of an identification with (or an imitation of) *what has taken place without taking place*, of a past that is not past but still to come, of a beginning so great that it dominates every future and remains still to be effected. (299)

Mimesis as *Wiederholung*, in this sense, is, properly speaking, anti-mimetic in its relinquishing of any concern for reflection, adequation, or truth. It is rather a bearing witness to the impossibility of representation and correspondence. In its impulse to repetition, it is always aware of the difference inherent in repetition, whereby all claims to adequation are relinquished.

"Mimesis has always been an economic problem; it is the problem of economy (Lacoue-Labarthe 124)."[15] Mimesis as *aletheia*, I would argue by elaborating on Lacoue-Labarth statement, is related to a restricted economy, while mimesis as *Wiederholung* is related to a general economy. They do not form an opposition, as Derrida has argued, but are mutually contaminated. In what follows I try to explicate the restricted economy of mimesis (and its dependence on a general economy) in relation to travel in general and Romantic travel in particular. In the second chapter, while trying to delimit the boundaries of my project, I will continue my discussions of the restricted economy of travel by analyzing three texts selected from the tradition of immigrant autobiography, whether fictional or non-fictional.

The dialectics of travel has almost always been posited within a restricted economy of exchange: an economy of life and profit, which denies or suppresses its own condition of possibility, i.e., its dependence on a general economy of excess, death and expenditure without return. The decision to leave home is motivated by a desire for a revenue, a return, in financial, epistemological, or experiential terms. One may distinguish, within the framework of a restricted economy of travel, at least two general evaluative approaches to travel. Travel can be construed to be a negative or "useless" undertaking when it does not provide any horizon for appropriation, any possibility of gain or profit. In Voltaire's *Candide*, after a series of misfortunes that befall characters in their peregrination around the globe, the "philosophical tale" ends in the didacticism: "it is necessary to cultivate our garden," the epitome of sedentariness (Van den Abbeele xvii). La Fontaine's famous fable "The Two Pigeons" also provides an eloquent example of this negative notion of travel: "In this satire of the urge to travel, one of the two pigeons, "crazy enough to undertake/ a voyage to some faraway land," suffers one disaster after another in his journey until, "half dead and half limping," he decides to return home" (xvii). In Attar's *The Conference of the Birds* (13th Century medieval Persia), a group of birds embark on a journey to mount *Ghaf* (an imaginary mountain) to find the *Simorgh* (the imaginary Greek *Phoenix*, who, when the time comes, sets fire to herself only to be reborn out of her own ashes, an heir to herself; also known as *Bennu* in Egyptian, *Milcham* in Jewish, *Garuda* in Indian, and *Karura* in Japanese mythology, all having their own separate story to tell). During the journey many die. Those who remain (their number is thirty, which is significant) reach a point where they can go no further due to hardship, fatigue and cold. In disappointment as well as in surprise, they find out, almost by chance, that they are the *Simorgh*, that is, Si ("Thirty" in Persian) Morgh ("bird"). The proper name is turned into a common name. They realize that it was they themselves that they were looking for. The external journey is revealed to be an internal one, a journey in search of the self. Know thyself and you will know the world. In this journey, there is no gain or profit since it is always already attained. Travel can also be experienced as a negativity of exile, the subject of which always desires a return back home. Many of the fables in Rumi's *Masnavi*, to bring another example from medieval Persia, as well as numerous stories told by mystics of the middle ages[16] are stories of exile and expatriation from the "original" union, whose roots, following de Certeau's argument, lie in their socio-material circumstances of their context of production.

Now, if there is an insecurity or anxiety associated with travel, it is that insecurity associated with the menace of irreparable loss. This loss can affect not only one's monetary assets but also one's very life or sanity. Or one can simply lose one's way, since the possibility of there being no return is always implied in travel. Every voyage is potentially a voyage into exile, a voyage to the "end of the night" (Van den Abbeele 1992: xvii).

One the other hand, there should be a positive notion of travel (the possibility of gain or profit), otherwise there would be no incentive to travel: from tourists' accumulation of "cultural capital" and "cultural experience" that then increases their social value within their home communities,[17] to voyage seen as an escape either in the banal urge to "get away from it all" or in the Baudelarean flight from *ennui*,[18] to imperialist and colonialist ventures (Abbeele xvii).

The positivity of travel lies in its "uses," which can cover a broad spectrum, from the nothingness of Barthes to Levi-Strauss's "principles of social life" to capital accumulation of 18th and 19th century colonial voyages. The revenue in the restricted economy of travel is not necessarily something taken, in the form of some knowledge, experience, etc, from the *real* world. The real world can be fictionalized, but it still participates in the economy of loss and return, even if it is the return of nothingness and the loss of meaning. Roland Barthes is not concerned with the real Japan: "Hence Orient and Occident cannot be taken here as 'realities' to be compared and contrasted. I am not lovingly gazing toward an Oriental essence — to me the Orient is a matter of indifference . . ." (Barthes 3). Japan becomes rather an "excuse," a pretext to think the possibility of a difference. It provides Barthes with a "reserve of features," put together imaginatively but always motivated by the real, whose manipulation allows him not only to "entertain the idea of an unheard-of symbolic system," but more importantly, to think "the very fissure of the symbolic" (4). The experience of a fictionalized foreignness allows Barthes to point to, without ontologizing them, the lacks and lacunas, the blindness of self/same, the other within: "Someday we must write the history of our own obscurity — manifest the density of our narcissism . . ." (4). The collapse of the symbolic, and with it the meaning in/of language in which one witnesses the emergence of nothingness, threatens the subject with madness. It places him/her outside him/herself, "causes knowledge, or the subject, to vacillate" (4). This is also "the situation of writing" in which the unveiling[19] reveals nothing; "there is nothing to grasp" (110). Barthes's restricted economy of travel comes, however, close to a recognition of its dependence on a general economy of excess without return: an excess of meaning as event, escaping representation, nomination or possession. After the traveler flees signification and loses it in the experience of the foreign, meaning somehow reasserts itself but with the traveler now passively receiving its flashes, no sooner perceived than erased. He can only bear witness to what exceeds him, without being able to capture it in any form of reified knowledge. This instant Barthes locates, but does not attempt to master, in the fragment called "So," in which he examines Japanese haiku: "Here meaning is only a flash, a slash of light...; but the haiku's flash illuminates, reveals nothing; it is the flash of a photograph one takes very carefully (in the Japanese manner) but having neglected to load the camera with film. Or again: haiku reproduces the designating gesture of the child pointing at whatever it is (the haiku shows no partiality for the subject), merely saying: that! . . ." (83).

For Levi-Strauss, the use of travel lies in the possibilities that it provides to "borrow" from others, not specific cultural practices, but certain "principles of social life": "However, by getting to know them better, we are enabled to detach ourselves from our own society . . . . But it is the only one from which we have a duty to free ourselves, using all societies, without adopting features . . . to elucidate principles of social life that we can apply in reforming our own customs . . ." (Levi-Strauss 1997:479). This is not far from what Barthes ultimately desires to be a "usefulness" of traveling, i.e. and to put it paradoxically, to see our own blindness, which is also to say, to clear a path, a *Lichtung*, for a future to come to pass. To the extent that this "future" resists reification or ontologization, the restricted economy of travel recognizes the excess on which it depends.

Carter's *The Road to Botany Bay* (1988) is ultimately concerned with the conditions of the possibility of blindness as well as the question of futurity. Let me unpack, through some quotations, some lines of his argumentation that bear on these notions:

> The basis of the explorer's interest in the landscape is neither objectively empirical nor is it merely literary or autobiographical: his stance is, rather, phenomenological in nature. It is grounded in his recognition that he, the observer, does not gaze on the world as through a window, but rather inhabits it. His perception of the world's appeal is inseparable from his own interest in it, from the 'intentionality' of his gaze. (82)

> Mitchell's geographical fantasies were essential to his notion of traveling. They were ways of rendering the country habitable — the grander project which distinguished the surveyor from the explorer. (108)

> So a spatial history does not go confidently forward . . . It advances exploratively, even metaphorically, recognizing that the future is invented. Going back, it questions the assumption that the past has been settled once and for all, suggesting the plurality of historical directions. (294)

> . . . it is by reflecting on their intentions, by understanding what lies behind the finished map, the elegant journal...that we recover the possibility of another history, our future . . . history of convicts. (295)

> An aboriginal history of space would, then, be a symbolic history. It would not be an anthropologist's account of the Aborigines' beliefs. Nor would it be a history of frontiers and massacres. Rather than seek by a newly ingenious means to translate the otherness of their experience into empirical terms, it might take the form of a mediation on the absent other of our own history. It might begin in the recognition of the suppressed spatiality of our own historical consciousness. (350)

The recognition of the suppressed spatiality of our historical consciousness is not to commemorate what is irretrievably past (it is not a work of mourning), but as a means to open a future, to give a chance to something as future to come to pass and that it is not a mere continuation or replication of a present or a past; to make sure that the past doesn't repeat itself. To do this one does not need the empirical other but a recognition, without ontologization, of the other within. To "recover the possibility of another history" is not a retrieval of what has been suppressed, e.g., a history of convicts or a history as the Aborigines might have narrated, a possible history outside our actual history. It is rather to come to terms with the contingency of "our" own history, how it could have been otherwise. Spatial history is to become hospitable to the materiality of history. Carter posits his spatial history within a phenomenological framework only to come across, somehow implicitly, the delimitation of that framework. If it is true that the subject's perception of the world is a function of his interest and his being in that world, it is also true that to the extent that the subject realizes the contingency or historicity of his perception, he experiences his own finitude, his own death.

Carter's distinction between an imperial history and a spatial history can be construed to correspond to the distinction between a restricted economy of travel and a general one. In both these cases, the former term territorializes on the latter one. In other words, spatial history can be understood to form the background on which an imperial history consolidates, ontologizes, or reterritorializes itself. The distinction is also that of a map and the markings of an itinerary.

> He [Mitchell] was the means of transforming the dynamic space of travelling into the fixed and passive space of settlement . . . . He viewed the country he passed through as if with the eyes of the future . . . writing over earlier names . . . Mitchell's reports were blueprints for the movement of people . . . . They made places where people could settle, could imagine settling. (120-22)

> The possibility of an imperial history and its map depends, however, upon the condition of a denial of time and difference. Its logic is a logic of possession and mastery, which suppresses the historicity of a spatialization of time and a temporalization of space; it is a forgetting of singularities of time and space, and the difference in their repetition. The logic of the map is based on a violence, which reduces the dynamic space of an itinerary to a rigid grid. It is a reduction that fails to acknowledge that "itinerary is the condition of the possibility of map." (de Certeau, 1984:119)

The "usefulness" of travel, a certain revenue gained in the experience of the foreign, stands central in the romantic theories of translation, a process which makes *Bildung* (or the Latin *Kultur*) possible by being mediated through travel. The concept of *Bildung* (process of formation as well as its result) is one of the central concepts of German culture at the end of the eighteenth century. It is related to nouns such as *Bild* (image), *Einbildungkraft* (imagination), *Ausbildung* (development), *Bildsamkeit* (flexibility, formability). It can be found everywhere: in Herder, in Goethe and Schiller, in the Romantics, in Hegel, and in Fichte. *Bildung* is always a movement toward a form, *one's own form* — which is to say that, in the beginning, every being is deprived of *its* form, every being homeless:

> In the speculative language of German Idealism, the beginning may be the particularity which lacks the determination of the universal, the unity from which the moment of scission and opposition is absent, the panic indifference lacking all articulation, the thesis without its antithesis or synthesis, the unmediated immediate, the chaos which has not yet become world, the position deprived of the moment of reflection, the unlimited which must be limited (or vice versa), the affirmation which must go through negation, etc. These abstract formulations also have a concrete and metaphorical side: the child that must become adult, the virgin that must become woman, the bud that must become flower and then fruit . . . . *Bildung* is also the process of an unfolding of freedom. (Berman 1992: 44)

Berman argues that at bottom all *Bildung* is triadic, which is to say that its structure is essentially "homologous" to what Heidegger defined as: "the principle of unconditioned subjectivity of the German absolute metaphysics of Hegel and Schelling, according to whose teaching the being-with-itself of spirit requires a return to itself which, in turn, requires a being-outside-itself" (Berman 44). The structure of *Bildung* is triadic because the movement towards the outside does not return to the same locus. It forms, therefore, an open triangle: three points, two lines.

To achieve *Bildung*, it is necessary to go through the detour of a certain voyage (*Reise*), or migration (*Wanderung*), "a 'same' unfolding itself to attain its full dimension" (44) in the experience of the foreign. This process is what is called "experience," a nothingness that desires to be everything. Its essence "is to throw the 'same' into a dimension that will transform it. It is the movement of the 'same' which, changing, finds itself to be 'other.' 'Die and become.' Goethe said" (44). Later, in the process of unfolding my argument, I will argue that the subject is always already dead as soon as (s)he decides to travel (or one could even say that subject of travel has to commit suicide in order for something as the event of travel takes place if the decision to commit suicide did not already presuppose positing a subject). The decision to travel is the decision of a dead (wo)man. But as a voyage, it is also "the experience of the *alterity of the world*: in order to have access to that which, in the guise of a becoming-other, is in truth a becoming-itself . . ." Novalis in *The discipline at Saïs*: "He lifted the veil of the Goddess at Saïs. But what did he see? He saw — miracle of miracles — himself" (45): the si morghs (the thirty birds) finding themselves the *Simorgh*, the miracle of miracles.

The problem of *Bildung* is the problem of mediation. Goethe's *Wilhelm Meister* is the story of the education of the young hero, a formation which passes through a series of mediations and mediators, one of whom is significantly called the "Foreigner." Because the foreign has a mediating function, translation can become one of the agents of *Bildung*. *Bildung* can never be the simple imitation of the foreign. Nevertheless, it maintains an essential connection with what is called in German *Urbild* (original, archetype) and *Vorbild*, the model of which it can be the reproduction (*Nachbild*). The foreign initially functions as a *model*, and then subsequently as *mediation*: first Wilhelm Meister attempts to identify with the people he encounters, but they eventually teach him to find himself. (47-48).

The process of *Bildung*, in its experience of the foreign, is deeply embedded in a restricted economy of travel. In Novalis, this economic revenue is called "potentiation," a movement that consists of going through everything. Novalis also called it *versability*. A great part of Nietzsche's reflection, in *The Gay Science*, is devoted to measuring the disastrous consequences of that "chameleonic" ability to creep into anything (Novalis: "The accomplished man must live, as it were, in many places and many people at once...then the true, grandiose present of the spirit is formed." (80)), to penetrate all spaces and all times without really inhabiting them, to ape all styles, all genres, all languages, all values — an (in)ability which, in its monstrous development, defines the modern Western world as well as its cultural imperialism and its appropriating voracity. Potentiation (what Benjamin calls "endangered semantic potentials") is a generalized translatability, which brings forth the "tendency" in the original. Novalis in a letter of 30 November 1797, addressed to A. W. Schlegel: "I am convinced that the German Shakespeare today is better than the English." This evaluation is to be explained in terms of the movement of translation constituting the original into a *potentiation*. The original itself, in what the Romantics call its "tendency," possesses an *a priori* scope: the Idea of the Work is what the work wants to be, *tends* towards (independently from the author's intentions or not), but empirically never is. In this respect, the original is only the copy — the translation, if you want — of this *a priori* figure which presides over its being and gives it its necessity. Now translation aims precisely at this Idea, this *"origin of the original."* Through this aim, it necessarily produces a "better" text than the first, if only because "the movement constituted by the passage from one language to another — the *Übersetzung* — has necessarily distanced, removed the work by force from the initial empirical layer that separated it from its own Idea." The translation, the second version of the work, brings it closer to its truth. For the romantics, criticism has the same status. F. Schlegel did not hesitate to call his review of *Wilhelm Meister* an *Übermeister*, an over-Meister. Every *Übersetzung* is a movement in which the *Über* is a potentiating going beyond: Thus one may say that A. W. Schlegel's Shakespeare is an *Übershakespeare*. The original is inferior to its translation in the same way "Nature" is inferior to "Facture." "The further one is distanced from the natural, the closer one gets to the absolute poetic core, the ether of its own infinity" (Berman 1992:108).

"Potentiation" is a gift of the other; the other gives what it does not have. Or rather, the gift is not given, but taken, which implies a certain violence in the relation to the other. *Bildung* gives itself the gift of the other, i.e., the origin of the original. Potentiation, however, can never be objective or innocent; it participates in what one might call "a politics of representation." Berman points out this politics of potentiation: "Thus foreign literatures become the mediators in the internal conflicts of national literatures and offer them an image of themselves they could not otherwise have. Goethe played this role, for example, in the conflicts between classics and romantics in Italy" (65). Hölderlin raises the stakes: the gift of the origin of the original, as soon as it arrives, is turned into an exchange; one has to pay for it. The price is, however, a linguistic one in case of translation. Hölderlin's translations, precisely because they do submit the German language to the "violent motion of the foreign language" (rather than preserving the contingent state of the German language), move to the center stage. For Hölderlin, the relations of languages are relations of mutual *differentiation*, of *confrontation* and *hybridization* (Berman 18). Hölderlin challenges the law of classical *Bildung*, i.e., the movement of leaving and returning to itself of spirit, what is one's own gains access to itself only be experience, namely the experience of the foreign. Hölderlin proposes something more profound and more risky: the movement toward what is one's own and the movement toward the foreign do not succeed each other in a linear fashion (136). The poem "The Journey" (*Die Wanderung*) shows the simultaneity of these two modalities of experience: ." . . the towns . . . by the Rhine, / All them affirm that / No dwelling-place could be better. But I am bound for the Caucausus!" For Hölderlin, both of these two experiences (the experience of the foreign and what is one's own) are necessary but none should be taken without the mediation of the other: the law of double mediation.

> On the one hand, 'the homeland devours him'; on the other, 'the shadows of our forests' save him. The movement by which the 'spirit' escapes the mortal (devouring) immediacy of the homeland is also the movement that threatens to consume it by the searing light of the foreign. Henceforth, as the experience [*épreuve*] of the foreign protects from the bad homeland, so does the apprenticeship of the homeland protects from the fire from heaven — from the foreign. The two movements are inseparable: The task of poetry consists in mastering the imbalances inherent to the experience of what is one's own and the experience of the foreign. (165)

The foreign, the fire from heaven, would burn to ashes the one who comes too close, but what is one's own, the homeland, is no less dangerous; it causes blindness.[20] In both cases there is the danger of pure "indifferentiation," a falling into "mortal immediacy." It is only through poetry that the "reign of the Differentiated is instituted" (165).

The potentiation of the original, in German romantic theory of translation, is also, at the same time, a potentiation of the other in the experience of the foreign; to see the Greek as they could never see themselves. The potentiation of the other is, however, eventually a means to an end, that is, the potentiation of the self; to reveal the suppressed element in it, the other within. A movement from S towards, not O but, O´ (a potentiated modality of O) in order to return to S´ (a potentiated modality of S). The relation to the foreign is therefore always inscribed within a politics of, or rather a political economy of, experience.

Although the German notion of "home" (*Heimat*), far from being a given term, is something to be achieved in the process of *Bildung*, it remains circumscribed within an economic point of view. To be able to talk about loss or gain also requires that something in the transaction remains unchanged, something in relation to which one can register a loss or a gain. What is in fact at stake is a certain property. In order to be able to have an economy of travel, some fixed point of reference must be posited. The economy of travel needs an *oikos* (the Greek for "home" from which is derived "economy") in relation to which any wandering can be comprehended (enclosed as well as understood). The positing of an *oikos*, or *domus* (the Latin translation of *oikos*) in domesticating the voyage by ascribing certain limits to it, abnegates the possibilities of non-return (either of or for the subject, i.e., either death or expenditure without profit) inherent in any act of travel.

Let us examine how the restricted economy of travel and displacement is at works in three immigrant autobiographies: Mukherjee's *Jasmine*, Rodriguez's *Hunger of Memory*, and Hoffman's *Lost in Translation*. But before any analysis, I need to contextualize the genre of immigrant autobiography and explore briefly the interrelationship between the concepts of home, identity, displacement and writing.

A major feature of postcolonial literatures is its concern with place and displacement. It is here that the special postcolonial crisis of identity manifests itself: the concern with the development or recovery of an effective identifying relationship between self and place. A valid and active sense of self may have been eroded by dislocation, resulting from migration, the experience of enslavement, exile, transportation, or "voluntary" removal for indentured labor. Or it may have been destroyed by cultural denigration, by conscious or unconscious oppression of the indigenous personality and culture by a supposedly superior racial or cultural model. The dialectic of place and displacement is always a feature of postcolonial societies whether they have been created by a process of settlement, intervention or an emancipation thereof. Beyond their historical and cultural differences, place and displacement and the related notions of home, at-homeness, as well as a pervasive concern with the myths of identity and authenticity are features common to all postcolonial literatures in English.

The discourse of displacement can be understood as the literary or cultural representations of the separation of people from their native culture either through physical dislocation (as refugees, immigrants, migrants, exiles, or expatriates) or the colonizing imposition of a foreign culture. This separation and dislocation is one of the most formative experiences of modernity. To take only one instance — the displacement of people as a result of Nazi policies and World War II — it is estimated that during the years of Hitler's rule over 30 million people were uprooted and forcibly moved, while the final redistribution of population in Europe alone after the end of the war resulted in the "permanent migration of another twenty-five million" (Kulisher 1948:305). All in all, World War II is estimated to have effected the greatest displacement of human population ever recorded in world history.

In the case of people who are not expelled from but displaced within their native culture by processes of external and internal colonization, no comparable counts or estimates exists. It is obvious that not all of the 23 million who lived under French imperial rule in Indochina, or the 340 million British imperial subjects from the Indian subcontinent can be said to have been displaced by colonial rule, even if one understands "displacement" in a metaphorical way. What is certain, however, is the effects of the totality of the colonial and imperialist policies on the lives of the indigenous people and the fact that these effects did not end with official decolonization. Among these policies were: the expropriation of land that often left indigenous people with a small, and mostly poorer, portion of their own land;[21] laws that controlled and regulated their physical movement; the economic shift that forced them into the centers of imperial employment thus creating new patters of migratory labor;[22] and the presence of a foreign ruling power that disappropriated local cultures.[23]

Displacements within the context of colonialism had also ramifications for our understanding of not only modernity but also modernism and postmodernism, the two main "periods" into which the cultural history of the twentieth century is typically divided. According to Fredric Jameson, modernism as it took shape in Western Europe between World War I and World War II is precisely predicated upon the structural displacement of significant parts of the Western world, which is "located elsewhere . . . in colonies over the water whose own life experience and life world . . . remain unknown and unimaginable for the subjects of the imperial power" (44). This simultaneously split and doubled existence — stretched across the multiple ruptures between "here" and "there" — constitutes the "new and historically original problem" of modernism: "the inability to grasp the way the system functions as a whole" (51). In our so-called postmodern time, one's identity is ineluctably, it seems, marked by a geography of identity: both here and there and neither here nor there at one and the same time. It is in this sense that marginality and otherness increasingly figure among the predominant signifiers of postmodern "identity." It appears that to "be" in the postmodern sense is somehow to be displaced, to be an Other. This, however, leads one to a theoretical difficulty: the relationship(s) between "displacement" as a theoretical signifier or a textual strategy, and a lived experience. Is "displacement" as a concept a metaphor for "displacement" as a lived historical experience? This is a major question, which, in a sense, summarizes the discrepancies between (certain trends in) the theories of the so-called postmodernism and postcolonialism. "Displacement" as a theoretical term is related to alterity, to become other than oneself, to be outside of one's "proper" place, to become Other. The subject is always already in displacement. In a postmodern theory of textuality, it is what makes meaning tremble. Meaning is always already deferred and differed (*différance*), never having a fixed and determinate identity. Displaced but not replaced, it remains a source of haunting; it keeps coming back (the return of the repressed). It cannot have a positive, determinate identity; it is a ghost. As a theoretical signifier, "displacement" carries resonances of both Freud and Derrida. For Freud, displacement (*Verschiebung*) was central to the operation of dream-work, the process by which uncomfortable thoughts and feelings ("latent dream-thoughts") are transferred to the safe remove of representational symbols ("manifest dream-content"). Displacement was thus, for Freud, similar to repression (*Verdrängung*): in both cases something was pushed aside. For Derrida, the interpretive (meaning-making) process is also a form of pushing aside, which, however, leaves the traces of this displacement within the text and is haunted by it.

But in certain trends of postcolonialism it is precisely the displaced subject who asks to be recognized as such, as a subject with a positive identity who has revolted against the colonial masters and is now trying to fashion an identity either through a recourse to the pre-colonial time or through characterizing him/herself as belonging to certain national, racial or ethnic formations. If as a theoretical term displacement is a critique of the metaphysics of presence, in historical experiences it is what results in a form of identity politics. Bensmaïa's text precisely tries to avoid constructing a positive identity for his character (his named being pronounced in different ways, he wants to get rid of his face, or passport?). It is in this context that Derrida begins his reflections on today's Europe with the question, "Is 'cultural identity' a good word for 'today'?" (Derrida 1992:13). He concludes by answering in the negative. For, as he maintains,

> Whether it takes a national form or not, a refined, hospitable or aggressively xenophobic form or not, the self-affirmation of an identity always claims to be responding to the call of the universal. There are no exceptions to this law. No cultural identity presents itself as the opaque body of an untranslatable idiom, but always, on the contrary, as the irreplaceable inscription of the universal in the singular. (72-73)

How should we understand this tension between these two incommensurable meanings of "displacement," where, on the one hand, it means a critique of the sovereignty of subjectivity and identity, a critique of the metaphysics of presence and, on the other hand, it constitutes a movement that ends in some form of determinate identity, whether cultural or political? For example, we could read a text like "The Ends of Man" against documents from the same period in which "Man" had a considerably different meaning.[24] I cannot claim to be able to resolve this incommensurability. All I can say is that the contradiction that this incommensurability brings about does not, however, need to be immobilizing. It can be construed as a symptom of what has always been the necessary dual strategy of an oppositional politics: negative systems critique and affirmative practical politics.

In this chapter, I will analyze the phenomenon of displacement in three immigrant autobiographies (fictional as well as non-fictional) in order to demonstrate the restricted economy of loss and gain at work in them. I will try to show that the stories of place and displacement as narrated by Richard Rodriguez, Eva Hoffman, and Bharati Mukherjee are characterized by a certain tendency to closure, a desire to build a home away from home, a re-fashioning of identity, and a settling down by creating an economic equilibrium between loss and gain. Let me explain what I mean by these and how I understand the relationships between (the economy of) writing and the desire to return or arrive in exilic and immigrant writings. I will try to show, in what follows, that many immigrant autobiographies are characterized by a tendency in which displacement and deterritorialization are overcome by a desire to settle down, reterritorialize and find a new home. This is the economy of loss and gain in immigrant autobiographies: the nostalgia for the past is balanced by a desire to capture the present; the loss of identity (through a process of displacement) is compensated by gaining a new one. Hoffman in "The New Nomad": "Is it then all pain and no gain? Of course not." In immigrant autobiographies, writing itself becomes a means par excellence for retrieving what is lost. The distancing from the past, combined with the sense of loss and yearning, can be a wonderful stimulus to writing. Joyce Carol Oates, in a striking formulation, has written that "for most novelists, the art of writing might be defined as the use to which we put our homesickness. So powerful is the instinct to memorialize in prose — one's region, one's family, one's past — that many writers, shorn of such subjects, would be rendered paralyzed and mute." In exile, the impulse to memorialize is magnified, and much glorious literature has emerged from it. *Native Realm* by Milosz or Nabokov's *Speak, Memory*, some of Brodsky's essays in *A Room and a Half* or even Kundera's much cooler take on transplantation in *The Book of Laughter and Forgetting*-these are works of lyrical commemoration informed by a tenderness for what is lost and by the need, even the obligation, to remember. For George Steiner reading and writing are closely related to the exilic condition.[25] He argues that writing (the book) enacts, as it were, the condition of exile. The Jewish diasporic consciousness is torn between, on the one hand, finding a home in writing and, on the other hand, finding a concrete, material "native ground."

> The tensions, the dialectical relations between an unhoused at-homeness in the text, between the dwelling-place of the script on the one hand (wherever in the world a Jew reads and meditates Torah *is* the true Israel), and the territorial mystery of the native ground, of the promised strip of land on the other, divide Jewish consciousness. (Steiner 1985:5)

In Diaspora, the Jew has carried, like a snail, the house of the text on his back. He is a "bookkeeper" or an "archivist of the revealed" (9) and precisely because of this custody, the accountant is accountable to God as is no other people. It is in the sense of assuming responsibility for the reading and writing of texts that the Jews are the chosen ones.[26] The Jew as an archivist of the word, finds his homeland and nationhood in his "prophetic and speculative addiction to insight" (20):

> How can a thinking man, a native of the word, be anything but the most wary and provisional of patriots? The nation-state is founded on myths of instauration and of militant glory. It perpetuates itself by lies and half-truths (machine guns and sub-machine guns). In his model of the social contract, Rousseau declared unequivocally that there is a contradiction between humanity and citizenship: "Forcé de combattre la nature ou les institutions socials, il faut opter entre faire un home ou un citoyen; car on ne peut pas faire à la fois l'un et l'autre." The consequence is stark: "a patriot is hard on strangers, for they are but men.[27] (20)

In *Minima Moralia*, Adorno is concerned with the same problem of homelessness[28] and the traumatic experience of it. For Adorno, the development of thought has reached a historical juncture at which one can claim that *Das Haus ist vergangen* — an enigmatic and hyperbolic claim that signifies "the house is gone," but also "the house is [in the] past" (Adorno 39); that is, the idea of the house, i.e., dwelling, is no longer viable. Under these circumstances Adorno declares, "it is part of morality not to be at home in one's own house" (*Es gehört zur Moral nicht bei sich selber zu Hause zu sein*).[29] For Adorno, homelessness becomes a moral imperative or a moral virtue (Israel 2000: 83).

In various places in *Minima Moralia*, Adorno seems to suggest that the act of writing itself provides a home, a kind of asylum, for the displaced subject. The following passage demonstrates Adorno's exploration of the "home-in-writing:"

> In his text, the writer sets up house. Just as he trundles papers, books, pencils, documents untidily from room to room, he creates the same disorder in his thoughts. They become pieces of furniture that he sinks into, content or irritable . . . for a man who no longer has a homeland, writing becomes a place to live. In it he inevitably produces, as his family once did, refuse and junk [Abfall und Bodenramsch]. But now he lacks a store-room, and...it is not easy to part with garbage [es ist . . . nicht leicht vom Abhub sich zu trennen]. She pushes it along in front of him, in danger finally of filling his pages with it. The demand that one harden oneself against self-pity [means that the writer must counter . . .] any slacking of intellectual tension with the utmost alertness, and eliminate anything that has begun to encrust the work. [This encrustation . . .] may at an earlier stage have served . . . to generate the warm atmosphere conducive to growth, but [it] is now left behind, flat and stale. In the end, the writer is not even allowed to live in his writing. (Adorno 2002:87)

Adorno thus tries to build a house out of writing, replete with intellectual furniture, but is evicted by the process of writing. The exilic writer is not allowed to live in his prose, because if exilic writing is indeed a place to live, it is a house suffering severe dilapidation; it is a house in ruin.

One of my goals is to try to show how most of immigrant or exilic literatures are characterized by a tendency toward what one might call a "homecoming." The displaced individual's desire to end a nomadic lifestyle (as well as a deterritorialized Self and its language) culminates in a will to write. There exists an analogy, which is more than a simple metaphor, between the traveling (whether immigrant or exilic) individual and the act of writing. Writing, as a "journey in words," is as much concerned, conventionally speaking, with arrival at a determinate meaning and a semantic closure as a traveler is with destination, arrival, or homecoming (return). The subject of travel departs from an alleged home only to return (or to find a home away from home). The writing of travel not only mimics this movement but is itself, more often than not, an attempt to semantically close what is in practice an open-ended experience. What constitutes an ethics of travel (including the different forms of voluntary or involuntary displacement) is also, by the same token, an ethics of writing: an ethics celebrating openness by resisting closure (any form of "semantic homecoming" or arrival at a determinate destination, whether geographical or semantic) and responding to the Other, the unknown, the outside. From the standpoint of a discourse on/of travel, this ethics marks a journey without return[30] (Byron as opposed to Goethe). I will come back to the ethics as well as politics of displacement in the concluding chapter.

Mukherjee's *Jasmine* and the *Aufhebung* of Memory

Jasmine tells the story of a young girl born in the village of Hasnapur, India, who undergoes enormous personal and cultural disruptions and revisions, changes which are not finished by the close of the action. A poor girl but a bright student, Jyoti is educated over the protests of her traditional father, and eventually marries a modern Indian husband, Prakash, whose dream becomes emigration to the U.S. to study and open an electronics business, a career which will include Jyoti, now re-named Jasmine by her husband. Already she has undergone major identity shifts, from feudal Hasnapur to urban Jullundhar, from her traditional cultural desire to have children early to Prakash's contempt for those desires: "We aren't going to spawn! We aren't ignorant peasants!" (77), and already she feels the tensions of trying to accommodate these changes: "Jyoti, Jasmine: I shuttled between identities," she says, and ." . . I felt suspended between worlds" (76-77).

Soon Prakash is killed, by a bomb meant for Jasmine and hidden in a portable radio by Sikh terrorists. Jasmine vows to complete Prakash's dream, to go to his intended school in Tampa, Florida and sacrifice herself on the campus. She manages to smuggle herself into America using false passport papers. There she is raped by her smuggler, after which she kills him and abandons her holy journey. She is befriended by an American woman, Lillian, who helps her learn to pass as an American woman and evade the INS and who calls her "Jazzy." She moves to New York, moves in with Prakash's old professor and becomes a live-in domestic, feeling desperately that she has moved back to Hasnapur. She gets a green card and an au pair position in Manhattan, which allows her to complete her Americanization by becoming an integral part of an American family and also by learning how to consume, which she does gleefully. However, her husband's killer appears in New York as well, and she flees to Iowa, where she marries Bud, a rural banker, becomes Jane Ripplemeyer, and adopts a Vietnamese refugee son, Du. The novel closes as Taylor, her now-divorced former employer in Manhattan, asks her to come with him and his daughter to California, where Du has already gone. Pregnant from her time with Bud, she leaves him anyway to be with Taylor in California. Such are the bare bones of the narrative, but its unifying theme is Jyoti/Jasmine/Jane's mutability, her adaptation to circumstances, expressed as a change from passive, traditional object of fate to active, modern, cross-cultural shaper of her future.

From the beginning, Jyoti rebels against her cultural inscriptions. A seer foretells her future, pronouncing "my widowhood and exile . . . I was nothing, a speck in the solar system . . . I was helpless, doomed" (3-4). In response she whispers "I don't believe you," and, claiming that a wound on her forehead is her "third eye" she proclaims herself a "sage," rewriting her position from passive object to empowered seer. Mukherjee establishes this mortal stasis as a component of the past, and it becomes Jasmine's goal to move away from the past at all costs, including the cost of self-knowledge, a stable identity. Mukherjee is plainly disinterested in the preservation of cultures, the hallowing of tradition, obligations to the past; at least, she is not interested in the nostalgic aspects of such preservation. Rather, her current work forwards a distinction between "pioneers" and pitiable others for whom attachments to personal and cultural pasts foreclose possibilities. These pioneering characters undergo personal changes in their movements from culture to culture, changes that Mukherjee characterizes in the strongest terms.

In many places throughout the text, Jasmine refers to herself, and her past selves, as ghosts, phantoms, or to herself as an astronaut, moving between worlds, never solidly attached to any. Often, she adopts the trope of reincarnation, describing her various identities as separate lives, lives which must be sealed off from each other: "For me, experience must be forgotten, or else it will kill" (33). She disdains her father's obsession with the vanished past, a past in which he was a wealthy farmer, before the Partition Riots. The family was violently dispossessed of their property, but her father has never been able to accept his new status, preferring to imagine himself as he was. Jasmine says of him, "He'll never see Lahore again and I never have. Only a fool would let it rule his life" (43). In the end she is seen to continue this protean narrative, never sure what the future will bring, but always knowing that it is preferable to the past: "Time will tell if I am a tornado, rubble-maker, arising from nowhere and disappearing into a cloud. I am out the door and in the potholed and rutted driveway, ... greedy with wants and reckless from hope" (241).

Mukherjee is so far from veneration of tradition that her works accept, and indeed, embrace, the violence that accompanies cross-cultural revision and personal change. Jasmine says: "There are no harmless, compassionate ways to remake ourselves. We murder who we were so we can rebirth ourselves in the image of dreams" (25). It is the willingness of Jasmine to murder her past self that enables her to actively advance into unknown but promising futures. The futures she propel herself toward, and even help to shape, are not guaranteed to be successful, but do have the potential for personal, material and spiritual success.

Jasmine has uprooted herself from her original culture and is now trying to reterritorialize in a new culture. She is now characterized by contradictory desires: on the one hand she would like her readers to believe that she is in a state of constant change and moving from one identity to another,[31] on the other hand, she is getting rooted in the new culture. Consider the following passage:

> Taylor, Wylie, and Duff were family. America may be fluid and built on flimsy, invisible lines of weak gravity, but I was a dense object, I had landed and was getting rooted. I had controlled my spending and now sat on an account that was rapidly growing. (179)

This can be, in spite of all the differences between Moll and Jasmine, a typical passage from Defoe's *Moll Flanders*: multiplicity of character, reinvention of self, measuring the world in terms of capital accumulation,[32] etc. What one sees here is the desire to settle down and find a home away from home. After going through a whole process of deracination and displacement, Jasmine wishes to settle down, a desire apparently not in contradiction with her constant shedding of skin and perpetual transformation. It is important to note, however, that Jasmine's self-determination is inflected with some of the same cultural narratives that she attempts to re-direct. Her present is a tense, contingent result of continual negotiations between her past and her future; her future self can never entirely escape her past inscriptions.

Two versions of history and narration emerge in *Jasmine*. For Jasmine, history is the discontinuity and rupture produced by material and political events and, as a result, the self becomes plural and contradictory. Her survival depends upon a flexible strategy of appropriation and transformation. For Bud, history is a straight line, a teleological and progressive ordering of existence where the phenomenological world is transparent and the self is unified and autonomous. These two versions of history require two distinct types of relations that the displaced subject establishes. Bud's "continuous history" is fundamentally different from Jasmine's "discontinuous" one. It is Jasmine's notion of discontinuous history that allows her to overcome the inhibiting structure of memory in her attempt at re-inventing herself. Memory, in a continuous understanding of history, constitutes the subject and tends toward totalization. In a discontinuous history, memory is not rejected but tamed, sublated. It is deprived of its power to determine identity and is instead put to use instrumentally as well as strategically. In her self-fashioning, Jasmine does not erase or discard the past, but subject it to a process of sublation: a simultaneous negation and preservation of the past. The past is negated in terms of its power of restriction and paralysis but preserved as a means of re-fashioning identity within the framework of an instrumental rationality. This sublated memory remains within an economy of loss and gain: memory is kept half-alive to produce profit in forming new identities.

The apparent absence of any sign of mourning, nostalgia, or melancholy in *Jasmine* is quite remarkable. Initially Jasmine cries on a book of photographs of migrant workers, something which is rather impersonal and is related to her only by association. She then quickly gathers herself together and concludes that she will not cry over Hasnapur ever again. "I remembered Kate's book of photographs of migrant workers that Lilian, the proud mother, had shown off to me back in Fowlers Key. That book had brought back such sharp memories of Hasnapur that I'd cried. It was now only a few months later, but I didn't think I could cry over Hasnapur, ever again" (160). There is a temporal ambiguity in this passage: it is not clear whether she promises herself not to mourn again as if mourning is an intentional act, or she is surprised by the event of mourning in which the subject is taken over by the intensity of memory.

As many people know, from their own personal experience or not, the process of deracination and uprooting is quite painful and is associated with a certain type of violence that leaves its traumatic traces on the subject. Freud in his "Mourning and Melancholia" argues for the fact that people "never willingly abandon a libidinal position" (244), even though the "reality-testing has shown that the loved object no longer exists, and it proceeds to demand that all libido shall be withdrawn from its attachments to that object" (244). The demand of reality to withdraw all libido usually arouses opposition in the subject. This opposition can be so intense that "a turning away from reality takes place and a clinging to the object through the medium of a hallucinatory wishful psychosis" (244). In Jasmine the libidinal cathexis is of a particular type and, I should add, a counter-intuitive one. Mourning and the intensification of memory is usually regarded, at least by Freud, as an event (with all the implications of surprise and unpredictability) rather than something that the subject has control upon or can manipulate at will. In other words, it appears as if, in *Jasmine*, we witness an absence of mourning when we expect one. The absence of mourning in *Jasmine*, however, might be explained in different ways. One "common sense" explanation would assume a "smooth" transition in the process of immigrating from one culture to another. One can simply relinquish one culture and embrace another as easily as one changes a piece of clothes for another: you barely mourn the loss of a shirt! Another explanation would assume that there is no need for mourning simply because nothing has been lost, or at least this is the way that the subject of immigration perceives the situation. Jasmine's narrative is structured in such a way that almost every other chapter is referring to the past and in a way very different from, for example, Eva Hoffman's. The past is constantly present in the text but without affect, without any capacity to invoke emotions. The narrated past is filled with memory, but a memory devoid of any capacity to invoke mourning. There is memory, but a castrated, domesticated one, an *aufgehoben* memory. Jasmine, therefore, seems to be able to subject her memory to an instrumental use and apply them as raw material in constructing new identities. In *Jasmine*, the eventful primacy of memory in a process of mourning over the loss of the object of desire (family bonds, friends, "natural" environments, etc.) is replaced by a calculated as well as calculating memory, always at the service of the subject as a repertoire to draw upon in an odyssey of identity formation (or rather moving from one to another).[33] Jasmine therefore implicitly says: "I *have* memory" rather than saying: "I am in the grip of memory." This sublated memory becomes capital in the hands of Jasmine, a capital that can be used in the process of constructing identities. In other words, in *Jasmine*, there is memory as standing-reserve rather than memory as event, which is more hauntological rather than ontological. Adorno describes this distinction in his short note on Jean Paul in *Minima Moralia*:

> The pronouncements, probably by Jean Paul, that memories are the only possessions which no-one can take from us, belongs in the storehouse of impotently sentimental consolations that the subject, resignedly withdrawing into inwardness, would like to believe the very fulfillment that he has given up. In setting up his own archives, the subject seizes his own stock of experience as property, so making it something wholly external to himself. Past inner life is turned into fur-

niture just as, conversely, every Biedermeier piece was memory made wood. The interior where the soul accommodates its collection of memoirs and curios is derelict. Memories cannot be conserved in drawers and pigeon-holes; in them the past is indissolubly woven into the present. No-one has them at his disposal in the free and voluntary way that is praised in Jean Paul's fulsome sentences. Precisely where they become controllable and objectifies, where the subject believes himself entirely sure of them, memories fade like delicate wallpapers in bright sunlight. (Adorno 2002:166)

I propose that Abraham and Torok's distinction between incorporation and introjection in the process of mourning can be used to shed light on Jasmine's instrumental rationality in capitalizing on her memory. Let me explain as well as support myself by invoking Derrida on Abraham and Torok.

Introjection, in an act of mourning the loss of an object of desire, is a process by which, according to Ferenczi, "autoerotic cathexes are extended" (Derrida 1986a:xvi). This means that through this process the object is included in the Self and contributes to the expansion of the latter. Contrary to the cases of melancholy (or Kristeva's discussion of depression) the Self, during the process of introjection, does not retreat but enlarges itself: the Self "advances, propagates itself, assimilates, takes over" (xvi). In fact the Self is usually believed to be nothing but a set of introjections, memories of lost objects assimilated. My first hypothesis, therefore, would be that this is what Jasmine wants her readers to believe, that she is undergoing a process of normal mourning or introjection, a process by which she assimilates the dead as a living part of her. Mukherjee's portrayal of Jasmine presents the latter as a "normal" individual undergoing "normal" mourning. But her readers know that introjection, although possible, is very improbable. They also know that introjection and incorporation do not form a binary opposition; one is always already contaminated by the other. One, therefore, has to move to another hypothesis: that there is no introjection but incorporation in Jasmine (or rather that the introjection is contaminated by incorporation). She has incorporated her earlier Self (a beaten and raped self) within her in a secret interior, but, by the same token, outside it, external to the interior.

The constant presence of the figure of death is an indication that there is incorporation rather than introjection in *Jasmine*. Jasmine feels the need to kill her former selves simply because they cannot be assimilated or used to contribute to the development or enlargement of the subject. If there was a complete mourning, i.e., loving the dead as a living part of her, there would have been no need to kill the former selves. If the figure of death somehow dominates Jasmine's narrative, it is because we have to do with a refusal of mourning, a process of incorporation through which Jasmine's earlier memories or identities form a cryptic enclave.[34] This cryptic enclave, which contains images of an earlier dehumanized Self, remains a foreign body preserved as foreign but, at the same time, excluded from the Self: "what the crypt commemorates, as the incorporated object's 'monument' or 'tomb,' is not the object itself, but its exclusion, the exclusion of a specific desire from the introjection itself" (xvii). In short, what we have in *Jasmine* is the portrayal of a character who is trying to convince her readers that she has overcome the past by assimilating it, somehow harmoniously, into her present Self. What is, however, left unsaid is that the present Self is being in fact haunted by the past it wishes to tame.

The incorporated object is the result of a process of *Aufhebung*: it must be both killed and kept safe. Incorporation into the Self becomes, as it were, an economic answer to the loss of the object: the memory is objectified and turned into a commodity by which a Cartesian subject like Jasmine can enter into transactions with the world around her. What is also important to notice, assuming that there is no introjection but incorporation, is the implicit and naïve claim in *Jasmine* that even though the subject undergoes a traumatic experience of the loss of her object of desire, an experience that disrupts the supposed coherency of the individual, she, somehow magically, can transform all these to something more positive: Jasmine, being in control of what puts her outside herself, is the epitome of an ideal capitalist, a pragmatically-oriented individual and an American heroine who faces the frontier (240) and who can fashion and refashion herself quite voluntarily. Incorporation in Jasmine is not outside the economy of self-fashioning: not only a capitalization on memory but also a positing of Jasmine as a subject in control and as an agent of the reinvention of the Self. In her dialectical economy of the invention of the Self, she makes sure that nothing remains (nothing is "wasted") in the sublation of the past.

If in *Jasmine* we witness an absence or a refusal of mourning, it can also be seen as an indication that in fact nothing has been lost. The act of writing (an autobiography) is itself a negation of loss or at least a promise of the recovery of what has been lost: "Signs are arbitrary because language starts with a negation (*Verneinung*) of loss, along with the depression occasioned by mourning. "I have lost an essential object that happens to be, in the final analysis, my mother," is what the speaking being seems to be saying. "But no, I have found her again in signs, or rather since I consent to lose her I have not lost her (that is the negation), I can recover her in language" (Kristeva 1989:43). What has been lost can be recaptured by the imagination. The writer "comes home" in the writing itself, transforming rupture into connection. By weaving "here" and "there" together in the space of the imagination, the writer uses language (and fiction) to resolve the terrors of displacement and anomie: a historical loss is compensated by an aesthetic gain. Before discussing the texts of Rodriquez and Hoffman I would like to say a few words on some of the general theoretical difficulties of immigrant autobiographies.

A comparison of texts by writers of different ethnic/racial background raises certain methodological questions. After a brief overview of the current debates over methodological concerns regarding critical writing about "ethnic" literature, I will compare and contrast the autobiographies of Eva Hoffman, a Jewish Polish immigrant to the United States, and of Richard Rodriguez, a Mexican-American. In doing so, I will not neglect the differences between the respective diasporic locations of the two writers. Other autobiographies by so-called visible minority writers born in the United Stated lend themselves to comparison with Rodriguez's *Hunger of Memory: The Education of Richard Rodriguez*. Maxine Hong Kinston's *The Woman Warrior: Memoirs of a Girlhood among Ghosts* and Zora Neale Hurston's *Dust Tracks on a Road*, like Rodriguez's autobiography, have been criticized for misrepresentation by members of their "own ethnic" groups. The similarities and differences between these autobiographies are instructive, and a comparison of the two can provide significant insight into the intricacies involved in comparing two texts that deal with problems of assimilation and that share a number of narrative strategies, even though their authors and the autobiographical selves represented in the texts belong to different "ethnic" groups.

The main question one needs to consider when comparing the texts of writers with different "ethnic" backgrounds is how one can read these texts as sharing ways of conceptualizing the pull of two or more cultural loyalties without losing sight of the fact that their "ethnic" communities have experienced different degrees of dislocation, colonization, and racism. Two approaches to ethnic literature have been prevalent in recent American criticism: the cultural pluralist approach, which claims that each ethnic group's experience within mainstream American society is different and that this difference is reflected in their texts, and the approach that assumes that all ethnic writing shares a collective experience. Proponents of the latter have been criticized for "relegating 'race' to a mere feature of some ethnic groups" (Wald 1987:22) and for disregarding the fact that European Americans are usually no longer exposed to racism.

The endeavor to look for similarities while discounting differences also obscures the distinction between first and second generation as is obvious, for example, in William Boelhower's *Immigrant Autobiography in the United States: Four Versions of the Italian American Self*. Boelhower attempts to prove that all immigrant American autobiographies deal with the protagonist's "transformation" or Americanization. As he sees it, the immigrant anticipates America as a country of hope and renewal, a fact that is reflected in the biblical language with which America is usually described in these autobiographies. Claiming general validity for this model, Boelhower maintains that the range of cultural strategies exemplified in the four Italian-American texts that he discusses could just as easily be illustrated by the texts of any other ethnic group. By testing Boelhower's typology with Chinese-American and other Asian American immigrant autobiographies, however, Sau-ling Cynthia Wong has found that many of these autobiographies deviate from the pattern Boelhower suggests in that they display "a pragmatic, matter-of-fact attitude towards the idea of going to America on the part of Chinese immigrant autobiographers" (Wong 1991:155). She concludes that while his typology may apply to European immigrant experience, it does not apply to that of non-European groups.

Like William Boelhower, Werner Sollors assumes that all ethnic groups share a collective experience. He claims that to understand American literature as "a poly-ethnic literature, it is essential to use comparative methods. Comparing Afro-American, Jewish-American, and Irish-American novels of the 1930s thus becomes as essential as comparing writings by immigrants and writings by their descendants" (Sollors 1984: 96). In *Beyond Ethnicity*, Sollors explores the similarities between "black" and Jewish writing. He points out that Charles W. Chesnutt's "The Wife of His Youth" and Abraham Cahan's *Yekl: A Tale of the Ghetto* resort to the same symbolism to depict the tension between the hereditary and the contractual (156), while James Weldon Johnson's *Autobiography of an Ex-Colored Man* and Abraham Cahan's *The Rise of David Levinsky* use similar literary strategies in doing so (168). Interestingly enough, Sollors foregrounds Jewishness in this latter comparison rather than Cahan's Lithuanian and Levinsky's Polish descent. By doing so, he fails to do justice to the complexity of "descent" and the relevance of potentially conflicting "loyalties."

Although I agree with Werner Sollors that criticism of "ethnic" writing requires comparative methods, it needs to be more observant of cultural differences. Mary E. Young, for example, in *Mules and Dragons: Popular Culture Images in the Selected Writings of African-American and Chinese-American Women Writers*, bases her comparison of these two groups of writers not only on their histories, "but also [on] each group's response to the stereotyped images that have become part of American cultural history" (ix). Thus Young claims that Native American women, Hispanic women, and Jewish women have also been stereotyped, but that none of these stereotypes has been as persistent as the stereotypes of African American and Chinese-American women. Likewise, Inderpal Grewal, in her comparison of Sara Suleri's *Meatless Days* and Gloria Anzaldua's *Borderlands/La Frontera*, observes that although both texts "share a concern with the breakdown of ethnocentric dualities, which they both see as sources of oppression" (251), the different diasporic locations of the two writers make it "impossible to analyze Anzaldua's 'borderland' through theories of Asian diasporas" (248). Finally, Shirley Lim in her study of the difference between Anglo American and Asian American poetry also takes an "ethnocentered" approach. She justifies her focus on stylistic and textual features that differentiate Asian American from Anglo American poetry by arguing that an emphasis on the differences is necessary to "correct" (51) "the inherent bias of the Anglo-American mainstream" (51). In her opinion, ethnopoetics asks for "an informed socio-cultural approach which counteracts the privileging of the dominant culture" (59).

Following Shirley Lim's call for an "informed socio-cultural approach," I suggest combining the methodologies of the two theoretical camps and to consider several questions before setting out to compare and contrast "ethnic" texts. First of all, do the authors of these texts have any antecedents in their "own ethnic' group, and do they choose to acknowledge them? Eva Hoffman, for example, can look back to a long tradition of Polish-American autobiography, Jewish and non-Jewish, as Magdalena Zaborowska has shown, and she does refer to some of these texts. Since intertextuality plays an important role in most "ethnic" writing, it would be worth asking if a text by a writer from one "ethnic" group serves as a model for a writer with a different "ethnic" background, as Richard Wright's *Black Boy* provided a model for Carlos Bulosan's *America Is in the Heart.* If a minority writer chooses to rework the text of a writer who belongs to a different minority, he or she, in doing so, might want to draw attention to the fact that the discrimination to which both groups are subjected is comparable. Consideration of whether the ethnic groups to which the two writers belong share a common experience of racism or a similar experience of discrimination and stereotyping is therefore important. If minority writers, on the other hand, write back to a text of the canon, they usually intend to "rupture" and destabilize this text to uncover its underlying ideologies.

Over the last few years, interest in literary predecessors has justifiably fallen into disfavor for being Eurocentric and essentialist. The discussion of predecessors, however, is not reductive as long as it is not preoccupied with verifying sources and influences rather than being concerned with exploring intertextual dynamics and diasporic locations. For, as Shirley Lim points out, "the differences in cultural contexts create significant differences between readers' expectations and authors' intentions, between the untrained readers' conventional, culture-bound responses and the trained readers' ethno-sensitive interpretations" (56). Therefore, if two texts such as Abraham Cahan's and James Weldon Johnson's exhibit "striking similarities," as Werner Sollors puts it, one needs to ask whether these two texts can be read as representative of their "ethnic" groups. This question leads to what is probably the most important question: Who is the intended audience, and how have the texts been received both by readers of the same "ethnic group" and by readers of the mainstream? As Gayatri Spivak has pointed out in a discussion of multiculturalism with Sneja Gunew, "the question 'Who should speak?' is less crucial than 'Who will listen?'" (194). Both critics agree that when a writer from the margin confronts the dominant culture, this audience will affect the construction of that writer's identity by virtue of the choices it makes in reading the writer's work.

Hoffman and Rodriguez: A Desire to Gain

Eva Hoffman's *Lost in Translation: A Life in a New Language* (1990) relates the experience of a Jewish Polish girl emigrating first to Canada with her parents and younger sister and eventually to the United States. The chapters that are concerned with her happy pre-adolescent and adolescent life in Cracow, her unhappy life in Vancouver (for the young Hoffman the word "Canada" had "ominous echoes of the 'Sahara'" (4)) and her Americanization, that is, assimilation into middle-class America through institutional education. Hoffman interrupts biographical chapters with essayistic meditations on the difficulty of living "between" two languages and her struggle to achieve fluency in English.

Although the three chapter headings, "Paradise," "Exile," and "The New World," seem to suggest that Hoffman is inverting the conventional immigrant model in which the "Old World" figures as a place of hardship or even persecution, and the "New World" is anticipated in utopian terms, a close reading of the text shows that the place where Hoffman finds her true fulfillment is New York and not Cracow. Cracow appears as a paradise only in comparison with her "exile" in Canada/Vancouver, not with her life in the United States. Cracow stands for all that Canada/Vancouver is not: her childhood. Cracow offered stability because of its long history, it was a place in which "the signifier" was not "severed from the signified" (106), and in which the self was one with its surroundings. Paradoxically, in Hoffman's retrospective description, the aura of Cracow is not significantly tainted by Polish anti-Semitism and the fact that her grandparents were victims of the Holocaust, a fate which her parents only narrowly escaped.

In Vancouver, the place of "exile," the adolescent autobiographer undergoes an unsettling Anglicization of her name, an experience described in many immigrant novels and autobiographies. Her family also moves considerably down the social scale, and her parents have even greater difficulty adjusting to the new life than their daughters. Their feelings of disorientation and displacement anticipate what has become another commonplace in immigrant literature, the role reversal in the parent-child relationship. The teenaged Eva explains: "I'm a little ashamed to reveal how hard things are for my family, how bitterly my parents quarrel, how much my mother cries, how frightened I am by our helplessness, and by the burden of feeling that it is my duty to take charge, to get us out of this quagmire" (112). Richard Rodriguez describes a similar role reversal in his own family once he and his siblings achieve fluency in the dominant language while their parents communicate in heavily accented and not always grammatically correct English.

The chapter entitled "Exile" concludes with a reference to Mary Antin's autobiography, *The Promised Land*. Hoffman points out that in certain details Antin's story so closely resembles her own that "its author seems to be some amusing poltergeist" (162). The parallels between the two writers' lives are uncanny indeed. *The Promised Land* is usually read as a narrative of success, a story of a model assimilation. Antin was born into a Jewish family in Polotzk, a town within the Russian Pale. Faced with czarist anti-Semitism, the Antins decided to emigrate to the United States, settling in Boston when Mary was thirteen—Hoffman's age when her family emigrated. Hoffman claims that the similarities between Antin's biography and her own end when it comes to the interpretation of their respective lives, especially Antin's reading of her new life as an untarnished success story: "For, despite the hardships that leap out from the pages, Mary insists on seeing her life as a fable of pure success: success for herself, for the idea of assimilation, for the great American experiment" (163).

However, contrary to what Hoffman seems to suggest, Mary Antin is quite aware of these hardships, of her older sister's less privileged life, and of the "sad process of disintegration of home life" (271). Furthermore, the similarities between Hoffman's text and her predecessor's are less tenuous than Hoffman is willing to admit. Like Antin, Hoffman gives credit to the American education system as the main assimilating force and she praises American education just as enthusiastically as does Antin: "For one thing, I've learned that in a democratic educational system, in a democratic ideology of reading, I am never made to feel that I'm an outsider poaching on others' property. In this country of learning,

I'm welcomed on equal terms, and it's through the democratizing power of literature that I begin to feel at home in America" (183-84). Thus for Hoffman, the PhD in English Literature, which she received from Harvard, becomes the "certificate of full Americanization" (226).

This ode to education is also reminiscent of the glorification of American education by eighteenth-century male American autobiographers like Benjamin Franklin. And like Franklin, "whose name [she has] never heard" (137), the teenaged Hoffman devises programs of "physical, intellectual, spiritual and creative" (137) self-improvement. Franklin's description of his achievements, raising himself "from the poverty and obscurity in which [he] was born . . . to a state of affluence and some degree of reputation in the world" (3), anticipates Hoffman's account of her own success. In both texts, conversion, the objective of spiritual autobiography, is translated into wealth and social prestige. Hoffman fails to acknowledge the inadequacy of an eighteenth-century male vision, which, among other things, assumes the absence of racial and sexual prejudice and discrimination in a classless society in the contemporary context. On the contrary, she discounts issues of race, class, and gender in her own description of school and university. Being also relatively unconcerned with her Jewishness, as I have mentioned before, she blames her struggles for Americanization on the fact that English was not her first language, discounting the possibility that her Jewish-Polish descent might have been an obstacle.

While similar life stories have been told by other European immigrants to the United States, especially Eastern European immigrants, the innovative technique of Hoffman's autobiography is its investigation of the role of language in the process of assimilation. It describes the tension between the "ethnic" language, which for Hoffman remains the language of privacy and intimacy, and the "New World" public language which Eva "learns from the top" (217) and which will ultimately separate her from Cracow and estrange her from her parents. Hoffman's privileging of the "public" over the "private," her refusal to reflect on the androcentric tradition of autobiography, her adoption of the male model of self-representation, and her endorsement of the American story of successful assimilation. The extent to which Hoffman values public over private is apparent in her comparison of her own position with that of her mother's. By claiming in a rather patronizing manner that her mother lacks the skill to address the public in English and therefore has no autobiographical self, Hoffman marginalizes and silences her. She also firmly believes in keeping separate the private and the public self: "I've developed a certain kind of worldly knowledge, and a public self to go with it. That self is the most American thing about me; after all, I acquired it here" (251).

This statement uncannily echoes Richard Rodriguez's Prologue to his autobiography where he claims, "my book is necessarily political . . . For public issues . . . have bisected my life and changed its course. And, in some broad sense, my writing is political because it concerns my movement away from the company of family and into the city. This was my coming of age: I became a man by becoming a public man" (7). Both authors imply that the only identity worth having is a "public" identity, steeped in middle-class "public" discourse. Why would the identity of an immigrant woman in Vancouver and the identity of a Mexican worker be less authentic, "public," or political than that of an urban writer? And how can Polish, and particularly Spanish, be conceived as languages that are less "public" than English in North America?

Like Hoffman, Rodriguez argues that literacy in the dominant language has social transformational power. Thus, he does not blame his Mexican descent for his struggle as a boy to fit into mainstream society, but his parents' lack of education and the fact that they spoke Spanish at home. In the Prologue, entitled "Middle-class Pastoral," Rodriguez assumes a representative voice by claiming that his experience is a typically American one: "This is what matters to me: the story of the scholarship boy who returns home one summer from college to discover bewildering silence, facing his parents. This is my story. An American story" (5). Rodriguez describes the scholarship boy, a term he borrows from Richard Hoggart, as a student who imitates his teachers in an attempt to become like them, tries as hard as he can to lose his accent, distances himself as much as possible from his ethnic heritage, and is not able to form an original thought.

By this definition, the scholarship boy seems to be a close relative of the "mimic man." For Frantz Fanon, mimicry is the result of colonial indoctrination through which the Caribbeans have been coerced into seeking cultural identity through the imitation of Western models. Derek Walcott considers the politics of imitation and the dilemma of the mimic man as endemic to all of America, not just the Caribbean: "The Old World, whether it is represented by the light of Europe or of Asia or of Africa, is the rhythm by which we remember" (7). Indeed, "melting pot" ideology is based on the idea of repetition and imitation, and as Robert F. Sayre has shown, the instinct of emulation, "which is imitation and something more" (154), has been identified as the main impulse in the making of self as described in many American autobiographies. Public figures like Benjamin Franklin, in addition to imitating classical and European models, also see their mission as providing role models through their autobiographies, "looking to the West and other directions to the new American who will one day imitate [them]" (Sayre 1980:167). For consent-oriented immigrants from Eastern Europe and members of so-called visible minorities, American models of identity seem to be equally alluring. The attempts of Eva Hoffman's autobiographic self to lose her accent and join the mainstream by imitating role models are just as desperate as those described by Rodriguez. The dialectics of loss and gain is here at work again

What seems to legitimate a comparison between Rodriguez's and Hoffman's texts is that in many ways the former asks to be read as immigrant autobiography. As William Boelhower points out, "immigrant autobiography is a schooling text, describing the transformation of the protagonist from an alien to a sovereign American self" (Boelhower 1990:303). Although Rodriguez, unlike European immigrants, is not able to relive the journey on the Mayflower, his move out of the family enclave, like Zora Neale Hurston's out of the black community of Eatonville, has a symbolic function similar to the trans-Atlantic voyage. What usually separates immigrant experience from that of the second generation is the fact that the American born do not have direct memories of the "Old World"; their understanding of the "Old-World" culture is mediated by their parents. Chicanas/Chicanos of the Southwest, however, live so close to the Mexican border, and Hispanic culture pervades American culture to such a degree, that it could be argued that Mexican-Americans' access to the "Old World" is at once synchronic and diachronic. On the other hand, it is important to keep in mind that Mexican-Americans are mestizas and mestizos, victims of various colonization processes.

The parts of Rodriguez's text discussing his life could easily be divided into the three sections that Eva Hoffman uses to describe her own assimilation. Although the paradise of Rodriguez's childhood was not in rural Mexico, but in a house on Thirty-ninth Street in 1950s Sacramento, Spanish, the language of family and intimacy, isolated him from the world. His fluency in English, the language of the classroom, finally made it possible for him, so he claims, to integrate fully into mainstream American society at the cost of estrangement from his parents and the loss of fluency in Spanish. He points out that what he needed to learn in school was that he had the right to speak the public language of the "gringos." His childhood "exile" then, similar to that of Hoffman, was created by his feelings of inferiority and alienation from the mainstream because of the lack of language fluency.

The comparability of Rodriguez's autobiography to immigrant autobiography is also partly indicated by his ambiguous discourse on race, his disavowal of Chicano heritage, and his refusal to engage in, and more importantly, to politicize ancestral memory. While Hoffman identifies to a certain extent with the autobiographical experiences of Antin, Nabokov, Kazin, and Podhoretz, all fellow Eastern European immigrants to the United States, Rodriguez does not acknowledge any of his predecessors in the long and rich tradition of Mexican American autobiography. By doing so he gives the impression that he sees himself as separated from the Mexican-American community and its political struggles, outside socio-historical reality and colonial history. At the beginning of his autobiography, Rodriguez claims: "Aztec ruins hold no special interest for me. I do not search Mexican graveyards for ties to unnamable ancestors" (5). Working on his PhD in English Renaissance literature, Rodriguez, when asked by "a group of . . . Hispanic students [who] wanted [him] to teach a 'minority literature' course" (161), replies that he "didn't think that there was such a thing as minority literature" (161). He confesses that after this encounter he "became a "coconut" someone brown on the outside, white on the inside . . . some comic Quequeg, holding close to [his] breast a reliquary containing the white powder of a dead European civilization" (162). He eventually refuses to accept a job offer from Yale because he suspects that his race had given him an advantage over other applicants. This conclusion has led him to become a fervent opponent of bilingual education and of affirmative action.

Paradoxically, in his autobiography, Rodriguez is very concerned with a skin color that reveals his "Indian" descent and describes himself as the least European looking in his family: "I am the only one in the family whose face is severely cut to the line of ancient Indian ancestors" (115). In "Complexion," he discusses the prejudice against dark skin within Mexican culture. He explains, for example, that some Mexican women risk abortion by taking "large doses of castor oil during the last weeks of pregnancy" (116) to lighten their unborn children's skin color and how "children born dark grew up to have their faces treated regularly with a mixture of egg white and lemon juice concentrate" (116), yet he discounts his experience of racism. Admitting that "in public [he] occasionally heard racial slurs," he minimizes their significance by pointing out that "in all, there could not have been more than a dozen incidents of name-calling" and by concluding that because of the paucity of racist evidence, he "was not a primary victim of racial abuse" (117). Consequently, he claims that he "didn't really consider [his] dark skin to be a racial characteristic" (125), but that he felt his "dark skin made [him] unattractive to women" (125) since the women in his family were so worried about giving birth to "dark-skinned" children. Rodriguez suggests that the panacea for his dilemma and that of fellow Mexican-Americans is monolingual education.

Apparently unaware of the interest postcolonial critics have taken in the figure of Caliban to demonstrate the complexities of relationships between colonizer and colonized, Rodriguez opens his book with the words: "I have taken Caliban's advice. I have stolen their books. I will have some run of this isle" and "in Beverly Hills will this monster make a man" (3). Although he seems to be alluding to Caliban's subversive potential with these words, Rodriguez puts his education to the service of the status quo. Like Hoffman, who, as mentioned above, refers to her Ph.D. as the "certificate of full Americanization," Rodriguez argues that education dismantles social and therefore "racial" and "ethnic" boundaries. For a consideration of Rodriguez's diasporic position, it is significant that he fails to problematize and, more important, to politicize his sacrifice, that is, his decision not to complete his Ph.D. and to turn his back on the academic world although he was a promising scholar and enjoyed teaching.

However, the important difference between Hoffman's and Rodriguez's diasporic locations comes to light when one considers how their texts are being read and by whom. As far as I know, no one has criticized Hoffman (or even Mukherjee) for discounting her Polish and her Jewish selves in favor of her public American self in the way Rodriguez has been attacked for selling out to "white America." Neither does she feel the need to define her audience in her text. Rodriguez, on the other hand, considers it important to draw attention to the fact that his reader is European American, well-educated, male, and "white": "All that I know about him is that he has had a long education and that his society, like mine, is often public (un gringo)" (182). Despite their similar educational backgrounds and academic and professional achievements, Hoffman will hardly ever find herself in a position where she is addressed by the mainstream as a member of a minority, while Rodriguez will always be constructed as insider informant of a culture that "grates against" (3) that of the United States, to use Gloria Anzaldua's words.

Hoffman's and Rodriguez's autobiographic selves, on the other hand, by making mainstream culture the center of their perception, view reality in terms of dichotomies: failure versus success, gain versus loss, chaos versus order, private versus public, family versus city, past versus future, insider versus outsider, communal versus individualistic, Old World versus New World, loyalty versus betrayal, masculine versus feminine, macho versus effeminate, and language of the past versus language of the present. They essentialize "English" as a monolithic structure that opens the door to privilege once the novice has "made some run of" it. Since Hoffman and Rodriguez believe in the separation of the private and the public, there is no discussion of homosexuality within the Mexican-American community (in other contexts Rodriguez identifies himself as a gay man). There is also no discussion of failed marriages between immigrant and non-immigrant Americans. (Hoffman only briefly mentions her divorce from her American-born husband). Neither of the autobiographical selves think that it is possible "to go home again," neither personally nor culturally speaking. Interestingly enough, both Hoffman and Rodriguez do go "home" physically in their subsequent autobiographical ethnographies *Exit into History: A Journey through the New Eastern Europe* (1993) and *Days of Obligation: An Argument with My Mexican Father* (1992), in which they assume the position of the American confronting the Eastern European and the Mexican Other respectively. By creating this alterity, Hoffman and Rodriguez prevent the dialogue between "collective ethnic memory and individual memory" (Browdy de Hernandez 1996) from taking place.

Hoffman and Rodriguez: An Awareness of Loss

The trajectory of Hoffman's fate may be viewed as a typical success tale: from the strict, prison-like Communist system of Central Europe to the free world of North America. But Hoffman destabilizes such neat divisions and complicates the popular picture by focusing on the charms and blessings of the System and the terrors and curses of the Promised Land. This problematization of formulaic descriptions of the two political, social, and cultural systems emerges as Hoffman re-visions and reconstructs her Polish self through her American identity, and re-examines her American subjectivity through the memory of her Polish selfhood. Hoffman's re-presentation of her experience becomes a deep probing into the phenomenon of exile in the second half of the twentieth century (10). The book speaks of the results of the loss of what poststructuralist wisdom would call a romantic illusion of unity and center and of the costs and rewards, the joys and the terrors, of being thrown into the postmodern world of constantly shifting boundaries and borderless possibilities.

It is precisely the question of borders and boundaries that is central to the exiled self. Paradoxically, in the Communist system, with its explicit rules and principles aimed at regulating every aspect of the citizens' lives, even their ideology and morality, Eva can perceive herself as a free agent. Felt as something imposed and external, the boundaries of the System are clearly defined, and as such they can be trespassed and broken, giving a feeling of freedom. Once in Canada and then in the United States, the narrator feels lost: the old familiar System with its clear network of rules has disappeared and the boundaries of the new world are invisible to her. Carrying the old System now within herself, she tries to impose its rules upon the new territory. Simultaneously, she stumbles upon imperceptible boundaries within the new culture and as a result is lost between the two systems' networks, or, as she puts it, she falls "out of the net of meaning into the weightlessness of chaos" (151).

To describe the moment of crossing the borders, of initiation into exile, Hoffman self-consciously employs two tropes typical of emigrant autobiography: that of division into two and of second birth. She compares her train journey towards the new destination with "scissors cutting a three thousand-mile rip" through her life (100). On the third night in the new country, she has a nightmare in which she is drowning in the ocean and, scared, wakes up in the middle of a scream which she calls "the primal scream of my birth into the New World" (104). Thus the physical and geographical separation from the mother country becomes also a symbolic separation from one's roots; the familiar, well-mapped territory gives way to an incomprehensible space.

To describe her emotional response to the New World, Hoffman repeatedly resorts to the image of flatness and desert. In her new world, she observes only sterility and absence of depth. The Canadian landscape appears "vast, dull, and formless" (100); the Canadian interiors seem "oddly flat, devoid of imagination, ingenuous" (102); the spaces are "plain" and "obvious"; even the Canadian accent is "flat." Smoothness is another term that Hoffman uses, in particular to describe her impression of Canadian and American faces. For her, the cheerful looks seem to be imitations of the expressions in ads and commercials, and as such they are strangely impersonal and unreadable. She senses danger in the matted look in the eyes of her new friends, because it "flattens [her] features" (147), obliterates her. She links this "open sincerity of the simple spaces, open right out to the street" (102) with lack of privacy, depth, interiority. Another image is that of a desert. At some point Hoffman refers to Canada as her "lush Sahara" and the oxymoron echoes Baudrillard's view of America: "Culture, politics — and sexuality too — are seen exclusively in terms of the desert, which here assumes the status of a primal scene. Everything disappears before that desert vision. Even the body, by an ensuing effect of undernourishment, takes on a transparent form, a lightness near to complete disappearance" (Baudrillard 1988: 28). Both the image of flatness and of a desert signal a terrifying rather than liberating disappearance of boundaries and imply an unmapped and therefore both unknown and unknowable territory.

Also the Promised Land's internal landscapes are arranged in different formations. The insertion into the Canadian culture forces Eva to suppress, or rather restructure, her emotional world. For instance, she learns that in English there is a prohibition against using uncharitable words. This knowledge makes her refrain from passing explicitly strong judgments at the cost of suppressing her instincts and her quick reactions. While in Polish she might have called the people she meets "silly" and "dull," in English she forces herself to call them "kindly" and "pleasant" (108). Her emotional life is invaded by the new taboos. Having to express gratitude for hand-me-down clothes and to make other gestures of kindness, Eva is "beginning to master the trick of saying thank you with just the right turn of the head, just the right balance between modesty and obsequiousness," but in her heart she feels "no gratitude at being the recipient of so much mercy" (104).

Eva's odyssey of comprehending the other culture is paralleled by her experience of her own otherness. Emigration forces her not only and not primarily to learn how to move in a strange external landscape; the inner landscape has to be remolded. Eva's thoughts, feelings, impressions have to be cast in language; but which one, if Polish does not cover the new physical world and English seems inadequate to describe the inner? Ironically, Eva's entry into the English language at the age of fourteen begins with a phrase of silencing: "shut up" is what she hears all around her on her first day in school. Years afterwards, a graduate student in English literature, Eva experiences a return of this "shud-dup" to silence her Polish self. Faced with the question of marriage, she is faced with the problem of making her choice in English or in Polish. In a dramatized dialogue between the two languages, two cultural systems emerge:

> Should you marry him? the question comes in English.
>
> Yes.
>
> Should you marry him? the question echoes in Polish.
>
> No.
>
> But I love him; I'm in love with him.
>
> Really? Really? Do you love him as you understand love? As you loved Marek?
>
> Forget Marek. He is another person. He's handsome and kind and good.
>
> You don't feel creaturely warmth. You're imagining him. You're imagining your emotions. You're forcing it .... (199)

For her, each language structures the process of decision-making along different coordinates and preferences: the Polish "no" to marrying an American is a response to an absence of (Polish) "creaturely warmth" towards the man; her English "yes" to the marriage question is rooted in a critique of her Polish understanding of love as a "romantic illusion" that has to "shuddup" (199). She realizes that "between the two stories and two vocabularies, there's a vast alteration in the diagram of the psyche and the relationship to inner life" (269). Making a choice in Polish means following one's passion and a sense of duty to oneself; a choice in English entails reasoning and calculating (and reasoning wins: she marries her American only to divorce him later on). No simple translation is possible between these two tongues; they belong to two different worlds. What Eva experiences here, far from being love in two languages, is an awareness of the incompatibility and heterogeneity of these two worlds, a translation from one to the other implies loss.

Language acquisition is far from an innocent intellectual activity; in *Lost in Translation* it is presented as a carnivorous process. From the start, English "invents" another Eva (121), not only changing her intellectual perception of the world, but inscribing itself into her body, becoming incorporated "in the softest tissue of [her] being" (245). Attuned to the noise of "the Babel of American voices" but lacking a voice of her own, Hoffman feels powerless against the invasion of other voices, voices of the Other: "They ricochet within me, carrying on conversations, lending me their modulations, intonations, rhythms. I do not possess them; they possess me," she writes (220). She is conscious of the experience of a linguistic construction of herself, a process that appears to her as a form of dispossession.

But by far the most painful form of exile is not the expulsion from her "natural" geographical, political, social, cultural, or linguistic milieu, but Eva's exile from her own gendered body. The physical and intellectual are always linked in Eva's account. "Telling a joke is like doing a linguistic pirouette," "laughter is . . . the eroticism of conversation" (118), she observes. In the New World, the gaze of others dislodges her perception of her own body. While in Poland, Eva is considered a "pretty young girl"; on the other side of the Atlantic she is suddenly found "less attractive, less graceful, less desirable," and "a somewhat pitiful specimen" (109). The othering of her body is most violent when she is subjected to actions aimed at making her body look like "typical" American female bodies. For others, her "other" body is intolerable, and it has to be acculturated, remolded to fit new categories of beauty and decency; it has to be harnessed to conform to the local norms of femininity. Eva's armpits are shaven, her eyebrows plucked, her hair set up in curls, her feet forced into high-heeled shoes and her breasts modestly bridled by a bra. This external acculturation of the body only augments the sense of alienation which, Eva feels, "is beginning to be inscribed in [her] flesh and face" (110).Thus her experience of exile becomes a lesson in what after Bourdieu may be called symbolic violence, a lesson in the legitimate ways of (re)presenting her body to others and to herself. Through social criticism and censorship she is taught the "right" gestures, manners, ways of walking, dressing, and looking at the world. New social power relations are inscribed onto her very body, turning her into a stranger to herself.

An outsider to the American construction of the feminine of the fifties, Eva has to consciously learn the highly standardized semiotics of dating and behavior towards the other sex in the New World. In comparison, the conventions of Polish dating seem "natural" because its rules have never been spelled out. In fact in both cultures the codes of sexual behavior are mediated through an elaborate social process of education. In Poland Eva is initiated into the world of sex by books: Sienkiewicz's *Quo Vadis?* with the scenes of Roman orgies and Boccaccio's *Decameron* with "scenes of hermits giving in to fleshly temptresses" (28). Eva's Polish world is filled with her childhood companion and first boy friend, Marek, and their "tousles and sex games" (40). Marek is the center of her erotic and emotional universe. While in Poland, she never questions her own femininity, she merely tries to find ways of expressing it. Faced with the Canadian feminine, Eva recognizes the fact that "the allegory of gender is different here, and it unfolds around different typologies and different themes. I can't become a 'Pani' [lady, mistress, madam, Mrs.] of any sort: not like the authoritative Pani Orlovska, or the vampy, practical Pani Dombarska, or the flirty, romantic woman writer I once met. None of these modes of femininity makes sense here, none of them would find corresponding counterparts in the men I know." Unsure of how to transpose herself "into a new erotic valence" (189), Eva is initiated into the rules and constraints of sexual behavior by her new friend Penny and the artifacts of American culture: ads, movies, literature. The male faces are understood as handsome because they resemble figures in cigarette ads (148); her first American boy friend's male beauty is mediated through the images she has seen on posters and in the movies (187). Ultimate Americanization means for Eva being able to "recognize sexuality in the American grain" (245). This recognition means for her not merely knowing about the sexual rules but first of all having them inscribed onto her body so that they stop being cultural and begin to feel "natural." But her becoming a woman in the American grain can never end in a return to "nature" — Eva's destiny is an awareness of culture-generated rules, principles, constraints, boundaries and borders which mark emotional life and relationships, especially between the sexes. Thus Hoffman's book registers a recognition not only of the impossibility of such a "return" but also of the fictionality of every construct of the natural.

Despite the constantly recorded pain of exile, *Lost in Translation* may be seen as an account of a relatively successful process of coming to terms with one's otherness. Writing her book, Eva speaks after all not from a socially marginal position but from what can easily be perceived as a center (the intellectual world of New York). One could argue that she merely recapitulates the process of marginalization and subsequent centralization. And yet, quite ironically, Eva's success trajectory means moving from one kind of marginality to another. In Poland her marginality was linked to her Jewishness and was a source of strength and pride. Not saying the words of the prayer at school, refusing to weep with the others to mourn the death of Stalin, eating Jewish bread — that is, resistance against the dominant group, stressing one's marginality, made her, in her mother's words, "perhaps better than others." Silence, lack of tears, matzoth became markers of difference, which she experienced as something positive. In the Polish Communist culture whose dominant ideology extols homogeneity, an individual's gesture of differentiation is an act of defying the centre, an act of courage. By a strange reversal, in the New World with its central ethos of difference, sameness seems to be the object of everybody's desire. In Eva's experience of herself the value of difference is shifted: "to be different" now means "to be worse," and as an emigrant she finds herself decentered and powerless. Paradoxically, her ultimately successful journey to the inner circles of New York's professional life results in yet another and more complex form of exile, that of a postmodern subject. That is, her sense of physical and emotional exile in geographical, social, and cultural terms is now overshadowed by her awareness of being exiled from selfhood into subjectivity (i.e., subject positions). Aware of being constructed by a variety of competing discourses, Eva finds herself in the precarious position of "always simultaneously [living] in the centre and on the periphery" (275).

Eva's poststructuralist world is first of all a world of awareness of the problematic nature of self-consciousness. The narrator suggests that it is in her awareness that her exile should be situated: "From now on, I'll be made, like mosaic, of fragments — and my consciousness of them. It is only in that observing consciousness that I remain, after all, an immigrant" (164). This closing statement of the middle section of the book (called "Exile") summarizes the experience of her physical and cultural expulsion from the native country and her socially and culturally successful adaptation to the New World. At the same time, the same observation marks the beginning of a permanent state of exile, an exile that she says she shares with her American generation. This form of exile may be called postmodern in its "acute sense of dislocation and the equally acute challenge of having to invent a place and an identity . . . without the traditional supports" (197).

Eva's narrative is full of marked tensions between her intellectual understanding of her condition and her experience of loss. The titles of the three parts of *Lost in Translation* (Paradise, Exile, The New World) bring forth a whole range of biblical and cultural associations, the most prevalent of which is a loss of innocence coinciding with leaving behind one's childhood and entering one's teens. Exiled from what she experiences as "nature" into the American culture, she loses the (seeming) immediacy of experiencing her self as herself. When, in an attempt to come to terms with the loss, Eva decides to undergo psychotherapy, she sees it as a cure against her "American disease," defined as "anomie, loneliness, emotional repression, and excessive self-consciousness" (268). Ironically, the homologue of her "talking cure," the cure of writing her book, turns out to be saturated with self-conscious reflections on her consciousness. Her autobiography, rather than (re)constructing a coherent Self, is in fact a testimony to its impossibility. Her vocabulary is surfeited with self-conscious references to literature and postmodern theory and philosophy. Sometimes with a touch of irony, sometimes in despair, Hoffman turns to the insights of Freud, Lacan, Jameson, Derrida and others to understand and name her condition. A product of her (postmodern) age, Eva tries to intellectualize even her suffering. She clearly posits a difference between her own distance from her feelings and her mother's total symbiosis with her emotions: "My mother cannot imagine tampering with her feelings, which are the most authentic part of her, which are her. She suffers her emotions as if they were forces of nature, winds and storms and volcanic eruptions" (269). Yet Hoffman's attempts to affirm a (poststructuralist) fragmented, decentered, and fictional self are subverted by outbursts of rage and an acute sense of loss. Eva's knowledge of her social and cultural subjectivity fails to offer her a satisfactory explanation of her experience of pain. Intellectually embracing subjectivity, she seems to create a space for selfhood when she phrases the following question: "Suffering and conflict are the best proof that there's something like a psyche, a soul; or else, what is it that suffers?" (273).

Throughout, *Lost in Translation* dwells on the question of relationship between lived experience, its textual representation, and theoretical discourse interpreting both the experience and its representation. For Hoffman, the space between the memory of her selfhood and her intellectual understanding of herself as a script becomes the space of exile. It is this exile that seems to generate Hoffman's writing, quite in keeping with Kristeva's view of exile as the very condition of writing: "How can one avoid sinking into the mire of common sense, if not by becoming a stranger to one's own country, language, sex and identity?" (Kristeva 1989:298). Eva's is a truly contingent mode of being. She feels caught between two incompatible narratives of being, the Polish story telling her that "circumstance plays the part of fate," the American story anchoring fate in character. This radical incompatibility generates the process of never-ending translation. Eva can never securely inhabit any one system: she is engrossed in a constant process of crossing boundaries. Unlike the fiction of Mary Antin's America with its central ethos of "a steady, self-assured ego, the sturdy energy of forward movement, and the excitement of being swept up into a greater national purpose," Eva's Promised Land offers a postmodern narrative of "the blessings and the terrors of multiplicity" (164), always reminding Eva of the contingent nature of (her)self.

In its mixture of various modes of expression, in its abundance of metacommentary, in its awareness of structuralist and poststructuralist theories, in its predominant concern with linguistic and cultural constructions of the self, *Lost in Translation* resembles such tales of exile as Maxine Hong Kingston's *The Woman Warrior* or Ihab Hassan's *Out of Egypt*. In its intellectual interest in the costs and rewards of exile, Eva Hoffman's book has much in common with the books by Milan Kundera, Stanislaw Baranczak, Czeslaw Milosz, or Julia Kristeva. A careful examination of the treatment of exile by Central European writers as compared to that of other ethnic exiles (for example, those from other Communist regimes: Central American, South East Asian, Chinese) bears the promise of yielding interesting insights into the various techniques of constructing a sense of self-identity. The striking generality of the phenomenon of exile in the present-day world should not obliterate the culture-bound specificity of the experience and representation of exile.

To conclude, what Hoffman and Rodriguez do have in common, in sharp contrast to Mukherjee for whom the past must be overcome, is their nostalgia for a pastoral past. This nostalgia prevents them from linking collective ethnic memory and individual memory in a dialogue, a narrative strategy that, according to Jennifer Browdy de Hernandez, is characteristic of "ethnic autobiography." Nostalgia, as bell hooks points out, is "that longing for something to be as once it was, a kind of useless act," which is different from "a politicization of memory," "that remembering that serves to illuminate and transform the present" (147). Hoffman's and Rodriguez's texts are problematic because they avoid the "politicization of memory." Their texts are caught between a persistence of a memory of the past and a promise of the future.

What is at stake here are competing notions of history and memory: In Mukherjee, as well as Rodriguez, memory is subservient to oblivion; they remember in order to forget. In Hoffman the relationship to the past is nostalgic, not necessarily in the sense of a desire to return but rather in terms of the persistence of the past as an untranslatable utopia, a loss that can never be retrieved.

Jasmine ends her story with an image of the frontier, a (apparently) perpetual movement forward, in a rather adventurous way, to forge identities on the condition that the past is suppressed or remembered strategically. Eva's story ends in a more subtle way: the past remains within Eva as an untranslatable crypt, while the present let her "breathe in the fresh spring air" (280), somehow appearing as being natural and necessary ("How could there be any other place"? (280)). She is therefore caught between two worlds, "two stories and two vocabularies" (269). Rather than causing her *Angst*, the "inbetweenness" leaves her with a form of *Glassenheit*, an imperturbability that allows her to conclude: "I am here now" (280).

What is, however, lacking in all these texts is a politicization of memory, that remembering that serves to illuminate and transform not only the present but also the future. Let me explain how I understand a "politicized memory" or a "politicized history," whether personal or collective. Walter Benjamin, in his "Theses on the Philosophy of History," writes the following: "Historical method is philological method, a method that has as its foundation the book of life. 'To read what was never written,' is what Hofmannsthal calls it. The reader referred to here is the true historian" (*"Die historische Methode ist eine philologische, der das Buch des Lebens zugrunde liegt. 'Was nie geschrieben wurde, lesen' heißt es bei Hofmannsthal. Der Leser, an den hier zu denken ist, ist der wahre Historiker"*). What does it mean to confront history as a reader and to read what was never written? This notion of history is closely related to what Benjamin, throughout all his life, calls "redemption." The event of redemption is concerned with a messianic moment of thinking, a thinking of the possibility of a future. It is in this moment that the past is saved, not in being returned to what once existed but precisely in being transformed into something that never was or was never written. One can understand the "not-written" of history in terms of the potentialities that were never actualized in the past. In this sense the task of the historian becomes that of a prophet facing backwards, to see the future in the potentialities of the past. For Agamben, what was never written is the fact that there is language, i.e., not the content of transmission but the fact that there is transmission. Language, in western tradition, has always been "presupposed." This, according to Agamben, involves an aporia: the fact that there is language and transmission cannot be communicated in the form of a particular statement simply because statements and utterances are possible only after language has already begun.

For Agamben the fact that there is language and that it is always presupposed is the unwritten of history, in which "sayability remains unsaid in what is said"

(Agamben 1999: 33). According to him, the task of philosophical, and I would say ethical, presentation is "to come with speech to help speech, so that in speech, speech itself does not remain presupposed but instead comes to speech" and in this way language reaches the "unpresupposable and unpresupposed principle (*arkhē anypothetos*)[35] that, as such, constitutes authentic human community and communication" (35).

History has always been transmitted in "a determinate mode" (60). The task of the coming philosophy, Agamben argues, is to liberate history, Being and potentiality from *presupposition* and to *expose* them (76). The exposition of presupposition is called philosophy (67). The liberation of language from presupposition, from any determinate or historical transmission of meaning is what Benjamin calls "pure language":

> To relieve it of this [meaning], to turn the symbolizing into the symbolized, to regain pure language fully formed in the linguistic flux, is the tremendous and only capacity of translation. In this pure language — which no longer means anything [nichts mehr meint] and no longer expresses anything [nichts mehr ausdrückt] but, as expressionless and creative word, that which is meant in all languages — all communication, all sense, and all intention finally encounter a stratum in which they are destined to be extinguished. (Benjamin 1968: 80)

I argue, in the final chapter, that Bensmaïa's *The Year of Passages* is concerned with and exemplify this redemptive and messianic moment of pure language in a performative gesture. For Bensmaïa, both history and memory have been redeemed of their burden of determinate meaning. The vision of history that Bensmaïa's *The Year of Passages* puts forth is fundamentally different from that of Mukherjee's *Jasmine*, or Hoffman's *Lost in Translation*. In *The Year of Passages* history (the personal or even collective history of the narrator) is not transmitted in a "determinate mode," whereby the subject puts himself back together in his writing. His writing, rather than being an achievement of a symbolic home away from home, is an ethical celebration of the imperative to remain "homeless." The ethics of displacement lies in the necessity of remaining homeless and refusing to reterritorialize, once the phenomenon of displacement has taken place. As for the politics of homelessness and displacement, Kristeva's position is quite revealing to when she argues that exile is a form of dissidence:

> Exile is already in itself a form of dissidence, since it involves uprooting oneself from a family, a country or a language. More importantly, it is an irreligious act that cuts all ties, for religion is nothing more than membership of a real or symbolic community which may or may not be transcendental, but which always constitutes a link, a homology, an understanding. The exile cuts all links, including those that bind him to the belief that the thing called life has A Meaning guaranteed by the dead father. For if meaning exists in the state of exile, it nevertheless finds no incarnation, and is ceaselessly produced and destroyed in geographical or discursive transformations. Exile is a way of surviving in the face of the dead father, of gambling with death, which is the meaning of life, of stubbornly refusing to give into the law of death. (Kristeva *1989:* 298)

Notes

1. Lyotard in his "Domus and the Megalopolis": "Perhaps thinking's lot is just to bear witness to the untamable, to what is incommensurable with it. But to say witness is to say trace, and to say trace is to say inscription" (197).

2. Edith Wharton's *Italian Backgrounds* (1905), *In Morocco* (1919), and *A Motor-Flight Through France* (1908); William Carlos Williams's *A voyage to Pagany* (1928); Aldous Huxley's *Along the Road* (1925), *Beyond the Mexican Bay* (1934); *Jesting Pilate: An Intellectual Holiday* (1926); John Dos Passos's *Brazil on the Move* (1963), *In All Countries* (1934), *Journeys Between Wars* (1938), *Orient Express* (1927); Saul Bellow's *To Jerusalem and Back: A Personal Account* (1976); Wyndham Lewis's *Filibusters in Barbary* (1932), *Journey into Barbary: Morocco Writings and Drawings* (1983), W. H. Auden and Christopher Isherwood's *Journey to a War* (1939), W. H. Auden and Louis MacNiece's *Letters from Iceland* (1973); William Golding's *An Egyptian Journal* (1985); Heinrich Böll's *Irish Journal* (1957); Nikos Kazantzakis's *England* (1941), *Japan/China* (1938), *Journeying: Travels in Italy, Egypt, Sinai, Jerusalem and Cypres* (1927); Le Corbusier's *Journey to the East* (1966); Antoine de Saint-Exupéry's *Wind, Sand and Stars* (1939) and Pier Paolo Pasolini's *The Scent of India* (1974).

3. Stephen Leacock, *My Discovery of the West*, 1937, 57.

4. Michael Kowalewski's introduction to his edited volume, *Temperamental Journeys: Essays on the Modern Literature of Travel*. Athens: The University of Georgia Press, 1992.

5. See Theroux's "Stranger on a Train: The Pleasure of Railways," in *Sunrise with Seamonsters: Travel and Discoveries, 1964-1984*, 126-35. Paul Fussell refers to such travelers as "stationary tourists."

6. It should here be emphasized that the distinction between a mimetic and a non-mimetic theory/experience of travel is not binary. There are, as I try to show bellow, numerous examples of transgressive, non-mimetic elements within a more mimetic, touristic experience, and vice versa.

7. See for example Maria Graham's *Three Months Passed in the Mountains East of Rome during the Year 1819* (London, 1820) and Lady Morgan's *Italy* (London, 1821).

8. The Romantic notion of travel, which lies, as we will see shortly, at the heart of the process of *Bildung*, might be seen as a movement toward the realization of the self through an experience of the foreign while affirming its danger and destabilizing power, but, ultimately, returning to the self/same.

9. Compare this with the following passage from Dostoyevsky's *Notes from the Underground*: "But man is a frivolous and unseemly creature and maybe, like a chessplayer, likes just the process of attaining the goal alone, and not the goal itself. And who knows (one can't be sure), maybe the entire goal here on earth toward which mankind is striving consists of nothing more than this continuity of process of attainment alone, in other words, in life itself and not actually in the goal proper, which, it goes without saying, cannot be anything except two times two makes four, that is a formula, and after all, two times two makes four is already not life, gentlemen, but the beginning of death" (Westling, et al 2074).

10. Compare again with Dostoyevsky's *Notes from the Underground*: "I not only did not manage to become nasty, but I did not manage to become anything at all; not nasty, not nice, not crooked, not honest, not a hero, not an insect. Now I am living out my life in my corner, taunting myself with the spiteful and pointless consolation that an intel-

ligent man cannot really become anything anyway — it takes a fool to become anything. Yes indeed, the intelligent man of the nineteenth century is obliged and morally bound to be basically characterless, the man of action, is apt to be basically a limited creature" (2057).

"I has long seen clearly that a great part of the pleasure of travel lies in the fulfillment of these early wishes, that it is rooted, that is, in dissatisfaction with home and family" (311)

11. She is mourning Shelley's death in 1822.

12. See Philippe Lacoue-Labarthe's *Typography: Mimesis, Philosophy, Politics*, 81.

13. Heidegger explicitly translates *poiesis* by *Herstellung* and *Darstellung* (Lacoue-Labarthe 72).

14. Mimesis in its impulse toward reproduction and counterfeiting becomes *unheimlich*, an estrangement of the familiar.

15. See Jacques Derrida's "Economimesis" in which he analyzes, among others, the relationship between mimesis and economy: "It would appear that *mimesis* and *oikonomia* could have nothing to do with one another. The point is to demonstrate the contrary, to exhibit the systematic link between the two" (264). Derrida further refuses to draw binary opposition between a restricted and a general economy: "And we are not yet defining economy as an economy of circulation (a restricted economy) or a general economy...this is the hypothesis — there is no *opposition* between these two economies. Their relation must be one neither of identity nor of contradiction but must be other" (264).

16. See for example Michel de Certeau's *The Mystic Fable* (1992).

17. For the theme of "cultural capital" gained in journeys see: Dean MacCannell's *The Tourist*; Jonathan Culler's, "The Semiotics of Tourism"; Abbeele's "Sightseers: The Tourist as Theorist"; Levi-Strauss's, *Tristes Tropiques*, Mary W. Helms's, *Ulysses' Sail: An Ethnographic Odyssey of Power, Knowledge and Geographic Distance*.

18. See Spacks's (Patricia Ann Meyer) *Boredom: The Literary History of a State of Mind* ; R. C. Kuhn's *The Demon of Noontide: Ennui in western Literature*

19. See Cixous and Derrida's *Veils*.

20. We will encounter a similar strategy of double negation when discussing Réda Bensmaïa's *The Year of Passages*.

21. For the issue of land ownership in the case of France see Sartre in *Colonialism and Neocolonialism*.

22. In the case of France see Maxim Silverman's *Deconstructing the Nation: Immigration, Racism and Citizenship in Modern France*; Alec G. Hargreaves's *Immigration, 'Race' and Ethnicity in Contemporary France*; Adrian Favell's *Philosophies of Integration: Immigration and the Idea of Citizenship in France and Britain*.

23. See wa Thiong o Ngugi's *Decolonizing the Mind: The Politics of Language in African Literature* as well as his earlier work, *Homecoming: Essays on African and Caribbean Literature, Culture and Politics* for both a particularly powerful description of the violence of cultural colonization and an eloquent argument for a cultural politics of resistance. Derrida also analyzes, in his *Monolingualism of the Other or the Prosthesis of Origin*, the "interdiction" of access to language in the context of the French colonial rule in Algeria.

24. For example one could read, in this context, essays and speeches of Martin Luther King, Jr. or other documents of the American Civil Rights movement. There the organizing slogan of Operation Push was "I am a Man."

25. George Steiner in his "Our Homeland, the Text:" "At the same time, doubtless, the centrality of the book does coincide with and enact the condition of ex-

ile...Reading, textual exegesis, are an exile from action, from the existential innocence of praxis...the reader is one who is absent from action...the text was an instrument of exilic survival..." (5).

26. Steiner argues that it is because of this "addiction to words" and this "bookishness" that the Jews have generated the provocative pre-eminence in modernity (17): "The bookish genius of Marx and of Freud, of Wittgenstein and of Levi-Strauss, is a secular deployment of the long schooling in abstract, speculative commentary and clerkship in exegetic legacy. The Jewish presence, often overwhelming, in modern mathematics, physics, economic and social theory, is direct heir to that abstinence from the approximate. from the mundane, which constitutes the ethos of the cleric" (17). The bookishness of the Jew is also revealed in the death camps, in his "correcting a printing error, emend a doubtful text, on his way to extinction" (18). Reading and writing are his homeland. It is "the false reading, the erratum that made him homeless" (20).

27. Steiner further continues: "The sole citizenship of the cleric is that of a critical humanism. He knows not only that nationalism is a sort of madness, a virulent infection edging the species towards a mutual massacre. He knows that it signifies an abstention from free and clear thought and from the disinterested pursuit of justice. The man or woman at home in the text is, by definition, a conscientious objector: to the vulgar mystique of the flag and the anthem, to the sleep of reason which proclaims "my country, right or wrong," to the pathos and eloquence of collective mendacities on which the nation-state ..builds its power and aggression. The locus of truth is always extraterritorial; its diffusion is made clandestine by the barbed wire and watch-towers of national dogma (21). Steiner concludes that the State of Israel, even though wholly understandable, is at the same time "an attempt to eradicate the deeper truth of unhousedness, of an at-homeness in the word, which are the legacy of the Prophets and of the keepers of the text." (24). The Boyarins's radical revision of the notion of peoplehood for Jews is similar to Steiner's. In their "Diaspora: Generation and the Ground of Jewish Identity," the authors seek to disentangle Jewish consciousness from nationalism and argue that Diaspora (and not monotheism) is the most important contribution of Judaism to the world. Diaspora, rather than territorial fixation, gives us the insight that peoples and lands are not naturally and organically connected. According to the Boyarins's formulation, America is home precisely because it is diasporic.

28. Adorno in fact replaces, in *Minima Moralia*, the Heideggerian homelessness (*Heimatlosigkeit*) with dwellinglessness (*Obdachlosigkeit*). Dwellinglessness is for him designating a more specifically socio-historical phenomenon (as contrasted to homelessness which relates to the idea of racial community), which is to say a more materialist phenomenon, to be disentangled via the work of the negative. The issue becomes more complicated when one remembers Heidegger using the term "dwell" (*wohnen*) in the 1951 essay "Building Dwelling Thinking" (*Bauen Wohnen Denken*). This is not a place to enter into a discussion of the interface between the thoughts of Adorno and Heidegger. Fred Dallmayr's *Life World, Modernity and Critique* (drawing on Hermann Mörchen's *Adorno und Heidegger: Untersuchung einer philosophischen Kommunicationsverwigerung* (*Examination of a Refused Philosophical Communication*)) discusses this issue in some detail.

29. In *The Gay Science,* Nietzsche too, quite joyfully, writes: "At the sea — I would not build a house for myself, and I count it part of my good fortune that I do not own a house [*Es gehört selbst zu meinen Glücke, kein Hausbesitzer zu sein*]. But if I had to, then I should build it as some of the Romans did — right into the sea. I should not mind sharing a few secrets with this beautiful monster" (214).

30. Death can be implicated in a journey without return, whether the physical or the symbolic death of the subject of travel. In an ethical journey, there is an imperative to die or to commit suicide.

31. "How many more shapes are in me, how many more selves, how many more husbands." (215)

32. Schorer calls *Moll Flanders* "our classic revelation of the mercantile mind" (Schorer 1976:123). An important point, which is somehow related to my discussion of Jasmine but I will not have time to develop here, is not Moll's actions but the reflection of these actions in her memory and the way she tries to understand them. To put this in other words which does justice to the dialectics between 'action' and 'character' in *Moll Flanders*: not Moll's actions 'in themselves', but the way they are understood and interpreted by Moll in her recollection of the past in her autobiography constitutes Moll's character. The specificity of Moll's character lies in her (mis) perception of her own actions. The interrelationship between action and character finds a symbolic co-relation in the narrative text itself: Throughout *Moll Flanders* it is assumed that the respectable reader abhors crime and despises thieves but in the case of Moll herself we are, paradoxically enough, invited to abhor her crimes but urged not to despise the criminal herself. In short, Moll wants to make sure that we see what she wants us to see. She controls her narrative and presents us with her own version and interpretation of events (which leads her to a life of imposture and theft).

33. Jasmine represents herself as being in control of her own destiny, or her own memory ("I rip myself free of the past" (208)), or even when to change and when not to: "I changed because I wanted to. To bunker inside nostalgia, to sheathe the heart in a bulletproof vest, was to be a coward. On Claremont Avenue, in the Hayeses' big, clean, brightly lit apartment, I bloomed from a diffident alien with forged documents into adventurous Jase" (185).

34. No matter how Jasmine desires a total erasure and disappearance of the past, death, in *Jasmine*, remains within the order of memory. One should understand death in *Jasmine* as being mediated by a process of *Aufhebung* whereby the "thing" is negated and preserved. Therefore, when Jasmine tells us that she has killed her former selves, what she means is that her past is "encrypted" as well as sublated. The figure of death, understood this way, is crucial for an economy of (incomplete) mourning as well as for a process of (instrumental) identity formation. What is left outside of this framework is the hauntological aspects of such a scene of murder. See Agamben in *Language and Death* as well as Kristeva's "Life and Death of speech" in her *Black Sun* for a similar argument.

35. Plato in his *Republic* presents "*arkhē anypothetos*, the unpresupposed principle, as the *telos*, fulfillment and end of *autos ho logos*, language itself: the 'thing itself' and essential matter of human beings" (47). According to Agamben, this "unpresupposed principle" is what is at stake when Benjamin talks about "pure language."

Chapter Three

Toward A General Economy of Travel

> Whoever cannot seek
> The unforeseen sees nothing,
> For the known way
> Is an impasse.
>
> Heraclitus, *Fragments*, 7

> This foreign death makes us die in the distress of estrangement.
>
> Maurice Blanchot in "Rilke and Death's Demand," 126

In this chapter I will explore the question of death as finitude and as excess, which is further analyzed in relation to both Dasein and language. The restricted economical aspects of the phenomenon of death (the death of the Object/Event) and the subsequent process of mourning in language (language as a topos in which death is incorporated and assimilated) are elucidated and critiqued in order to reveal the underlying general economical forces. Within the framework of a general economy of representation, death is non-sublatable. The haunting memory (memory as event, as elaborated below, or ghostly memory) of the death of the Object/Event, therefore, disrupts and disjoins the temporality of mimesis, and language as *oikos* of *oikēsis* (the house of death) becomes rather a haunted house. In other words, I will try to refute the claim that one (as an exile or a displaced subject) can find one's home in language (Heidegger, Aciman, etc.). I further analyze in details Kader Abdolah's *Spijkerschrift* and Kiarostami's *The Taste of Cherry* in order to explore the extent to which the general and restricted economical moments/forces are at work. While analyzing the former in terms of the crisis of representation in its relation to secrecy and the latter in terms of the crisis of representation in relation to death, I will argue that in Kader Abdolah's *Spijkerschrift*, even though it acknowledges the textual excess, the final strategy is in fact a restricted economical one. Kiarostami's *The Taste of Cherry*, on the contrary, foregrounds a general economy of representation by positing death as an outside, to which one has no relation, and is therefore cannot be sublated. But first let me explain how a restricted economy of travel and displacement might be theorized.

In *Sein und Zeit* (sections 50-53), in an attempt to further investigate the fundamental characteristics of Dasein, Heidegger opens a discussion of the relationship between Dasein and its death. The discussion of death does not refer to the death of animals or to a merely biological fact, since the animal, the merely-living (*Nur-lebenden*) does not die but ceases to live. It is only Dasein who dies simply because Dasein is the only being who is aware of the possibility and the eventuality of its own death. Death is, however, not something that is waiting at the end of life or even something that is going to be actualized; it always already belongs to the very structure of Dasein: Dasein is a being-toward-death, a being-for-the-end: "The ending that we have in view when we speak of death, does not signify a being-at-an-end of Da-sein, but rather a *being toward the end* of this being. Death is a way to be that Da-sein takes over as soon as it is. 'As soon as a human being is born, he is old enough to die right away'" (Heidegger 1996a:228).

The death of Dasein is not simply one "outstanding" something among others. Heidegger tells us that the structural factor of care is revealed as outstanding things that have "not yet become 'real' as [a] potentiality-of-its-being" (219). In a familiar Sartrean formulation, Dasein is an unfinished project whose existence always precedes its essence. This Sartrean formula, and indeed the whole existentialist phenomenology, falls, however, short of an understanding of finitude and death. In fact, Sartre chooses not to think death since it is incompatible with his notion of human freedom and a "privileged selfhood" that he advocates. The Sartrean formula, in its temporal insistence, is limited, inasmuch as it fails to comprehend the immanence of death at every moment, that being is always already contingent:

> Despite taking so much from modern philosophers of death like Heidegger and Kojève, Sartre finally has to eliminate death from the finitude of being. He takes the Heideggerian nothingness into self, making it the basis of freedom, but he also privileges selfhood in a way which Heidegger emphatically did not, and resists Heidegger's embrace of death. Sartre knows that to take death so profoundly into being, as did Heidegger and Kojève, threatens the entire project of human freedom as praxis, which is the most important aspect of Sartre's existentialism. (Dollimore 1998:168)[1]

There is always a this or that (a becoming this or that) that is anticipated in life as potentialities waiting to be actualized, before Dasein attains the essence of its constitution, its own "wholeness." For Heidegger, it is impossible to experience Dasein ontically as an existing whole simply because there is always something outstanding in one's potentiality-for-being. Dasein reaches its totality only in death, but then it "simultaneously loses the being of the there" (221): as along as Dasein is as a being, it has never attained its wholeness, but as soon as it does, this "gain becomes the absolute loss of being-in-the-world" (220). Does this economy of loss and gain, at the limits of life, mean that only the dead, or for that matter, history or "histories" (indicating particular narratives within history), can have totalities? Heidegger does not ask this question but to imagine his answer in the negative, i.e., history should first come to an end before it can have any totality, would sound a too Hegelian interpretation of Heidegger. But another way of approaching the question would be to say that, as in the case of Dasein, the finitude of the world is not something at the end of the road but an *"eminent imminence"* (232) in the world. Death is not *of* the world (of Dasein, history, etc) but, rather, *in* the world. Nowhere does one have access to any totality; it is fundamentally eluding being experienced simply because there is the work of negativity (of death) at work: the dialectical opposition of being and nothingness cannot be sublated.

Dasein is characterized by *Angst*, not as something accidental or contingent, but as primordially constitutive of the being of Dasein. Dasein is delivered to its death as its "ownmost nonrelational possibility not to be bypassed" (232). The awareness of the imminence of death as "certain, and yet indefinite" (239) is what puts Dasein in the "attunement of *Angst*" (232). Angst or dread, as Heidegger makes it clear in *History of the Concept of Time* (section 30), is not to be confused with fear, or horror, or even terror. "Angst can befall us right in the midst of the most familiar environment" (289) One feels *unheimlich* in his or her domestic environment (*oikos*) not because anything has been changed or disoriented in any definite way: "the of which of dread is nothing" (290), that is to say nothing that takes place in the world, nothing definite, nothing worldly. Dasein's *Angst*, its *Unheimlichkeit in* the world is precisely a "cultivation of Dasein itself as being-in-the-world, so much so that it let itself be determined primarily *from* [my emphasis] the world" (293). The "from" has a double genitive structure here: Dasein's *Angst* is both related to his being-in-the-world as well as his flight from it to the "Anyone" (293) or "the they" (240) as a flight from authenticity: "It is precisely in the Anyone that Da-sein is its discoveredness as uncanniness" (293). In sum, Dasein's *Angst*, his *Unheimlichkeit*, is not something contingent; it is constitutive of his being, an effect of his awareness of his finitude, his being-toward-death: "In *Angst*, Dasein finds itself faced with the nothingness of the possible impossibility of its existence" (245). Man is not at home in the world because his home is a haunted one. It is haunted by something, which is actually nothing, a nothingness that puts Dasein outside itself. Dasein's being "outside" itself need not indicate spatial implications; it is simply the announcement of Dasein to itself, as the not-self or other of the self, yet erupting from within and in excess of the self.

Dasein is not simply mortal; it should rather become mortal, "become free for one's own death" (243). To say that death is a real thing and that it is possible and then go on and forget its possibility, i.e., that it can happen at any moment, is, argues Heidegger, inauthenticity par excellence. Dasein as a being-toward-death "should relate itself to that *death* so that it reveals itself, in this being and for it, as possibility . . . *as possibility of the impossibility of existence in general*" (242). Death "individualizes" (243) Dasein as the ownmost, freed possibility that Dasein takes over from itself: "Death does not just 'belong' in an undifferentiated way to one's own Da-sein, but it *lays claim* on it as something *individual*" (243). Therefore, it is through a certain relationship to death, one's own death, that one is individualized, or in non-Cartesian terms, becomes a subject, a subject who is always already haunted by the imminent possibility of its own impossibility, a subject always already outside itself.

For Heidegger, therefore, death is always a gift, beyond an economy of exchange. The gift of death cannot be recognized or phenomenolized as such, simply because it is nothing, but a nothing that individualizes and proffer identity: "The identity of the oneself is *given* by death, by the being-towards-death that *promises* me to it" (Derrida 1995: 45). This identity is by no means Cartesian or phenomenological. It should rather be understood, on the one hand, as singularity and irreplaceability of one's being, and therefore one's responsibility, and, on the other hand, as a gift, non-determinate, non-phenomenolizable: "To have the experience of one's absolute singularity and apprehend one's own death, amounts to the same thing. Death is very much that which nobody else can undergo or confront in my place. My irreplaceability is therefore conferred, delivered, "given," one can say, by death. It is the same gift, the same source, one could say the same goodness and the same law. It is from the site of death as a place of my irreplaceability, that is, of my singularity, that I feel called to responsibility. In this sense only a mortal can be responsible" (41).

At the same time, the gift of death is also the *gift* of death, poisoning and contaminating Dasein with something, which is nothing, that is absolutely exterior and foreign to its whole constitution as being; it gives and takes away at the same time². The gift/*gift* of death is not only constitutive of Dasein but also of its understanding of its being-there as it is expressed in language and discourse. In *Sein und Zeit*, section 34, Heidegger asks the following questions about language/discourse and its mode of being: "Is it an innerworldly useful thing at hand or does it have the mode of being of Da-sein or neither of the two? What kind of being does language have if there can be a 'dead' language?" (Heidegger 1996a:155). Heidegger does not give us an explicit answer to these questions, but, by way of formulating a tentative hypothesis, we might say or assume the following: that language is not a being-at-hand but has a mode of being analogically similar to that of Dasein itself; that language, as with Dasein, is permeated and radically constituted by the gift/*gift* of death; that language, like Dasein, carries death within itself. The relationship between language and Dasein is, to put it succinctly, a matter of non-synonymous substitution, a spectral link between two dissimilar "things," which is nothing other than *différance*. That is to say, language as the *différance of* Being, and Being as the *différance in* language. In other words, one needs to understand language as a cryptonymy whose inhabitant is "always a living dead, a dead entity we are perfectly willing to keep alive, but as dead, one we are willing to keep, as long as we keep it, . . ., intact in any way save as living" (Derrida 1986a:xxi).

Agamben formulates the question of death, and more generally the problem of negativity, with reference to Hegel and Heidegger:

> If this is true, if being its own Da (its own there) is what characterizes Dasein (Being-there), this signifies that precisely at the point where the possibility of being Da, of being at home in one's own place is actualized, through the expression of death, in the most authentic mode, the Da is finally revealed as the source from which a radical and threatening negativity emerges. (Agamben 1991:5)

The "thereness" of Dasein, being the source of its negativity, is analogically related, according to Agamben, to the Hegelian sense certainty's attempt at *das Diese nehmen* (This-taking). In the first chapter of the *Phenomenology*, Hegel addresses the problem of sense certainty through an analysis of *das Diese* and of indication. In spite of the appearance of being the richest kind of knowledge, sense certainty is characterized with an emptiness. Its attempt to grasp and define the concrete content of its object proves to be mediated by a universal, which negates the singularity of the indication. The answer to the question: "What is Now?" can, e.g., be: "Now is Night." We write down this truth, but when later we look again at the written truth we find it empty:

> The Now that is Night is preserved, i.e., it is treated as what it professes to be, as an entity [Seiendes]; but it proves itself to be, on the contrary, a nonentity [Nichtseiendes]. The Now does indeed preserve itself, but as something that is not Night; equally, it preserves itself in the face of the Day that now is, as something that also is not Day, in other words, as a negative in general. (59)

The desire to demonstrate or indicate something proves to be permeated by a realization that sense certainty is in fact a dialectical process of negation and mediation: "'the natural consciousness' (*das natürliche Bewusstsein*) one might wish to place at the beginning as absolute, is, in fact, always already a 'history'" (12). An analysis of the indexicals and indicators reveal that, before they designate real objects, they refer to the event of language; that language takes place without taking place, i.e., without its content being ever present. Agamben proceeds to argue that the problem of *deixis* is the problem of the voice and its relation to language. Without intending to enter, in more details, into his analysis of this problem, it would suffice for now to say that the voice, as a supreme indicator or shifter that allows us to grasp the taking place of language, is a negative ground, "the originary negativity sustaining every negation" (36). The voice is, therefore, always the voice of death. Here again we have a double genitive, both objective and subjective at the same time: "the voice is death, which preserves and recalls the living as dead, and it is, at the same time, an immediate trace and memory of death, pure negativity" (45). That is to say, discourse is both the death of the object and the memory of that death. "Death and voice have the same negative structure and they are metaphysically inseparable" (86). Therefore, to consent to the taking place of language is "to consent also to death, to be capable of dying (*sterben*) rather than simply deceasing (*ableben*)" (87). This paradox is also reflected in Greek tragedy. In the words of the chorus in *Oedipus at Colonus* we can find the essence of the tragic experience of language: "not being born overcomes all language; but having come into the light, the best thing is to return as soon as possible whence one came" (90). Philosophy, precisely presented as a surpassing of this tragic experience, constitutes the voice as a foundation for man's most proper dimension. The overcoming of this experience is to think the absolute:

> The Absolute is the mode in which philosophy thinks its own negative foundation. In the history of philosophy it receives various names: *idea tou agathou* in Plato, *theoria, noeseos noesis* in Aristotle, *One* in Plotinus, *Indifference* in Schelling, *Absolute Idea* in Hegel, *Ereignis* in Heidegger; but in every case, the absolute has the structure of a process, of an exit from itself that must cross over negativity and scission in order to return to its own place. (92)

The structure of the absolute is therefore the structure of language, carrying death and negativity within itself: to kill the real object and retain the memory of that death. Is the Absolute a crypt? Does it engage in incomplete mourning? This dialectical *Aufhebung* brings the Absolute to its own proper place, its *oikos*.

> To think the absolute signifies, thus, to think that which . . . has been led back to its ownmost property, to itself, to its own *solitude*, as to its own *custom*. For this reason, the Absolute always implies a voyage, an abandonment of the originary place, an alienation and a being-outside. If the Absolute is the supreme idea of philosophy, then philosophy is truly, in the words of Novalis, nostalgia (*Heimweh*); that is, the 'desire to be at home everywhere' (*Trieb überall zu Hause sein*). (92)

The *oikos* is therefore a place to which one returns having incorporated/introjected the negativity of death. Homecoming and philosophy are the different names of this domestication of death. What is usually called "home" should undergo a process of experiencing, and incorporating, death in order to become itself:

> And yet the Oikos in the Greek tradition (domus in the Latin tradition) is not, and I insist on this, the place of safety. The Oikos is above all the place of tragedy. I recall that one of the conditions of the tragic enumerated by Aristotle is precisely the domestic condition: relationships are tragic because they occur in the family, it is within the family that incest, patricide, and matricide occur. Tragedy is not possible outside this ecologic or ecotragic framework. (Lyotard, 1993:97)

To philosophize is therefore the desire to dwell in an *oikos*, but *oikos* is not itself if it has not incorporated and domesticated death in itself. The desire to philosophize is the desire to become immortal by becoming mortal: only through a detour of experiencing death, one can overcome death.

I would like to argue for the impossibility, in spite of the necessity, of *oikos*, homecoming and philosophy, all carrying an incorporated death within themselves: the possibility of the impossibility of Dasein is non-sublatable. Language bearing death within it, is also always haunted by the memory of the murder it has committed, *oikos* is always already an *Öffentlichkeit*, open to its outside, and homecoming always (the beginning of) another journey. In sum, to return to Heidegger, the gift of death cannot possibly be a foundation for an *oikos*. If death can give Dasein its totality, it is always a totality for the other and for the "I." Death, in a general economy of peregrination, is something that places the subject outside itself and forecloses the certainty of the latter to return home after recuperating the negativity of death.

Derrida's analysis of the Hegelian semiology brings to light some of the fundamental aspects as well as contradictions of the relationship between language and death. The sign, as we know, unites a signifier (a sensory perception) and a signified (concept); Hegel calls them "intuition" and "independent representation" respectively. In intuition "a being is given, a thing is presented and is to be received in its simple presence. It is there, immediately visible, indubitable" (Derrida 1986b:81). But then in the formation of a sign this intuition is welded to a *Vorstellung*, a representation, which is in fact "a representation (in the sense of representing) of a representation (in the general sense of conceptual ideality)" (81) This ideality is a *Bedeutung*, a signification, the content of a meaning: "Hegel accords to the content of this meaning, this *Bedeutung*, the name and rank of *soul (Seele)*. Of course it is a soul deposited in a body, in the body of the signifier, in the sensory flesh of intuition. The sign, as the unity of the signifying body and the signified ideality (concept), becomes a kind of incarnation" (82). Therefore, the opposition between the signifier, the intuition, the sensory, and the body, on the one hand and, on the other hand, the signified, the representation, the intelligible, and the soul is sublated in the sign itself: through the dialectics of *Aufhebung* a "body (*Körper*)" inhabited by *Geist* becomes "a proper body (*Leib*)" (82). This is true for Saussure as well as Husserl. The living word is a *geistige Leiblichkeit*, a spiritual flesh, as the latter has put it (82).

The sign is, therefore, the unity, or rather the sublation, of the signifier and the signified, body and soul, life and death. It opposes, denies, and murders the sensory object in order to subsequently incorporate it within it as a living dead; it is the scene of an originary mourning, albeit an incomplete one.

> Hegel knew that this proper and animated body of the signifier was also a *tomb*. The tomb is the life of the body as the sign of death, the body as the other of the soul, the other of the animate psyche, of the living breath. But the tomb also shelters, maintains in reserve, capitalizes on life by marking that life continues elsewhere. The family crypt: *oikēsis*. It consecrates the disappearance of life by attesting to the perseverance of life. Thus the tomb also shelters life from death. It *warns* the soul of possible death, warns (of) death of the soul, turns away (from) death. This double warning function belongs to the funerary monument. The body of the sign thus becomes the monument in which the soul will be enclosed, preserved, maintained, kept in maintenance, present, signified. (82)

This is a quite complicated passage requiring some explication, in which one should think about the relationship(s) between the proper, property, economy, *oikos*, on the one hand, and *oikēsis*, the crypt, the secret, memory, death and mourning, on the other hand: the economy of death. The sign is a tomb, an *oikēsis* in Greek, which is akin to the Greek *oikos*, from which the word "economy" derives. In "Différance" Derrida brings *oikēsis* and *oikos* into relationship with each other: "The *a* of *différance*, thus, is not heard; it remains silent, secret and discreet as a tomb: *oikēsis*. And thereby let us anticipate the delineation of a site, the familial residence and tomb of the proper in which is produced, by *différance*, the *economy of death*" (4). What I would like to demonstrate is that there is a certain analogy, or rather a homology without origin, between the sign and the *oikos* in relation to death and finitude: both are monuments of mourning and commemoration, sites of secrecy, and, following Derrida's deconstruction of the Hegelian thanatology, subjected to a hauntology which, rather than overcoming finitude, inscribes infinity within the finitude: the eternal return of the ghost.

The Hegelian version of the story is something like this: the sign is a double negation (double affirmation): a negation of life (affirmation of death), the sensory object, the living breath, the singularity of the here and now (where and when?), but also, at the same time, a negation of death (affirmation of life, another life), the perseverance and continuation of the immediate and the sensory, in a rather transcendent way, in the pyramid of the concept (the proper locus of life, albeit another life) in which an eternal repetition of the "same" would reveal itself as an *Überwindung* of temporality and finitude. This is the conception of immortality, which implies that the "self [sign] comprehends itself as withdrawn from the naturalness of existence and as resting on itself" (85). If the object is dead, it can live on (sur-vive) as a living dead in the life (the crypt) of the concept. The sign as "the monument-of-life-in-death and the monument-of-death-in-life" (83) is therefore the proprietor of the proper essence of the world in its withdrawal from it. The sign is also the sign of the freedom of spirit: "the production of arbitrary signs manifests the freedom of spirit" (86). To this Hegelian version of death, one can oppose (without any opposition) death as *différance*. The sign, inasmuch as, in being always already separated from any origin, is always re-marked as the iterable originary sign of death. Death as *différance* is an indication of the impossibility of any presence, any *parousia*, in the first place, to be negated afterwards.[3]

The sign as the *oikos* of *oikēsis*, as the house of death, is marked by the operation of *différance*: the economy of death is produced by *différance* (4). This implies that the sublation of the object is a result of a differing/deferring process: what is supposed to be a reproduction or re-presentation is marked by difference: the living soul that is "transposed" or "transplanted" into the concept, as a living dead, is radically different from either the signifier or the natural object itself: "The soul consigned to the pyramid is foreign (*fremd*). If it is transposed, transplanted into the monument like an immigrant, it is that it is not made of the stone of the signifier; neither in its origin nor its destination does it belong to the matter of the intuitive given. This heterogeneity amounts to the irreducibility...of two representations (*Vorstellungen*)" (84). And this is how one understands the arbitrariness of the sign, "the absence of any natural relation of resemblance, participation or analogy between the signified and the signifier, that is, here, between the representation (*Bedeutung*) and the intuition, or further between what is represented and the representative of representation by signs" (84). The sign also defers the presence of the natural object itself by constantly evoking the possibility of its presence. According to a classical semiology or even a metaphysical, dialectical, Hegelian interpretation of the economy of *différance*, the sign, which defers presence, (*ousia, parousia*) presupposes the presence that it defers. Derrida argues for an economy without economy of *différance*, gift economy of *différance*: "For the economic character of *différance* in no way implies that the deferred presence can always be found again, that we have here only an investment that provisionally and calculatedly delays the perception of its profit or the profit of its perception" (Derrida 1986c: 20).

There is an analogy between the movement of language and the experience of the foreign: language in mourning the absence of the event (the object, the sensory, or the immediate) promises a restoration of it. Language as the *oikos* of *oikēsis*, as the house of death, is also a house of life by keeping the possibility of the memory of the object open. That is to say, language as the house of death is constantly haunted by the ghost of the Object/Event. What is also crucial to recognize is that language is haunted by that memory rather than in control of it. This haunted language, I would argue, is also the structure of exilic and diasporic writings in which the subject of displacement, in his/her attempt at representing home, goes through a process of mourning in which he/she is haunted by the memory of the event of the loss of home and is thereby placed outside him/herself. In what follows, I would like to show that the relationship between representation, death and mourning is contingent on two different notions of, or rather relationships to, memory.

On the one hand, memory might be viewed as a standing-reserve of images, a reified memory (in which the subject remains intact and unaffected), a type of memory that John Donne calls "remembering" and according to him is the murderer of memory : "of our powers, remembering kills our memory"[4]. Memory as standing-reserve is a product of a restricted economy of representation and, to many, is an offshoot of the instrumental rationality predominant in post-industrial societies under capitalism. It is what Proust called *mémoire volontaire* as contrasted to *mémoire involontaire*[5]. It is associated with what Benjamin calls the "collector" as contrasted to an "allegorist" (Benjamin 2004: 211). Adorno describes the distinction between these two relations to memory as follows:

> The pronouncements, probably by Jean Paul, that memories are the only possessions which no-one can take from us, belongs in the storehouse of impotently sentimental consolations that the subject, resignedly withdrawing into inwardness, would like to believe the very fulfillment that he has given up. In setting up his own archives, the subject seizes his own stock of experience as property, so making it something wholly external to himself. Past inner life is turned into fur-

niture just as, conversely, every Biedermeier piece was memory made wood. The interior where the soul accommodates its collection of memoirs and curios is derelict. Memories cannot be conserved in drawers and pigeon-holes; in them the past is indissolubly woven into the present. No-one has them at his disposal in the free and voluntary way that is praised in Jean Paul's fulsome sentences. Precisely where they become controllable and objectifies, where the subject believes himself entirely sure of them, memories fade like delicate wallpapers in bright sunlight. (Adorno 2002:166)

Memory has long been compared to a container, a box, in which the individual stores images. Memory — a coffer, an armoire, or a jewel box — became a *book* in the fourteenth and fifteenth centuries: "In the miniature accompanying the section devoted to Flowering Memory (Flourie memore) in *Les Douze Dames de Rhétorique*, a late fifteenth century treatise on poetics, Memory is shown seated, with her eyes lowered, writing in a book. A small coffer is open at her foot" (Cerquiglini-Toulet 1997:123). Then we read the following: "I have carried a basket since I was a child, which I have filled with various things . . . By long travail and incessant care, I have filled the coffer of my memory" (qtd in Cerquiglini-Toulet 123).

Thus memory was a coffer that one fills with images of objects and events, an act of accumulating treasures, which then can be safeguarded and secured. This image of thought in which memory is posited as a repository of fixed images of the past reveals the restricted economy of travel and displacement in its fundamental strategy.

On the other hand, memory can be viewed as an event. It is a spectral and haunting memory that places the subject outside him/herself, and is akin to what the *punctum* of a photograph does to the subject. Hillis Miller is talking about "memory as event" when he says: "Our memories are out of our control. We remember only what our memories, acting on their own, happen to think it worthwhile to save" (in Derrida 2003: 202). In Deleuze when he describes Resnais: "In Resnais too it is time that we plunge into, not at the mercy of a psychological memory that would give us only an indirect representation, nor at the mercy of a recollection-image that would refer us back to a former present, but following a deeper memory, a memory of the world directly exploring time, reaching in the past that which conceals itself from memory" (Deleuze 1997:39). In his *Memoires: for Paul de Man* (1989) Derrida, remembering de Man remembering Hegel, discusses the aporia of memory by distinguishing two kinds of memory and the oscillation between the two. On the one hand, there is *Erinnerung* as an interiorizing memory that defines the coherent self by its ability to assimilate and fully contain a lost other. Its aim is what Freud describe in 1915 as the work of complete mourning, a process of introjection through which we sever our attachments to the lost one by cannibalistically devouring them. In this way we preserve them inside us until they can finally be declared dead and abolished. *Erinnerung* is also what Freud calls "complete mourning." *Gedächtnis*, on the other hand, arrests this sense of completion. As an exteriorizing memory, it defines the other not by its ability to interiorize a lost other but by its relation to an other that can never be fully contained. This "thinking" memory, or memory of "inscription" and difference, "disrupts the simple inclusion of a part within the whole." It recalls to thought "the other as other, the non-totalizable trace which is in-adequate to itself and to the same. This trace is interiorized in mourning as that which can no longer be interiorized, as impossible *Erinnerung*, in and beyond mournful memory — constituting it, traversing it, exceeding it, defying all reappropriation" (Derrida 1989:38).

Closely related to the theme of memory and the above distinction is another "aporia of memory" which can be described as follows: on the one hand, there is the almost irresistible urge to remember the past, "no one wants to forget. More accurately, no one wants to be forgotten. Or more peacefully, people bring children into the world to carry their name, or to bear for them the weight of the name and its glory. It has had a long history, this double operation of searching for a place or a time on which to put a signature and untie the knot of the name facing the long caravans of oblivion" (Darwish 1995:15). On the other hand, memory, more often than not, is associated with, as well as an agent of, death and oblivion. The inscription of memory in language, as we discussed Agamben, can be construed to be a scene of murder (or at least a mutilating reduction of the event represented by selective determinations and perceptions) and, in cases of Primo Levi and Charlotte Delbo, is reminiscent of death and the "unthinkable." For Delbo, as she was writing *Days and Memory* toward the end of her life, the challenge to future readers was how to remember those years whose "unthinkable" incidents no one wishes to reawaken from the slumber of forgetfulness. The urge to remember, in its overcoming the desire to forget, places the subject outside him/herself. Delbo began *Days and Memory* with the words *Expliquer l'inexplicable*, "explain the inexplicable," and like Primo Levi, she was still trying to do it forty years after the event. She spoke of two selves, her Auschwitz self and her post-Auschwitz self, and used the image of a snake shedding its skin to conjure up a sense of her new nature emerging after the camp years.

> Unfortunately, unlike the snake's skin, which shrivels, disintegrates, and disappears, what Delbo called the skin of Auschwitz memory remained. 'Auschwitz is so deeply etched on my memory,' she wrote, 'that I cannot forget one moment of it. So you are living with Auschwitz? No, I live next to it [*à coté de*]. Auschwitz is there, unalterable, precise, but enveloped in the skin of memory, an impermeable skin that isolates it from my present self. Unlike the snake's skin, the skin of memory does not renew itself . . . . Thinking about it makes me tremble with apprehension. (Delbo 1995:XI)

Delbo developed a distinction to help us discriminate between two operations of memory, speaking of the "me" of now, living under the control of what she called *mémoire ordinaire*, or "common memory," and the "me" of then, the Auschwitz "me," living under the dominion of *mémoire profonde*, or "deep memory."

> Common memory urges us to regard the Auschwitz ordeal as part of a chronology, a dismal event in the past that the very fact of survival helps to redeem. It frees us from the pain of remembering the unthinkable. 'I am very fortunate,' Delbo writes, 'in not recognizing myself in the self that was in Auschwitz . . ., I feel that the one who was in the camp is not me, is not the person who is here, facing you.' Deep memory, on the other hand, reminds us that the Auschwitz past is not really past and never will be, although on occasion Delbo seems to believe that the two kinds of memory can remain insulated from each other. But her own experience, as well as that of countless other survivors, violates her theory. (XI-II)

The second operation of memory, the "deep memory," is not, however, a repressed memory that can be retrieved from the layers of the past by a conscious, instrumental act. It comes close to what I called "memory as event" and about which Delbo can write:

> As far as I am concerned
>
> I'm still there
>
> Dying there
>
> A little more every day
>
> Dying over again
>
> The death of those who died (XV)

Memory as Event, Eruption of the Past, Logic of Haunting

Freud discusses the logic of haunting most directly in his "The Uncanny" as well as in *Beyond the Pleasure Principle*. In both essays, Freud shifts his emphasis from the distinction between the conscious and the unconscious to one between the coherent ego and the repressed. In other words, in these two essays Freud is no longer concerned with successful defense mechanisms against the past, something that the pleasure principle presupposes (the pleasure principle is also a principle of forgetfulness). Instead he focuses on unsuccessful defenses in which the repressed returns into conscious awareness and haunts the subject. The term he uses for the haunting and overpowering of the present by the past is "traumatic neurosis." The difference between traumatic neurosis and other forms of neurotic illness (i.e., the difference between successful and unsuccessful defense against the dead) corresponds to what Freud, in his "Mourning and Melancholia," calls complete and incomplete mourning and is further elaborated by Abraham and Torok.

It should also be remembered that in other neurotic processes (such as dreamwork) the working defense does not escape the past, but instead generates forms and structures in which the force of the past is lived, i.e., mediated. It is in fact a sublation (preservation and cancellation) of the past through acts of memory.

> Thus, since the defenses are themselves modes of the past's preservation, traumatic neurosis must be understood as a conflict between two modes of history, one mediated by forms of defense and the other antagonistic to such mediation. In traumatic neurosis, in other words, the past takes its revenge against the very possibility of a mediated relation to it, against, that is, the possibility of memory. (Horowitz 2001:123)

It seems that we are again dealing with two distinct ways of understanding memory: the first is encountered in non-traumatic neurosis in which the past is tamed, sublated, and mediated. Following what I proposed earlier, I would like to distinguish this way of understanding memory, which intimates an act of complete mourning, and might be called "memory as standing-reserve," from a second understanding encountered in traumatic neurosis, in which the past erupts and storms the fortified present. In this second understanding, which might be called "memory as event," the dead refuses to stay dead and the past haunts the subject as something untamable and unmediatable. The time of this second type of memory is out of joint, because the apparently surmounted past is reappearing in a time to which it does not belong. Traumatic neurosis, Freud seems to argue, is the derangement of historical time.

> The aftermath of the traumatogenic event is not a life full of recollections, but a life deformed by eruptions of the past which cannot be recalled. As past and present penetrate one another, traumatic repetitions *interrupt* the present and thereby disable the formative impulses of the pleasure principle (hence, Freud's formulation of trauma as 'beyond' the pleasure principle). Trauma is a break in the order of experience that blasts apart the great project of psychical life, the binding of past, present, and future. (Horowitz 2001:124)

The traumatic event, taking place without being remembered, points to a crisis of representation as well as a crisis of inheritance. The traumatic event cannot be represented because it cannot be remembered and mediated. It is also deprived of the capacity to weave time together in order to live and inherit from the past. In other words, the traumatic event is the ruination of inheritance and the representational relation.

The haunting power of the memory of/as event, and the differential representations of its loss is the theme of Pasolini's *Theorema* (1970). Before discussing Pasolini's *Theorema*, let us first see how the latter understands cinema. In an interview with Oswald Stack, Pasolini proposes the following understanding of cinema:

> In my view cinema is substantially and naturally poetic . . . because it is dreamlike because it is close to dreams, because a film sequence and a sequence of memory or of a dream . . . are profoundly poetic: a tree photographed is poetic, a human face photographed is poetic because the physical is poetic in itself, be-

cause it is an apparition, because it is full of mystery, because it is full of ambiguity, because it is full of polyvalent meaning. (Pasolini 1969:153)

Pasolini in his *Heretical Empiricism* argues for a deontologization of cinema:

> It is necessary to create ideology; it is necessary to destroy ontology. Audiovisual techniques are in large measure already a part of our world, that is, of the world of technical neocapitalism, which moves ahead, and whose tendency it is to deprive its technique of ideology or to make them ontological; to make them silent and unrelated, to make them habits; to make them religious forms. We are lay humanist . . . . We must therefore fight to demystify the "innocence of technique" to the last drop of blood. (71)

This statement, which concludes one of Pasolini's most important essays on film, "The Written Language of Reality," may be understood not only as one of his fundamental theoretical principles but also as the declaration of a radical political agenda, something that he could not quite realize by the time of his assassination in 1975. Ricciardi (2003) characterizes Pasolini's theory of artistic production as "spectropoetic," borrowing Derrida's word in *Specters of Marx*. Pasolini's heretical "spectropoetics" is manifested through a mournful relation to the past and a melancholic devotion to certain traditions. The past, in Pasolini's work, is not to be viewed as a historical truth, but rather as a metaphor for a radical new beginning. Pasolini's "spectropoetics" is a "poetic encounter with the specters of history" in which he bears witness to "not only the *revenants* of the past, but also the *arrivants* of the future" (Ricciardi 127). Pasolini's poetics of spectrality is also inscribed by a principle of hospitality to and of the Other. Pasolini, Ricciardi argues in quite some details, is preoccupied by the specters of history but not in the form of individual memories to which the subject has uninhibited access. In *The Ashes of Gramsci*, Pasolini creates an imaginary world where the figures of the past seem quite independent of authorial intervention. Pasolini's obsession with the word "ashes" is also explicit in his autobiographical poem "Poet of ashes" [*Poeta delle ceneri*] (1966). Pasolini wrote *The Ashes of Gramsci* during the same years in which Adorno expressed his skepticism regarding the writing of poetry after Auschwitz. These were also the years that Paul Celan reevaluated the meaning of the German word *Aschen*. Derrida, taking as his point of departure Celan's poetry, elaborated a philosophy of traces that likens memory to a process of incineration. Pasolini appears to take himself as a poet of ashes insofar as he believes in the necessity of working through a mourning of the past and the dead, a mourning that has little to do with memory as a standing-reserve of images and their reproducibility (which is nothing more than a reified memory) but with traces and ashes that keep returning to haunt the subject and announce a future to come. Pasolini reverses the function of the image toward its spectral and messianic potential. In this sense, Pasolini's cinema of spectrality is a radicalization of the spectropoetics developed in his lyric texts. Cinema seems to offer Pasolini a chance of not merely an aesthetic recovery of collective memory and tradition, but for the projection of the past into the future of ethical and political hopes. His chief achievement, Ricciardi argues, is his increasing awareness of the necessity of hospitality to the revenants of history (whether ideological, religious or political) who are to become the future restitution of justice, the apocalyptic event of a Marxism to come (139). It is in his *Theorema* that Pasolini most clearly demonstrates the logic of the spectral *arrivant* who, in fact, disappears as soon he arrives. The departure of the ghostly guest in *Theorema* initiates whole different processes of mourning in different characters. These processes, or rather events, of mourning (since they are somehow imposed on characters), places each subject (in both senses of he who is subjected as well as an agent of the mourning process) outside him/herself. One of the crucial issues that *Theorema* puts forward is that it is in a relationship to a spectral, incinerated past that the future is written. The movie represents, in other words and to borrow from Ricciardi, a "spectralization of messianic time" (140), a conjunction of spectropoetics and messianism mediated through mourning. "The spectralization of messianic time" mourns, as it were, the unfulfilled utopian promise of the future.

Another related theme in *Theorema* is that of absence and emptiness that triggers a process of mourning. Pasolini moves Antonioni's principle of empty space[6], that is, a dehumanized space, a space emptied of human figures, to another level. Pasolini much like Antonioni, believed that the absence of human figures from the cinematic field of vision brings about a greater gain in meaning than their presence. For him "the world is presented as if regulated by a myth of pure pictorial beauty that the personages invade, it is true, but adapting themselves to the rules of that beauty instead of profaning them with their presence" (Pasolini 1988:179).

Theorema is one of Pasolini's most significant films in terms of its ability to find a narrative framework for its allegorical content. It is also a movie that is emblematic of cinema as time-image. Deleuze has suggested that the cinema of time-image is inherently "theorematic"[7] in the sense that it has the mental effect of a theorem, that is, "it makes the unrolling of the film a theorem rather than an association of images, it makes thought immanent to the image" (Deleuze 1997:173). *Theorema*, as well as *Salo*, is theorematic because it has achieved a (mathematical) rigor that no longer concerns the image itself but the thought of the image, the thought in the image. It has become a cinema of cruelty of which Artaud said that "it does not tell a story but develops a sequence of spiritual states which are deduced from one another as thought is deducted from thought." (Deleuze 174). Deleuze further distinguishes between the two mathematical instances of "the theorem" and "the problem," which constantly refer to each other:

> A problem lives in a theorem, and gives it life, even when removing its power. The problematic is distinguished from the theorematic (or constructivism from the axiomatic) in that the theorem develops internal relationships from principle to consequences, while the problem introduces an event from the outside . . . which constitutes its own conditions and determines the 'case' or cases . . . this outside of the problem is not reducible to the exteriority of the physical world any more than to the psychological interiority of a thinking ego. (174)

What is important to note in Deleuze's argument is that Pasolini's *Theorema* is a theorematic film but its deduction is not theorematic but rather "problematic."[8] The guest from the outside is the occasion toward which every member of the family experiences an affect, event, or disruption: the girl is "paralyzed," the mother is "fixed in her erotic quest," the son blindfolded, urinating on his painter's canvas, the maid becoming a victim of a "mystical levitation," and the father is "animalized, naturalized" (Deleuze 175). All the members of this Milanese family are responding to one problem originating from the outside, i.e., the ghostly guest, but the consequence or deduction is different, and always uncertain, in each case. Therefore, the leitmotif of the film: "I am haunted by a question to which I cannot reply."

Theorema (1970), in telling the story of a mysterious guest who enters the lives of the members of a wealthy Milanese family only to vanish after disrupting their complacent, domestic, bourgeois routine, provides us in fact with the very "theorem" of Pasolini's aesthetics of cinema as a mode of mourning and a poetics of haunting. The guest brings about, on his departure, traumatic experiences in the lives of all the members of this Milanese family: Paolo, the paterfamilias and the owner of a local factory, gives away his factory to his employees and retreats to the desert; Lucia, the mother of Odetta, tries to substitute her lost object of desire with randomly picked-up men who strike her as bearing some resemblance to the guest; Odetta becomes literally paralyzed in her refusal to substitute the absence and the loss caused by the separation from the visitor; Pietro, the son, perpetuates the artistic curiosity passed on to him as a gift by the stranger; and Emilia, the maid, after a failed attempt at suicide, retreats into a mystical trance and is shown as levitating above the local rooftops.

From the very beginning, the structure of repetition that Freud associates with the work of mourning is apparent. Emilia's reaction to the guest, for example, immediately manifests the mechanism of repetition in her running back and forth from the garden to the house a few times before attempting to commit suicide in the kitchen. Repetition also decisively informs Lucia's behavior after the guest's departure, when her succession of meaningless liaisons with young men marks her sense of bereavement. In Odetta's case, the theme of repetition is played out in the substitution of the guest for the father.

Theorema is not only an allegory of mourning but also a diagnosis of the exhaustion of the bourgeois culture after the failure of the Enlightenment metanarratives of rational historical progress. The bourgeois culture as represented by this Milanese family is simply incapable of coping with the vicissitudes of life in the wake of the disappearance of the sacred. In an appendix to the first part of the novel, the individual members are assigned confessional monologues in which they all express their despair of ever finding a replacement (*Ersatz*) for the nameless stranger. The host becomes a hostage[9]. Their attestation to the impossibility of completing the work of mourning for their messianic guest is also a manifestation of their feelings of displacement and dislocation that will resist any definite utopian resolution. After he vanishes, all of the household's members pursue, in a manner reminiscent of Nietzsche's notion of the death of God and the proliferations of the will to power and interpretation, their own personal spiritual or material response in their mourning the disappearance of the object they were cathecticly invested in. In the extraordinary cases of Paolo and Emilia, *Theorema*, like much of Pasolini's oeuvre, dramatizes the emergence of the miraculous and the spiritual as the result of a spectral encounter with the Real. The impossibility of mourning in *Theorema* is directly related to the namelessness of the guest and the ambiguity surrounding his identity, history or his domicile. Because he has no legible, personal history of his own, he can be given to place or location in memory: "without a fixed [*arrête*] place, without a determinable *topos*, mourning is not allowed. Or what comes down to the same thing, it is promised without taking place, a determinable place, so henceforth promised as an interminable mourning, an infinite mourning defying all work, beyond any possible work of mourning. The only possible mourning is the impossible mourning" (Derrida and Dufourmantelle 2000:111).

The guest/host relationship in *Theorema* is best captured by citing Derrida on Antigone:

> It is *as if*, then, the stranger could save the master and liberate the power of his host; it's *as if* the master, *qua* master, were prisoner of his place and his power, of his ipseity, of his subjectivity (his subjectivity is hostage). So it is indeed the master, the one who invites, the inviting host, who becomes the hostage — and who really always has been. And the guest, the invited hostage, becomes the one who invites the one who invites, the master of the host. The guest becomes the host's host. The guest (*hôte*) becomes the host (*hôte*) of the host (*hôte*).
>
> . . . the master of the house is at home, but nonetheless he comes to enter his home through the guest — who comes from outside. The master thus enters from the inside *as if* he came from the outside.   (Derrida and Dufourmantelle 123-25)

Paolo, the father, the master of the house, the one who supposedly lays down the laws of hospitality, becomes, in his relationship to the visitor, a guest himself, who subsequently relinquishes his property and home and heads toward a desert. And the visitor, in his turn, becomes hospitable to those who host him. Even though, in a conventional sense, one cannot be hospitable without being sovereign in one's home, Paolo becomes perhaps truly hospitable by relinquishing his home. The injunction of hospitality is to become homeless.

In *Theorema*, the memory of the guest haunts the hosts and places them outside themselves: it is a memory beyond remembering, a memory as event. A more ethical relationship to the (alterity of the) other becomes possible when the individual, rather than voluntarily remembering and representing the experience of the foreign, is displaced in his/her subjectivity by a memory that keeps coming back while intimating the impossibility of representation.

The notion of memory as standing-reserve is analogous to what Benjamin, in his *The Arcades Project* (2004), discusses under the act of collecting, something that implies not only the historicity of any relationship to memory but also a sign of death:

> What is decisive in collecting is that the object is detached from all its original functions in order to enter into the closest conceivable relation to things of the same kind. This relation is the diametric opposite of any utility, and falls into the peculiar category of completeness. What is this 'completeness'? It is a grand attempt to overcome the wholly irrational character of the object's mere presence at hand through its integration into a new, expressly devised historical system: the collection . . . everything remembered, everything thought, everything conscious becomes socle, frame, pedestal, seal of his possession . . . collecting is a form of practical memory, and of all the profane manifestations of 'nearness' it is the most binding. (204-5) . . . With individuals as with societies, the need to accumulate is one of the signs of approaching death. (208)

The allegorist is, as it were, the polar opposite of the collector, although it is not always possible to draw a sharp line between the two. The allegorist has given up the attempt "to elucidate things through research into their properties and relations. He dislodges things from their context and, from the outset, relies on his profundity to illuminate their meaning. The collector, by contrast, brings together what belongs together; by keeping in mind their affinities and their succession in time, he can eventually furnish information about his objects. Nevertheless — and this is more important than all the differences that may exist between them — in every collector hides an allegorist, and in every allegorist a collector" (211).

In order to understand the past, Benjamin seems to say, one should open oneself to the possibility (and the actuality) of being disrupted. By saying that it is not us who go to the past, but rather the past that comes to us, Benjamin denies any intentionality in our relationship to the past and the mediating role of memory:

> The true method of making things present is to represent them in our space (not to represent ourselves in their space). The collector does just this, and so does the anecdote.) Thus represented, the things allow no mediating construction from out of 'large contexts.' The same method applies, in essence, to the consideration of great things from the past — the cathedral of Chartres, the temple of Paestum — when, that is, a favorable prospect presents itself: the method of receiving the things into our space. We don't displace our being into theirs; they step into our life. (206)

In memory as standing-reserve, the collection of images one calls memory undergoes a reification or a commodification process. Memory as event, on the other hand, is *our* memory but we do not possess it. The following passages from Marx can help us understand, in a rather figurative and allegoric way, the difference between the two types of relationships to memory. Marx in his *Der historische Materialismus*: "private property has made us so stupid and inert that an object is *ours* only when we have it, when it exists as capital for us, or when . . . we *use* it." (Benjamin 2004: 209). Also, in the same work: "All the physical and intellectual senses have been replaced by the simple alienation of all these senses, the sense of *having* . . ." (209). To think about memory in terms of what Marx understands as an impulse toward possession or even the use-value, would be to argue that it is not necessary to own or possess a collection of images about the past in order to be able to have a relationship to the past or inherit from it. The commodification of memory can, as it were, be construed as part of a more general problem of reification under capitalism.

Benjamin's distinction between trace and aura is another way of understanding a possessive and a haunted relationship to memory. According to Benjamin "the trace is appearance of a nearness, however far removed the thing that left it behind may be. The aura is appearance of a distance, however close the thing that calls it forth. In the trace, we gain possession of the thing; in aura, it takes possession of us" (447).

Memory as event can be further elucidated by Benjamin's notion of the reading (and writing) of history in which the historian reads what was never written.[10] He calls this "Copernican revolution in historical perception" a new "turn of remembrance."

> The Copernican revolution in historical perception is as follows: Formerly it was thought that a fixed point had been found in "what has been," and one saw the present engaged in tentatively concentrating the forces of knowledge on this ground. Now this relation is to be overturned, and what has been is to become the dialectical reversal — the flash of awakened consciousness. Politics attains primacy over history. The facts become something that just now first happened to us, first struck us; to establish them is the affair of memory . . . what Proust intends with the experimental rearrangement of furniture in matinal half-slumber, what Bloch recognizes as the darkness of the lived moment, is nothing other than what here is to be secured on the level of the historical, and collectively. There is a not-yet-conscious knowledge of what has been: its advancement has the structure of awakening. (389)

> The new dialectical method of doing history presents itself as the art of experiencing the present as waking world, a world to which that dream we name the past refers in truth. To pass through and carry out what has been in remembering the dream ! — therefore: remembering and awaking are most intimately related. Awakening is namely the dialectical, Copernican turn of remembrance. (389)

To further elaborate the distinction between memory as standing-reserve and memory as event, I would like to turn to the works of writers in exile. Exilic writers, in representing their sense of displacement, make literary capital out of their loss. Since for them "home" has either transformed beyond recognition, is unavailable, or is a site of ineluctable disappointment, they turn to memory as compensation for loss and a source of renewed identity and self-knowledge. It is through memory and writing that they built a home away from home. To be sure there are writers for whom nothing can compensate for the loss of home and the familiar. But for many exilic writers, nevertheless, the memory of home becomes the ground of creativity and invention exactly because of its remoteness, intangibility and inaccessibility. For an exiled writer like the Belgian Luc Sante, in his *The Factory of Facts* (1998), a disrupted past allows him the freedom not to be confined by it, but to become an inventor of that past and of the self, precisely because the past seems so ungraspable. André Aciman in his *False Pa-*

pers (2000), is less concerned with facts, and like Sante and the Nabokov of *Speak, Memory*, knows that exile bestows a curious freedom to remake and refashion the past. In the state of exile we remember as we wish. It is not history or the past that Sante or Aciman uncover, but the self in the present, a remembering self who substitutes for the disappearance of the remembered.

Gini Alhadeff's memoir demonstrates a profound indifference to loss; indeed she like Aciman regards loss as a form of gain. In fact, for Aciman, Alhadeff, Sante, Darwish and others, Adorno's aphorism about the advantage of homelessness applies: "For a man who no longer has a homeland writing becomes a place to live." [11]

André Aciman's *Out of Egypt* (1994) depicts his Jewish-Egyptian family in Alexandria over several generations, beginning with its move from Constantinople in 1905, and concluding with the departure of his family from Egypt in 1956 when Aciman was an adolescent and Nasser came to power, expelling Alexandria's Jews in the first wave of Egyptian nationalism. The family fled to Italy, then to France, and eventually to America, where Aciman was educated at Harvard and became an essayist, presently teaching French literature at Bard College. Aciman's narrative is a collection of portraits of family members and his visits of family members in his search to confirm his memories of a displaced culture. He returns to Alexandria twenty years later, imaging that everything will be the same. "Return" is a central motif in his memoir, both the literal or physical return which fills him with disappointment, as well as a mental return, which lies at the origin of memory. Aciman learns Greek from an elderly scholar and when they read *The Odyssey* together, the scholar tells Aciman that he agrees with the Alexandrian Greek poet Cavafy, who claimed the Odysseus never returned to Ithaca but succumbed to Calypso, voluntarily exiling himself on the island. Aciman cites Cavafy, who has Calypso say to Odysseus: "Why spurn my home when exile is your home? The Ithaca you want you'll have in not having…you're made thus, to yearn for what you lose (Aciman 1994:290).

What lies at the heart of Aciman's autobiography is his belief that his identity as exile will never end,[12] for he believes there is no way to recover home, or if by chance home is reached, it will provide little contentment. The only pleasure is from the act of memory rather than any physical return or arrival. Condemned to remember, he discovers that stability is elusive, and he can never really establish a new home anywhere. For Aciman nostalgia and homesickness are the existential conditions that endure and he has to find ways of dealing with them. Aciman, like Cavafy's Odysseus, loves the act of remembering more than the thing remembered. It is through his writing that Aciman tries to recuperate home. In fact, for Aciman, the ability to recreate the lost place in writing is not mere compensation but a significant value for any exiled person. Exile becomes the condition of the possibility of writing. One can see, once again, the restricted economy of exilic writing, and its concomitant notion of capitalization on loss, at work here. In exile memory becomes a standing-reserve for the subject to which the latter has immediate access and can use as a commodity in his/her refashioning of the self. It should, however, be noted that in order to avoid constructing a binary opposition, one needs to identify "moments" of capitalization on memory and loss, in an otherwise non-economic work.

Aciman's belief in the permanence of exile and the impossibility of return make him into a diaspora: not that he literally wanders the earth, but that he cannot be at home anywhere. Perpetually displaced, Aciman's initial exilic condition becomes diasporic. When he is temporarily back in Alexandria he is thinking of New York, not because New York has become his refuge or because he believes that New York is "better," but because in New York he had found a place of mourning that make him think longingly of Alexandria. In Alexandria he longs to be in New York as the only place Alexandria become compelling. Aciman's diasporic experience of loss and longing makes him the least faithful of men: to feel and understand a place he must be somewhere else, so that paradoxically he is home only when he is not home. Aciman's relation to home, to borrow from Benjamin, is, as it were, based on figuration and allegory: home cannot be understood on its own terms but it needs the mediation of another experience and another time/place.

Since memory is a powerful tool for (re)construction of identity, both the totalitarian regimes as well as Western, Liberal democracies have contributed to, what Tzvetan Todorov calls, the "blotting out of memory" (11). The totalitarian regimes have understood that both the transformation as well as the erasure of memory are powerful tools in their conquest of men and territories. The traces of what once existed have been either completely erased or is replaced by lies and fabrications, inventions and myths. In concentration camps bodies are dug up in order to be burnt in order to avoid or prevent worrisome memories. History is rewritten according to the exigencies of the dominant powers and ideologies. The totalitarian regimes are, however, not the only enemies of memory. Neoliberal democracies have also contributed to the "extinction of memory" (11) by celebrating and promoting consumerism and short-lasting pleasures: "Cut off from our traditions and deadened by the demands of a leisure society, deprived of spiritual curiosity and familiarity with the great works of the past, we are condemned cheerfully to celebrate forgetting and be content with useless pleasures of the moment" (12). In their march toward forgetting, both the totalitarian and the democratic regimes "are leading their people toward the same end" (12).

We must first of all keep in mind the fact that memory is in no way the opposite of forgetting. According to Todorov, the two terms that contrast with each other are *disappearance* (forgetting) and *preservation*. Memory is always and necessarily an interaction of these two. The complete reconstitution of the past is obviously an impossibility (but something a Borges could imagine in a story like "Funes the Memorious") and moreover, it is frightening and undesirable. Memory itself is necessarily a selection: certain characteristics of the event will be retained, while others forgotten. What we blame Hitler and Stalin for is "not that they retain only certain elements of the past, for we ourselves cannot do otherwise, but that they appropriate for themselves the right to control the choice of the elements retained" (12).

Todorov further distinguishes between "the *recovery* of the past and its subsequent *use*" (12). These two are not necessarily connected: to know about the past does not give us ethical guidelines on how to use it. The ethics of memory is necessarily, according to Todorov, related to the rejection of an economy of memory. The past is made up of multitude of events (and each event with multitudes of attributes) and of contradictory meanings and it is an ethico-political decision of those acting in the present that certain ones are chosen for commemoration and others are passed over. Todorov, in the following passage, argues that a repudiation of an economy of memory is a precondition of an ethics of memory:

> To remember an action in which I was the cause of something bad or in which I benefited from another's heroic exploits, to see these others as victims or benefactors, brings me no direct benefit. However, it is only in this way that I can put the happiness of others and my own perfection above personal interest and engage in a moral act. In other words, there is no moral benefit possible for the subject, whether he be an individual or a group, if his remembering the past puts him in a sympathetic role (hero, or victim), but only if, on the contrary, it makes him realize his weaknesses and his follies. (Todorov 2001:16)

Todorov, therefore, seems to say that what makes a memory an ethical act is to remember against oneself. This is contrasted to a politics of memory (or rather a political economy of memory) in which one remembers a particular selection from among the totality of events, one that assures its protagonist of maintaining the role of hero or victim when faced with any other selection that might assign him/her a less glorious role. Todorov's ethics of memory, it should be noted, is still inscribed within a Cartesian framework: memory is still something over which the subject has control, in such a way that one part of the ego can work against another. In other words, the splitting of the ego implies the possibility of self-regulation within the ego itself.

To sum up, I tried to elucidate some of the theoretical/philosophical underpinnings as well as to delineate the contours of what I understand under a general economical framework of travel (discourse). The principle of death (as that with which one has no relation) and the event of memory have been discussed as two exemplary figures through which the supposed subject's will to representation and knowledge is disrupted. In terms of the exilic/diasporic experience, the dialectical *Aufhebung* of return is arrested by excess and transgression.

I would now like to turn to Kader Abdolah's *Spijkerschrift* and Kiarostami's *The Taste of Cherry* in order to explore the extent to which the general and restricted economical moments/forces are at work. While analyzing the former in terms of the crisis of representation in its relation to secrecy and the latter in terms of the crisis of representation in relation to death, I will argue that in Kader Abdolah's *Spijkerschrift*, even though it acknowledges the textual excess, the final strategy is in fact a restricted economical one. Kiarostami's *The Taste of Cherry*, on the contrary, foregrounds a general economy of representation by positing death as an outside, to which one has no relation, and is therefore cannot be sublated.

In the past decades and within the social sciences scholars have become increasingly aware of the dangers of an essentialist approach towards concepts like culture and identity. An essentialist understanding of identity refers to an understanding of individuals or groups which is static and fixed in reference to their cultural and social contexts. In this way, concepts such as culture and identity became "things" which people "have." A constructionist approach is critical of the ways in which these concepts have been defined in a static and artificially coherent manner. Fredrik Barth's 1969 book, *Ethnic Groups and Boundaries: The Social Organization of Cultural Difference*, opened a door for a more critical examination of these concepts. His emphasis on ethnic boundaries instead of "the cultural stuff that it encloses" (Barth 1969:15) had a great impact on the perception of identity as a changing process. Within his analysis individuals were not captured within their social and cultural settings, but were construed to be individuals who consciously pursue goals. In this way, Barth "offers a model of ethnic and other social identities as somewhat fluid, situationally contingent, and the subject of perpetual negotiations" (Jenkins 1996: 23). Within this constructionist framework identity has been defined as a process and as "multiple" (Appadurai 1986, Friedman 1994, Giddens 1991). Shami describes it as "constructed, multi-faceted, negotiated, situational," (Shami 1993:9) while Fischer understands identity as "a pluralist, multidimentional, or multifaceted concept of the self" (Fischer 1986:196).

It seems that these new approaches did not quite satisfied scholars, since some have tried to replace it with alternatives. Essed prefers to talk about multiple identifications "in order to emphasize that subjectivities are not static but always in the process of being constructed in relation to perceived material, political or social interest" (Essed 1995:100). Fischer-Rosenthal (1995) finds the term "identity" so problematic that he proposes to withdraw it from use altogether. Identity, he argues, is a static term based on a simplistic approach to the individual. The term identity gives room for the old myth of the Enlightenment, which saw the subject merely as a rational being. In Fischer-Rosenthal's eyes, identity emphasizes the illusion of a coherent and integrated subject who is able to cope with the uncertainties of the outside world. He asks:

> Is identity just another 'modern' relic of Cartesian thought where methodological doubts produce the arrogant sum cogitans who by stepping outside the concrete life-world, gains an objective world — a field of observation and rational manipulation, while losing his own position within the same world? (Fischer-Rosenthal 1995:253)

By placing identity within a broader philosophical background, Fischer-Rosenthal shows the inadequacy of the term and proposes to replace identity with biography: "Biography refers to an interpretatively open process of 'becoming.' Identity, on the other hand, focuses on a fixed state of 'being' or 'having'" (258).

Another important dimension related to the process of identity formation is multiplicity, which challenges the unitary and coherent aspect of identity. Accepting identity as multiple carries the perceived danger of seeing the self as fragmented. There have been some attempts to argue against this fragmentation. R. Turner, for example, talks about the "basket of selves"[13] where the individual is the container and uses these selves, somehow voluntarily and differentially, when needed. The rhetoric of the "basket of selves" is, one might argue, what Mukherjee uses in representing the process of the reinvention of her character, Jasmine. Epstein (1978) puts it differently: identity "represents the process by which the person seeks to integrate his various statuses and roles, as well as his diverse experiences, into a coherent image of self" (Epstein 1978:101). In these two approaches the myth of the-powerful-subject-in control is recreated. It is the subject who is aware of his/her selves and makes the combination and creates an integrated self. More recent theories of identity emphasize identity not as an autonomous, self-contained and static term but as a narrative which is about "living a biography" (Giddens 1991:14). Somers and Gibson (1994) argue that narratives give individuals the possibility of understanding their surrounding world and of constructing their identities, even if these narratives are sometimes ambiguous and often contradictory. Homi Bhabha criticized the idea of multiple identities from a different angle. According to him, the term "multiple identities" gives a voluntaristic illusion of individuals who may choose between a collection of identities. He argues that although identity may be about negotiations of identifications, the whole process is an ambivalent one. He replaces the term "multiple identities" with "the doubleness of identity."

> When I speak about the doubleness of identity, I don't mean two: I mean to suggest the negotiated iterability of identity, its constant repetition, revision, relocation, so that no repetition is the same as the preceding one.   (Bhabha 1984:12)

For Bhabha, the term "multiple identities" can create the illusion of freedom of choice. It is as if people may always choose what they want to be, while in reality they face limitations. Kader Abdolah *Spijkershrift* might be read as a novel posing the problem of the necessity of fashioning multiple identities in exile and the dilemmas associated with it. Before we turn to Kader Abdolah *Spijkershrift* and analyze his resolution for the crisis of identity he encounters in The Netherlands, I would like to talk about some of the socio-psychological causes underlying this crisis through some reflections on the question of the relationship between home and exile as well as the aporias of that of immigration, integration and cultural difference.

The concept of home is inevitably related to migration and exile and is reflected in the works of writers, artists, scholars and film-makers in exile. One of the central themes of these works is the link between the present and the past, in which the latter overlaps with, and more often than not is transformed into, the experience of the past: " . . . the past is home, albeit a lost home in a lost city in the mist of lost time" (Rushdie 1992: 9). There is a sense of loss associated with home and one's relationship to the past but there is also the acknowledgment that "we will not be capable of reclaiming precisely the thing that was lost; that we will, in short, create fictions, not actual cities or villages, but invisible ones, imaginary homelands, Indias of the mind" (10).

When home is equated with the past, it can easily become something static and fixed. Home becomes synonymous with the country of origin where people are supposedly rooted and which they have left behind. Scholars within the field of refugee studies have also contributed to this way of approaching home by making the assumption that the homeland or country of origin is not only the normal but the ideal habitat for any person. In this way, home is directly equated with the national borders of the country of origin. Malkki (1995) disputes this so-called "sedentarist bias" that assumes that rootedness in a culture and a geographic territory is a normal feature of human life. Malkki, in her refutation of "the sedentarist bias," deterritorializes the concept of home:

> But if 'home' is where one feels most safe and at ease, instead of some essentialized point on the map, then it is far from clear that returning where one fled from is the same thing as 'going home.' (Malkki 1995:509)

While an exilic approach to home is based on national boundaries, in a diasporic approach home is not linked to a certain physical space; it is rather transnational in character and is a constructed space in the present through contacts, memories and activities[14].

The two dominant relations to home, i.e., exilic and diasporic, are, however, not voluntaristic options open to all immigrants or displaced people. My hypothesis is that the tendency toward an exilic relationship to home (the longing to return to a particular geographic place and the country of origin) is stronger in cases of Iranian immigrants in most European countries where the prospects of integration into the host country are limited. On the other hand, the Iranian immigrants in US tend toward a transnational, diasporic relation to home (the Iran of their minds) precisely because it is much easier for Iranians in US to integrate into the society at large. Halleh Ghorashi, in her dissertation, compares the Iranian immigrants in the Netherlands with those in US. One can easily see that the Iranian immigrants in the Netherlands are more exilic compared to the Iranian immigrants in US who are more diasporic. Iranians in the Netherlands, as she tries to show, have a more contradictory relationship to their past and their home too. These contradictions are obvious in Leila's story. She lives in the Netherlands with her child and most of the members of her family are in the Netherlands as well. She works hard and studies and is rather an optimistic person. When Ghorashi asks her about her Iranian identity, she hesitates for some moments before replying:

> I am not a nationalist person who puts emphasis on Iranian identity. I do not believe in nationalism. I think that I can live in this society as a person, not so much as an Iranian . . . I do not want to emphasize my Iranian side and I do not want to show that I am not Iranian either. I am a person living in a society by chance, I am an Iranian living in the Dutch society. (Ghorashi 2001:186)

On another occasion, when she talks about her life in the Netherlands and her possibilities, Leila refers to Iran as her place. Iran in this sense becomes a physical homeland, which was hers and still is.

> The most important problem I have here is that I have no certain future as a migrant. You do not have the same rights in this country, you can not find a job and you can not be sure about your future financially....You become tired of the situation. Even if I feel that I have adapted myself to the new situation here, I sometimes feel that . . ., how can I say that, . . . I feel that my roots are there [Iran]. I think then that some day I will go back, because I prefer to live in my place [Iran], everybody likes to live in their own country. (187)

Leila's feeling of being a stranger in the new country fills her with a desire to search her roots in Iran. She becomes an exile.

On the other hand, Iranians in US usually claim to feel at home. Most of them are able to see home in a diasporic way by defining home based on the achievements and contacts they have in the new country. There are of course emotional investments with the past, but the final choice is for their life in the new country. They mention explicitly that home is where people can improve themselves. They are specifically critical of the Iranian nationalists (and royalists) in Los Angeles whose network and media in concentrated on the past and is obsessed with nostalgic and nationalistic feelings toward Iran. Naficy describes how the ideas of home and homeland as well as the relationship with the past are (re)constructed and fetishized by the Iranian media in Los Angeles. They present similar contradictions as the Iranian immigrants in the Netherlands:

> On the one hand, Iranian exiles have created via their media and culture a symbolic and fetishized, private, hermetically sealed, electronic communitas infused with home, past, memory, loss, nostalgia, longing for return, and the communal self; on the other hand, they have tried to get on with the process of living by incorporating themselves into the dominant culture of consumer capitalism by means of developing a new sense of the self and what can be called an "exilic economy." (Naficy 1993:xvi)

I would now like to turn to some of the social causes of the crisis of identity and address some of the problems associated with the questions of immigration, integration, as well as cultural difference, which I will put in a comparative framework.

The history of immigration in the US is closely linked to assimilation theory which has a hierarchical base of departure. The assumption is that there is a dominant culture (of the host society) and a subordinate culture (of migrants). The assimilation theory takes a strong unitary standpoint in which it is expected from the immigrants that they will change, when entering the host society, and adopt the dominant culture. Immigrants, with their assumed subordinated culture, were supposed to start at the bottom of the society and gradually move up. By the end of the twentieth century, this way of approaching migration had changed in the US (Waldinger and Bozorgmehr 1996:17). Diversity among the new immigrants has influenced this change. Among the new immigrants entering the US, there are many people with higher education and high skills who do not start from the bottom of the society, but claim a placer higher in the hierarchy.

These new kinds of immigrants have challenged their new society rather than adapting to it. Because of their high profile, they consider their migration a beginning point of negotiation with the new society. They can mostly start a new life within the host society by minor changes in language and diplomas they received from their homelands. With their compatible background they communicate and negotiate with the new society. They do not see themselves as inferior; on the contrary, they see themselves as having a lot to offer and are not ready to disregard their background. Their condition is to negotiate between their background and the new society they are entering into. The changing in the type of immigrants who entered the US has undermined the importance of assimilation theory in current immigration research to the extent that certain long-standing metaphors of the US society do not hold anymore:

> Certain metaphors long thought to accurately describe the United States — such as the 'melting pot' and the 'salad bowl,' with their connotation of conformism, homogenization of differences, and benign pluralism — no longer hold. (Naficy 1993:3)

This change necessitates the adoption of theories of immigration in which there is more space for negotiations between the immigrants and their host society. But this still does not mean that immigrants are considered equal to the members of the host society. Immigrants still have to try harder to achieve levels that suit their qualifications.

> The same proficiencies and skills yield better rewards for whites than for immigrants . . . Yes, the high-skilled immigrants are doing well, the argument goes, but having run into a glass ceiling, they do not do as well as they *should*. (Waldinger and Bozorgmehr 1996:20)

Nevertheless, new ideas regarding migration in which an assimilation standpoint is replaced by stimulation of ethnicities have been effective in the acceptance of cultural difference in the US. The existence and the process of acceptance of variety of cultures in a society have links to discourses related to national identity. These discourses are partially related to what Behdad calls "an ambivalent concept of the 'nation-state'" in which "displacement is the precondition of the formation of national consciousness in the United States. [. . .] In short, exile and displacement are not the opposite of nationalism, but the necessary prerequisite to imagining a national community in America (Behdad 1997:158). In this context I want to adopt Rawls's concept of thin universality and thick particularity related to discussions around pluralism, in order to delineate the place of difference in national discourses. It seems that the national discourse in the US consists of a thin notion of national identity in which there is room for thick particularities. American national discourse allows thick cultural differences within its understanding of a thin notion of national identity. It is possible to be considered American — both by yourself as by others — with diversity in physical appearances, language and cultural background. Thus, it seems, the notion of American identity is more of an umbrella, which includes different particularities. However, this does not mean that there are no boundaries related to American identity. On the contrary:

> Despite the fact that the United States is an 'immigrant country', there is a strong sense of the nation and of national boundaries which have to be protected against diseases (such as communism and AIDS) brought in by immigrants, a sense best expressed by the huge, impenetrable bureaucracy, the Immigration and Naturalization Service. (van der Veer 1995:2)

However, the limitations and the protection of the boundaries focus on the new migration. The existence of a thin American notion of national identity allows settled immigrants to feel that they are part of the new society. In spite of the differences, the existence of thick particularities in the US means that various cultures can co-exist together. But it also means more than that: the thickness of particularities and the thinness of general national identity give room for multiple identifications. One can argue that the history of Black struggle in the US has made an important contribution towards heterogeneity of national identity. The inclusion of difference within American national identity makes space for various ethnic and hyphenated identities. However it must be emphasized that not all immigrants have equal access to the public space. Also, hyphenated naming does not automatically imply a rejection of essentialism. As Friedman has argued, "mixed race movements" could become as essentialist as the "single-race movement" they are fighting against (Friedman 1997: 83).

The situation in the Netherlands is rather different. As both Wekker (1995) and Ghorashi (2001) have tried to show, the Dutch notion of identity is exclusive and thick, even though they claim not to be nationally oriented. By the thickness of national identity I mean that there is a common understanding of Dutchness, which excludes difference. This notion of Dutchness is based on color, "roots," and certain codes of behavior. These codes of behavior are in many ways related to the Calvinist background. This thick notion of national identity leads to a process of exclusion and a dichotomous relationship between "us" and "them."[15] The consequence is that people from different backgrounds who are even born in the Netherlands, or have lived most of their lives there and have Dutch nationality, are not included as "one of us."

Related to this notion of Dutchness is the approach towards difference. The most commonly used term in Dutch society regarding the issue of immigration is the concept of integration. The definition of integration is less strict than assimilation; however, the implicit understanding of both terms in the Dutch context do not differ much. Within the recent policies regarding immigrants, even the old understanding of integration which gave room to one's own identity is replaced by the fact that the immigrant's native identity should limit itself to the private domain.[16] While in the US the assimilation theory has lost prominence, it still persists in the Dutch society. Alongside the imperative to assimilate, there exists, in debates on multiculturalism in The Netherlands, contradictory demands such as the fear of loss of "our culture" and the temporary basis if immigrants.[17]

After WWII the Dutch society was characterized by pillars (*zuilen*), meaning "own worlds" (Duyvendak 1994:5). Pillars were social organizations based on religious affiliations. In those years "religious divisions were important in daily life, and were even increasingly so, mainly stimulated by inter- and intra- denominational divining lines. To many people, politics was first and foremost church politics" (De Rooy 1997: 33). In the period of pillarization, children were raised exclusively within the boundaries of their religious communities. Religious belief determined the choice of school, social contacts, etc. During this period, pillars functioned as an intermediary between individuals and the state, particularly in areas of health care and education. Van der Horst (52) argues that pillars were in many ways emancipation movements. In his view the role of the modern state based on social security was built up through the work of the pillars during post-war governments. From the 1960s the Netherlands went through a reverse process, namely de-pillarization (*ontzuiling*). The secularization of the Dutch society and the increasing role of the state in social affairs made the existence of the pillars unnecessary. The contemporary spirit of de-pillarization strongly disliked religioun-based group formations of the pillarization period. Nevertheless, the pillarization period has some persisting residual elements at the heart of which is the concept/practice of tolerance: the existence of different pillars necessitated a degree of tolerance (of the other) in order to create a peaceful state based on consensus. Tolerance has been a key term in contemporary debates regarding foreigners (in daily discussions) and discussions about multicultural society (in scholarly debates). Influenced by the historical context of Dutch society, tolerance has been mainly seen as letting others be. In this relationship to the other, boundaries and distance play an essential role. There is not much space for interaction between different ideas; there is rather respect for boundaries. The "other" should be tolerated: "leave them as they are." In this way tolerance becomes a sign of indifference which excludes interaction between groups and is likely to lead to a fear of the unknown. It is this fear that is expressed in statements in favor of assimilation: "foreigners live in our country and therefore they should adjust to our culture." The contradiction between these two statements cannot escape attention: on the one hand, the Dutch is proud of its practice of tolerance and on the other hand, there is an increasing pressure to assimilation. In fact, tolerance in its emphasis, within the Dutch context, on distance and boundaries rather than respect or interaction, can lead to the process of "othering" as well as an either/or situation in which multiple identification is structurally excluded.

Within the Dutch context tolerance is closely linked to the protection of the "self," which leads to the belief that the "other" is by definition an outsider and a threat. This process of othering creates a homogenous idea of "Dutchness," which excludes difference. Even when, for example, ex-refugees are legally designated as Dutch citizens, they are socially excluded as being "one of us." This thick notion of Dutchness also makes the existence of hyphenated identities, linked to multiple positioning, virtually impossible. There are examples of hyphenated designations in the Netherlands such as *Indische-Nederlanders* (Indo-Dutch, from the Dutch East Indies) who have long been considered as perfect examples of assimilated immigrants. However, the perspectives of the Indo-Dutch themselves present another picture (Willems, Cottaar en van Aken). While the first generation tried silently to assimilate into the Dutch society, the second generation in the 1970s and 1980s felt that the Dutch society still considered them as the "other." The third generation, as a result, started to search for their "roots." This shows that the hyphenated naming did not lead to multiple positioning and the immigrants, even when they are born in the Netherlands, remained the "other" because of their background. The general dilemma is captured in the following statement when an apparently assimilated Indo-Dutch says: "I did not know what the Dutch people expected from me. It was as if there was a secret code that only the white Dutch knew."[18]

In short, the conundrum of the immigrants in the Netherlands can be summed up by reference to the following two requirements: first, multiple identification is not accepted, one is either this or that and second, the conditions of a transition from one to another, i.e., from an alien to an equal citizen of the society is wrapped in layers of secrecy to which the immigrant is denied access. It is within this context that Kader Abdolah writes.

In Kader Abdolah *Spijkershrift* (2000) one witnesses the beginning of a crisis of identity that the protagonist implicitly undergoes. Life in exile, in a foreign land, requires major adjustments, revisions, and relocations of identity that for the protagonist of *Spijkerschrift* are intimately related to one's relation with the past. By switching back and forth between the memories of home and his current life in the present as a refugee in the Netherlands, Abdolah attempts to bridge the gap between the past and the present, between memory and consciousness, and between home and exile. In this "fusion of horizons" (*Horizontsvershmeltzung*), to use Gadamer's terminology, Abdolah seeks to avoid a crisis of identity prevalent in exilic experiences by trying to refashion, relocate, revise or update his identity. Abdolah's *Spijkerschrift*, in its anti-essentialist stance, also foregrounds some of the fundamental problems concerning memory as well as historical representation (and historicity).

Kader Abdolah's *Spijkerschrift* is the story of Agha Akbar and his son Ismael who is now living on the Ijssel (in the Netherlands) and wants to settle accounts with his past and his feeling of guilt towards it, in order to be able to go on with his life in a new land "*Als ik mijn boek af heb, ben ik niet meer in dienst van mijn vader. Ik zal voor mezelf leven*" (238) [If I finish my book, I will no more be at the service of my father; I will live for myself]. Agha Akbar was deaf and uneducated but he wrote his memoirs in a secret, cuneiform language. One day, Ismael, who is now living in Holland, receives a package from Iran that contains the notebook of his late father. The writing of the novel *Spijkerschrift* is in fact the reading and translating of Agha Akbar's notes. What is, however, interesting is that what remains from the deciphering of the secret text is nothing but the apparently most ordinary surface of everyday life.

The novel becomes a sharing of the secrets of Agha Akbar with/between Ismael (or the narrator) and the readers. We share with him what cannot be shared, a secret we know nothing about, neither him, nor us. "To share the secret is not to know or to reveal the secret, it is to share we know not what: nothing that can be determined. What is a secret that is a secret about nothing and a sharing that doesn't share anything" (Derrida 1995: 80). "If the other were to share his reasons with us by explaining them to us, if he were to speak to us all the time without any secrets, he wouldn't be the other, we would share a type of homogeneity" (57)

Ismael, the protagonist of *Spijkerschrift*, in a manner reminiscent of the story of Isaac in the Scriptures, is the bearer of the still Jewish experience of secrecy and absence. In the story of Abraham, a secret, absent, or mysterious God ("the one who decides without revealing his reasons" (58)) is demanding Abraham that most cruel and impossible gesture: to sacrifice what is most dear to him. Abraham decides to offer his son Isaac[19] as a sacrifice[20]. Everything goes on in secret, God keep silent about his reasons, and so does Abraham. Kierkegaard's *Fear and Trembling*, as a meditation on the experience of secrecy and sacrifice in Abraham, Derrida reminds us in his *The Gift of Death* (1995), is not signed by Kierkegaard but by Johannes de Silentio. According to Derrida, the pseudonym that keeps the real name secret ("like all pseudonyms, it seems destined to keep secret the real name as patronym, that is, the name of the father of the work, in fact the name of the father of the father of the work" 58) reminds us that "a meditation linking the question of secrecy to that of responsibility immediately raises the question of the name and of the signature" (58). Abraham has promised to keep secret the sacrifice of Isaac/Ismael, which is in fact a double secret: that between God and Abraham but also that between the latter and his family. Abraham must keep the secret without knowing it, or knowing its ultimate "rhyme and reason" (59). But of course in some respects Abraham speaks: "He speaks in order not to say anything about the essential thing that he must keep secret. Speaking in order not to say anything is always the best technique for keeping a secret" (59). The philosophical and ethical imperative is, however, to reveal rather than hide and keep secret. For philosophy and dialectics in general, from Plato to Hegel:

> The ethical as such is the universal; as the universal it is in turn the disclosed. The single individual, qualified as immediate, sensate, and physical, is the hidden. Thus his ethical task is to work himself out of his hiddenness and to become disclosed in the universal . . . the Hegelian philosophy assumes no justified hiddenness, no justified incommensurability. It is, then, consistent for it to demand disclosure . . . a refutable demand for manifestation, phenomenalization and unveiling.   (Derrida 1995:62)

Derrida argues that ultimate ethical responsibility involves an aporia: on the one hand the demand for unveiling, for a translation of oneself or the event into generality, hence the idea of substitution, which is also related to the idea of representation, and, on the other hand, absolute singularity, hence nonrepetition, silence and secrecy (61). I argue that this aporia stands as a central concern for

Abdolah's *Spijkerschrift* and, in fact, the novel in its formal and thematic structure is an attempt to come in terms with, or reflect on, this aporia. Ismael, on the one hand, desires to respond to and be responsible towards his past, his father, and what seems to be threatened to be forgotten, especially within an exilic context. On the other hand, a complete revelation and representation of the past is a betrayal of its singularity as much as it is unethical, and not to say impossible. Ismael knows the fate of the Islamic mystic Al-Hallaj and what befell him when he revealed secrets. The dilemma of the responsibility to the dead is therefore translated into a textual context in which he inherits a secret text from his father, which he subsequently tries to decipher. In other words, Ismael in Kader abdolah's *Spijkerschrift*, is haunted by the ghost of his father who speaks to him in a secret language (*"Je kunt niet uit de schaduw van zulke mensen komen, zelfs niet als ze doodgaan. Het wordt juist erger als ze doodgaan, ze keren sterker dan ooit in j eleven terug"* (211)) [You cannot get away from the shadow of such people, not even when they die. It even gets worse when they die, because they come back again in your life stronger than ever]. He takes it as his responsibility toward the past and the dead father to revive and reawaken what is threatened to be forgotten forever. In Abdolah's *Spijkerschrift*, the diasporic condition becomes a pretext for the injunction of the past, the recognition of the dead, and the work of mourning. The reawakening of the past is however paradoxically to occur not in one's own language but in the language of the other. Abdolah's own language, if it ever was his, becomes irrelevant within the exilic situation where he finds himself an outsider. In a poem by the Dutch poet Margryt, he finds an eloquent expression of his existential condition:

> Geen taal. Geen oud verhaal om op terug
> Te vallen. Ruimte die voor het oog oneindig is.
> Een kaart, waarop het spoor is uitgezet, en bruggen
> Die het niets met niets verbinden. Geen word
> Dat zegt dat wij hier een veilige woonplaats kunnen vinden. (125)
> [No tongue. No old story to
> Fall back on. Space which in front of one's eyes is endless.
> A map on which the trace is marked, and bridges
> Which connect nothing to nothing. No word
> That says that here we can find a safe dwelling place.]

One can read these lines and its imagery through Heidegger's discussion of the bridge. For Heidegger, in his "Building Dwelling Thinking" ["Bauen Wohnen Denken"] (1954) the bridge not only unconceals the banks in their being, ("it does not just connect banks that are already there. The banks emerge as banks only as the bridge crosses the stream" 152), it also gathers to itself different elements (earth and sky, divinities and mortals). This gathering or assembly, which is called "thing," makes possible a relation to location, and then through the latter, to space: "Thus the bridge does not first come to a location to stand in it; rather a location comes into existence only by virtue of the bridge" (154). It is, therefore, only through the mediation of locations that man enters into a relationship with space. ("spaces receive their being from locations and not from "space" (154); "spaces, and with them space as such — "space" — are always provided for already within the stay of mortals. Spaces open up by the fact that they are let into the dwelling of man. To say that mortals *are* is to say that in *dwelling* they persist through spaces by virtue of their stay among things and locations" (157)).

In Margryt's poem the space (*ruimte* in Dutch, *Raum* in German) does not become a location, or a thing, simply because it is incapable of bringing other elements together; it rather brings nothingness together. As a result dwelling becomes impossible, something that also marks the exilic condition. In fact for Heidegger this exilic or homeless condition is universal and constitutes the "real plight of dwelling" (161). For him, man has not yet learned how to dwell and his homelessness lies precisely in that.[21]

The experience of exile is not only the experience of one's inability to dwell in the present, it also problematizes one's capacity to dwell in the past, i.e., it triggers the necessity of a renewal of relationship with the dead and one's own past. Ismael is well aware of the difficulty of this task. If he is going to remain absolutely faithful to the past, he must remain silent by acknowledging the impossibility of writing a novel that brings together the two horizons of the past and the present: "Everything is new here, the earth smells like fish . . . but in the notes of my father everything is old . . . that is why I do not dare to put my pen on the paper. I think that on this new land one can write no novels." [*Alles is hier nieuw, de grond ruikt nog naar vis . . . maar in de aantekeningen van mijn vader is alles oud . . . daarom durf ik mijn pen niet op papier zetten. Ik denk dat op deze nieuwe bodem geen roman te schrijven is*, 124]. But remaining silent is obviously more unethical than any attempt at establishing a relationship with the past and the dead, i.e., a work of mourning. Abdolah, therefore, in a manner reminiscent of Benjamin, undergoes a process of mourning history and the dead in order to be able to think about his future. Walter Benjamin's "Theses on the Philosophy of History" (1940) might be described as a treatise on the political and ethical stakes of mourning the remains of history. According to Benjamin, to mourn the remains of the past is to establish an active and open relationship with history. This practice — what Benjamin called "historical materialism" — is a creative process, animating history for future significations as well as different empathies. For the historical materialist, to relive an era is not to bring memory to the past, that is, to blot out everything one knows about the later course of history; it is rather to bring the past to memory. It is to actively invoke a tension between the past and the present, between the dead and the living. In this manner, Benjamin's historical materialism establishes a continuing dialogue with loss and its remains.

Kader abdolah's *Spijkerschrift* may also be read as a work of mourning. Freud, in "Mourning and Melancholia" (1917), distinguishes between a complete mourning and an incomplete, endless mourning, i.e., melancholia. Although Freud endeavors to characterize the melancholic sustained devotion to the lost object as pathological, he also casts doubts on the inevitability of this distinction. Were one to understand melancholia better, Freud implies, one would no longer insists on its pathological character. For instance, we might observe that in Freud's initial conception of melancholia, the past is neither fixed nor complete. Unlike (complete) mourning in which the past is declared resolved, finished and dead, in melancholia the past remains alive in the present. By engaging in countless struggles with loss, melancholia might be said to constitute, as Benjamin would describe it, an open and ongoing relationship with the past, bringing in ghosts and specters, its flaring and fleeting images, into the present. In this sense, we find in Freud's conception of melancholia's persisting struggle with its lost objects not simply a grasping and holding on to a fixed notion of the past but rather a continuous engagement with loss and its remains. While complete mourning abandons lost objects by laying their histories at rest, incomplete mourning, or melancholia, allows us, by haunting us, a rewriting of the past and opening up new perspectives and understandings on the lost object. Ultimately we learn that the work of mourning is not possible without melancholia. In *The Ego and the Id* (1923), Freud comes to this conclusion by understanding that the ego is constituted through the remains of abandoned object-cathexes. As a psychic entity, the ego is composed of the residues of its accumulated losses. The ego is in fact a patchwork. In *The Psychic Life of Power*, Judith Butler expands upon this revised notion of melancholia, arguing that the incorporative logic of melancholia founds the very possibility of the ego and its psychic topography. Butler observes that melancholia is "precisely what interiorizes the psyche, that is, makes it possible to refer to the psyche through such topographical tropes. The turn from object to ego is the movement that makes the distinction between them possible, that marks the division, the separation or loss, that forms the ego to begin with" (170).

Agamben approaches melancholia through a detour of the medieval culture. According to Agamben, "We ought to say that melancholia offers the paradox of an intention to mourn that precedes and anticipates the loss of the object. This prescient melancholia emerges as the imaginative capacity to make an unobtainable object appear as if lost, opening a space for the existence of the unreal — a politics of ideality" (20). Here apprehensions and attachments to loss and its phantasms never simply dwell in the past, for the very process of narrativizing loss implies an impulse toward the future. Agamben's medieval melancholia, in a manner akin to Benjamin's, materializes, and therefore gives it a future, the ghostly remains of an unrealized potential in the past. For Agamben, melancholia, by producing an unreal image of an unobtainable object that never was[22] and hence was never lost, imagines a space for the remains of the past to emerge and have a future as motivating forces.

Abdolah's fusion of the horizons of the present and the past (Gadamer's *Horizontsverschmelzung*) is mediated by both a process of mourning that promises to become melancholic as well as by the process of reading a text written in a secret language and inherited from the father.

In many ways Abdolah's *Spijkerschrift* can be read through the mediation of Alan Resnais's *Hiroshima Mon Amour*, one of the masterpieces of the French

New Wave cinema. In their concern with memory and recollection, the claims of the past and the possibility of its representation, these two works reveal certain similarities.

From different perspectives it was the year 1959 that launched the "New Wave," a loosely knit group of French filmmakers who brought new and often subversive styles, visions, and politics to commercial cinema. That was the year that gave the world Godard's *Breathless*, Truffaut's *The 400 Blows*, and two films by Claude Chabrol, *Les Cousins* and *A double Tour* (Leda). It was also 1959 that saw the release of *Hiroshima Mon Amour*, directed by Alain Resnais who, at forty-seven, was older than most of the New Wave directors, and who had a tenuous connection at best with his New Wave colleagues. By 1959 Resnais had already produced a few movies, all of them documentaries, the most famous of which is his 1955 *Night and Fog*, which Godard has called a documentary on the memory of Auschwitz.

Initially *Hiroshima Mon Amour* was likewise intended as a documentary, this time on the horrors of the atomic explosion that ended World War II. But Resnais, for various reasons, changed course, commissioning a fictional screenplay from Marguerite Duras, one of the major figures in France's *Nouveau Roman* (New Novel) movement, who, starting in 1967, would go on to direct a number of her own films. The collaboration resulted in Resnais's first feature-length narrative film, after which he rarely returned (directly) to the documentary. Two of his subsequent films, *Muriel ou le temps d'un retour* (1963) and the particularly well received *La Guerre est Finie* (1966), continue to reveal the director's obsession-with recreating war-time situations out of memory, *Muriel* with France's Algerian situation and *La Guerre est Finie* with the Spanish Civil War. Two other Resnais films, the forever-controversial *Last Year at Marienbad* (1961), based on a screenplay by another New Novelist-soon-to-be-filmmaker, Alain Robbe-Grillet, and the English-language *Providence* (1977), deal, in both their montage and their labyrinthine narrative structures, with the themes of time and memory in such an enigmatic way that they come across as almost abstract. In his neglected masterpiece from 1968, *Je t'aime, je t'aime*, Resnais actually resorts to the sci-fi gimmick of a time machine.

Hiroshima Mon Amour, which seems to take place over a twenty-four-hour period in 1958 Hiroshima, is divided into five panels (not labeled, as such in the film itself): Prologue, Night and Morning, Day, The Café by the River, and Epilogue. The Prologue offers a perfect example of the ways in which filmmakers such as Resnais were challenging the standards of commercial cinema (not just Hollywood) and its eternal need for clarity and linearity. With Giovanni Fusco's incredibly poignant, solo-piano theme playing on the music track, the screen shows two nude, interlaced, and anonymous human bodies, one notably darker than the other — no faces, mostly arms and legs, and almost nothing with which to even identify the gender of these two beings, whose slight movements possibly suggest lovemaking. A glittery, powdery substance falls upon the bodies. It is described in the screenplay as atomic ash, but it could just as well (again according to the screenplay) be rain, dew, or sweat. Eventually, as the film dissolves to a glitter-less shot of the bodies, we hear the voice of a man (Eiji Okada) saying, "You saw nothing in Hiroshima. Nothing," to which the voice of a woman (Emmanuèle Riva) replies that she has seen everything. As viewer/listeners we cannot be sure whether these voice-overs even belong to the bodies on the screen, much less whether the dialogue takes place in the past, present, or future . . . or whether it even takes/took place within the narrative.

And thus does *Hiroshima Mon Amour* not only introduce its principal theme — the impossibility of clearly "reading," of ever deeply knowing the substance of images that we see and hear — it also immediately and literally involves the audience in the ambiguities of reading, in the impossibility of bringing the past into the present. As the film finally cuts away from the bodies, it begins to show us what the woman says she "saw": the Hiroshima hospital, and the Hiroshima museum, with its various documentary photographs, its artifacts, even its quasi-documentary recreation on film of the day of the bomb.

At this point it becomes apparent that the various denials proposed by the man's voice (for instance where he says that she has seen nothing, that she has invented everything, that she knows nothing, or that she has no memory) are based on the fact that all that the woman and almost all other people in the world at the time have seen or know of Hiroshima — the Hiroshima of August 6, 1945 — is based on images. *Hiroshima Mon Amour* presents some of these images, and some of them in fact are quite horrible. But, as the music in particular seems to tell us, what these provide is more of a tourist attraction than anything remotely close to the reality itself. And as the film constantly demonstrates, the past becomes a series of images the constant stream of which we have no idea how to read. For instance, the audience of *Hiroshima Mon Amour* in some instances cannot even tell whether it is witnessing documentary footage or recreations: the nurses and patients in the hospital, for instance, look into the camera, but is this real or staged, or both? At another point later in *Hiroshima Mon Amour*, the man and the woman find themselves caught up in a peace march that may or may not be part of the movie that the woman, wearing a nurse's uniform, has come to Hiroshima to act in.

All of this would seem to leave both the main characters of *Hiroshima Mon Amour* and the film's audiences trapped in a reality in which a rather sterile, eternal present offers the only knowable reality. Indeed, in spite of moments of warmth, the sexual affair between the French actress, who is married, and her Japanese lover, an architect who is also married, may be nothing more than a one-night stand in what has become a rather glitzy, Westernized city, in spite of the ruined presence of the Atomic Bomb Dome, where she is only a visitor. But then the film undergoes a remarkable transformation. Just at the moment when it seems as if the two lovers are moving rapidly toward their separation, their conversation subtly turns toward Nevers, a small city in the center of France that was the home town of the actress, who is now a Parisian. At this point *Hiroshima Mon Amour*, intermingling its dialogue in the present with a disconnected series of dialogueless flashbacks that include a number of highly evocative shots of Nevers itself, begins to reconstruct the war memories of the actress who, at the age of eighteen, had fallen in love with a German soldier who was part of the enemy forces occupying Nevers (Brown 2003).

The results, including the death of the German soldier and the humiliation and temporary madness of the young woman, are predictably tragic. It is a personal tragedy that seems far removed from the devastation of Hiroshima, yet it gives the couple a strange sense of solidarity. It is not that she has succeeded where Hiroshima's museum has failed in making the wartime past readable in the present, but rather that she, once again allowing herself a forbidden love, has made real a second tragedy that superimposes itself over the tragedy of war: the tragedy of forgetting. But in another way, through the retelling of the story — orally for the actress, cinematically for the film as a whole — memory acquires a nonhistorical reality of its own that owes as much to the present as to the past in which it originated but did not entirely disappear.

The couple will, of course, separate, he bearing the name of Nevers, she the name of Hiroshima, with both bearing the imprint of a barely noticeable transformation. *Hiroshima Mon Amour* has practically no narrative, yet, nearly forty-five years after its release, it remains, for all of its unresolved turns and twists, for all of its enigmas, and for all of its, yes, unreadability, one of the cinema's most engaging films. Like many of Resnais's films it is a documentary about both memory and forgetting. Yet *Hiroshima Mon Amour*, Resnais's first narrative feature, is also the story of a man and a woman who, through their ephemeral sexual encounter, through what may or may not be love, come out briefly on the other side of the unreadability of history and the fragility of memory. It is also the visual tale of two different cities, one destroyed and rebuilt in the image of its destroyer, the other a surviving monument of its country's past, deeply tied in, at opposite ends of the world and human psychology, with the horrors of war. With its — once again — unresolved twists and turns, with its enigmas on both the visual and the narrative levels, and with its unreadability, *Hiroshima Mon Amour* also allows its audience to confront the same problems, the same mysteries, in a way that no linearly narrative film could hope to do.

In Hiroshima in 1959 the past erupts and inundates the French woman's present life in the same way that the memories of the dead lover displaces Gretta in Joyce's *The Dead*[23]. In a moment of emotional crisis, in *Hiroshima Mon Amour*, the French woman attempts to come in terms with her memories the same way that Abdolah tries in *Spijkerschrift*. In both these works the processes of associative memory becomes a central focus of the narrative. In Abdolah's *Spijkerschrift*, Ismael is frequently taken back in time through the process of association in order to bring the past to memory, i.e., reconciling the past with his present. In the case of *Hiroshima Mon Amour* one might see in the process of associative memory the transposition of the psychology of Henri Bergson and Marcel Proust to the celluloid medium. There are however differences in the ways in which the process of associative memory attempts to establish a relationship with the past. In *Spijkerschrift*, Ismael seems to be in control of his memory and his discourse, although he acknowledges, from the very first page, that there are things inherited from the past that cannot be translated or read.[24] In

Hiroshima Mon Amour, on the other hand, the associative memory becomes hauntological and the sudden invasion from the past (already a sign of incomplete mourning) a source of terror. Once again there is a memory that places the subject outside herself. Freddy Sweet in his comments on *Hiroshima Mon Amour*, puts this point in the following way: "The imposition of the past on present events is painful, in spite of the fact that Riva needs to remember her experiences. There is a personal and psychological "nécessité de la mémoire" for the establishment of the continuity of the self. Yet, because of the suffering that memory produces, there is an equally strong need to forget. In matters of love and history, the entire film is an attempt to rediscover through memory the intensity of earlier experiences; yet, when unleashed, this recollection makes the character recoil for self-preservation" (Sweet 25).

The resolutions that *Hiroshima Mon Amour* proposes for the aporia of memory and forgetting is also different from that of *Spijkerschrift*. While the latter is moving within a hermeneutic context in which, following Gadamer, the horizons of the past are fused with those of the present (*Horizontsverschmeltzung*), in the latter the resolution of the aporia of memory is achieved through a process of naming. The man and woman have become emblematic of greater social tragedies. But it also shows the process of taming the untameable, of fixing into determinate nominal identities, things that otherwise are indeterminate and ghostly. In this way, and through a fantasy of closure, the eruption of the past is contained and the subject retains its sanity.

In certain respects Abdolah's *Spijkerschrift* resembles Mukherjee's *Jasmine* in terms of its articulations of a restricted economy of representation. As with Jasmine, the hero in *Spijkerschrift* seems to be in control of his memory and his past. He makes an instrumental use of his memory and his past in order to be able to survive in a foreign land: "That is why I delve into my father's notes, because what he has written is also my history. If I can structure a little bit my writing in Dutch language, I would be able to live easier in this new society" (*Daarom verdiep ik in de notities van mijn vader, want wat hij geschreven heeft, is ook mijn geschiedenis. Dus als ik mijn schrift een beetje kan ordenen in de Nederlandse taal, kan ik makkelijker in deze nieuwe sameleving verdergaan* (130)). But what makes this novel interesting is its open embracement of the possibility of the unrepresentable in the protagonist's relationship to his memory as well to his past. The past is inherited by Ismael in the form of a text written in a secret, cuneiform language and is therefore subjected to all the problems of indeterminacy, polyvalency and multi-interpretability that one encounters in one's dealings with the textual. At certain times, the past is also suspected to be fake, fictional, or fabricated: "Now I doubt the reality of the story; Kazem Khan might have fabricated that story . . . ." (*Nu twijfel ik aan de echtheid van de verhaal. Misschien had Kazem Gan dat verhaal verzonnen . . .* (130)). In fact Ismael's whole world as well as his *Weltanschauung* is mediated by a textual experience in which meaning is not assumed but made. For him, the past is essentially devoid of meaning, a secret without content, unless it is translated into the horizons of the present (*Dat die notities geen enkele betekenis hadden, maar alleen maar krabbeltjes waren van Agha Akbar...Ismael ging achter zijn schrijftafel zitten, bladerde erin en dacht: hoe zal ik ooit achter het geheim van die notities kunnen komen? Hoe kan ik dit boek laten spreken? Hoe zal ik het in leesbare taal kunnen vertalen?* (104), *... want ik moet mijn verhaal baseren op de onduidelijke en onleesbare gedachten van een ander* (141)).[25] The past is also written in a language and in a way that exceeds the horizons of the past itself and points toward the futurity of an event as well as an eventuality of the future. (*Wanneer hij [Agha Akbar] in zijn boek schreef wist niemand. Waarover hij schreef al helemaal niet. Dat hij moest schrijven over de dingen die hij niet begreep en die hij niet in gebarentaal kon uitleggen. Over onbereikbare, onbegrijpelijke, ontastbare dingen die hem in eens grepen en waar hij machteloos naar bleef kijken*(94)).[26] But Ismael is also aware of the possibility of failure in his attempt at reawakening the dead, whose centrality is apparent in the story of kahaf[27] that appears both in the beginning and at the end of the story. The reawakening of the dead may also be read as a secular, this-worldly rendering of the question of resurrection: the dead will be reawakened in *this* world.

Kiarostami's *Taste of Cherry* and the Unrepresentable

In this section I will approach the problem of representation and the unrepresentable through an analysis of Abbas Kiarostami's *Taste of Cherry*. If Kader Abdolah's *Spijkerschrift* is about the (un)representability of the past in its totality and an emphasis on the excess of the remains of history, Kiarostami's *Taste of Cherry* is about the (un)representability of the event of death, which, as I argued, is a fundamental component of a general economy of travel and displacement. Before a detailed analysis of this film, I would first like to provide the readers with a short history of the development of Iranian cinema and then after a discussion of the problem of fictionality arrive at my argument concerning the (un)representability of death by references to Blanchot's "Death as Possibility."

In the 90's the international film festivals around the world witnessed the emergence of new types of films from Iran. The history of film production in Iran, however, dates back to the early 30's. The first Iranian talkie, *The Lor Girl* (1934) was the first of several feature films made in India by an Iranian expatriate, Abdol-hossein Sepanta, for the Iranian market. After more than a decade of lethargic inactivity (due to WWII), film production in Iran resumed in 1949. From 1949 to 1979 (until the Islamic revolution), the Iranian cinema was dominated by commercial films, except for a few cases such as Dariush Mahrjui's *The Cow*. Mehrjui's *The Cow*, which appeared in the decade preceding the Islamic revolution of 1979, heralded the emergence of an Iranian New Wave, a movement producing films of high cinematic quality and social consciousness. *The Cow* portrays the life of a peasant who owns the only cow in a village. After the mysterious death of the cow, its owner undergoes a mental breakdown. *The Cow* was immediately banned because of its implacable depiction of poverty and despair in rural Iran. The film was, however, conditionally released only after it won a prize at the Venice Film Festival. Mehrjui was not the only director working during the decade preceding the revolution. Abbas Kiarostami, Bahram Bayzai (*Bashu, the Little Stranger*), Masud Kimiai (*Ghaisar*), Amir Naderi (*The Runner*), Parviz Sayyad (*The Mission*), and Sohrab Shaheed Sales (*Still Life*) are among the filmmakers who started their careers in this period.

In the first years following the 1979 Islamic revolution, very few dared to make films for a precarious market and an audience preoccupied with acute sociopolitical tensions. The confusion as to what was permissible to show on screen brought about the largest number of movies ever reedited in the history of Iranian cinema. Scripts endorsed by an official were rejected when the finished productions were shown to his successor. The release permits of many productions were quickly revoked. However, in spite of all the socio-political confusion, as well as the Iran-Iraq war, the newly established Islamic government decided to pay attention to matters of culture and art, and to encourage investment and talent into this field by assuring a secured economic environment. In 1983 the minister of Culture and Islamic Guidance declared a ban on the activities of video clubs, which were believed at that time to hinder domestic film production. The thousands of video clubs across the country had attracted funds which could now be used for production. They had also shaped the public's taste and functioned as a bridge-head for cultural imperialism, as the argument went. It was only with the establishment of the Farabi Cinema Foundation (FCF) that domestic production gained momentum. The FCF, as the executive branch of the cinema department of the Ministry of Culture and Islamic Guidance, supported film production by distributing film-making equipment among production groups as well as facilitating investment in the film industry.

Several major developments in early 1984 had a determining effect on the economy of Iranian cinema. In February 1984, all available copies of old Iranian and imported movies were removed from distribution, giving the FCF a monopoly on importing movies. While Iranian productions have always been at a disadvantage in the competition with imported ones, the drastic drop in the latter's importation is believed to have saved the domestic film industry. Another development was a 15% reduction in municipality taxes on the revenues of Iranian films, while increasing that on imported films from 20 to 25%. In addition, filmmaking equipment imported by the Ministry of Islamic Culture and Guidance were exempted from custom duties.

In this period of qualitative growth, the credible directors of the prerevolutionary days such as Dariush Mehrjui, Bahram Bayzaie, Massoud Kimiai, Abbas Kiarostami, Nasser Taghvai and Ali Hatami returned to resume their interrupted careers. The newcomers of this era were women directors. In late 80's Iranian productions began to attract attention at international film festivals and the first steps were taken to secure a share of foreign markets. In this period, new themes as well as forms were explored: psychodramas, science fiction and animated films for children, to mention only a few. As cultural critic Hamid Naficy puts it in his "Islamizing Film Culture in Iran": "Major repositionings and shifts have occurred in attitudes and perceptions toward both cinema and working in the motion-picture business. Cinema, rejected in the past as a frivolous *superstructure*, has been adopted as part of the necessary *infrastructure* of Islamic culture" (Mulvey 1998:26).

The Islamic revolution of 1979 was initially a fatal blow not only to film-production but also to poetry and literature. In an attempt to form an "Islamic, anti-imperialist" cinema, a new set of highly restrictive censorship codes brought film production under the tight control of the government. In an indictment reminiscent of Plato's charges against literature, many filmmakers were accused of "corrupting the public." One of the censorship codes imposed by the new post-revolutionary policy concerned the strict Islamic dress code that required women to cover their hair and wear loose-fitting outer garments in public. Also, women could only be intimate with the immediate members of their family. Therefore, actors playing couples could not be intimate on the screen unless they were married in real life. According to this new cinematic aesthetic, fiction is irretrievably connected to real, actual life. In other words, what is happening on the imaginary level of a work of art is, in fact, a continuation of real life. It seems as if the Iranian post-revolutionary aesthetic of the artistic form somehow refuses to subject the work of art and its fictional representations to the so-called temporary "suspension of disbelief." The philosophy of "als ob"[28] ("as if"), which characterizes one of the dominant modes of the aesthetic reception of art in the West, is apparently non-functional in post-revolutionary Iran. The rather recent example of Salman Rushdie's *The Satanic Verses* testifies to this theoretical underpinning of the aesthetic ideology of the Islamic authorities in Iran. Putting aside all the political and religious tumult around this book, what interests us here, which is rather of a theoretical nature, is to show the remarkable absence of any clear-cut border between fiction and reality: fiction is always already not only about reality but also referring to reality. As Saul Kripke[29] has argued in his discussion of the semantics of possible worlds, fictional objects, especially those with a co-relate in the external world, refer to the same objects in the real world. Let's examine this argument in more details.

Literature and art (and *mutatis mutandis* cinema) as a fictive discourse can be considered as a representation of both the real (actualized possibility) and the possible (unactualized possibility). In its act of representing the real, art distorts rather than imitates. As a matter of fact, the notion of distortion is implicit in the notion of imitation. Pierre Macherey puts it in the following way:

> . . . the idea of imitation, correctly understood, implies distortion, if, as Plato suggests in *The Cratylus*, the essence of resemblance is difference. The image that corresponded perfectly with the original would no longer be an image; it remains an image by virtue of its difference from that which it resembles. (Macherey 1978:61)

The distortion of the real is the distortion of its attributes and properties through which the designation of an object does not necessarily change. A unique fictional proper name with a co-relate in reality, a name like "London," designates the real London but presents it under certain attributes which are not necessarily the same as those occurring in reality. Therefore, in other words, fictional proper names with a co-relate in reality may be dealt with according to the "principle of minimal departure"[30] according to which the reader construes the fictional world as being the closest possible to the external reality. The immediate epistemological implication of this argument is that the reader uses his/her historical as well as social knowledge of the real to interpret the imaginary.[31]

The larger framework that informs my preceding argument is related to the questions of realism and representation. Since I am interested in arguing for the possibility of "political art," I need, theoretically speaking, some kind of realist framework in which what happens on the aesthetic level can directly be brought to relate to "empirical" political issues. But the so-called "empirical" issues are, as the postmodern critics of realism have showed us, nowhere simply given as a positive content in themselves. Our access to them is always already mediated through symbolic discourses. Here I would like to argue that should one wishes to have political art, one must postulate the possibility of some rigid reference, at least in case of proper names. If Syberberg's movies claim to be political, the occurrence of allusions to proper names like Hitler or the Nazi should be construed as strictly referential:

> But this must know be reformulated in terms of Syberberg's filmic system and of what we have described as his political project, his cultural revolution, or collective psychoanalysis. In order for his method to work, these films must somehow continue to "take" on the real world, and his Hitler puppets and other Nazi motifs must somehow remain "referential," must preserve their links as allusions and designations of the historically real. (Jameson 1992:79)

To agree with the postmodern critique of realism and representation, i.e., that the Thing (or the *"ding an zich"* as Kant calls it, or the Event) cannot be "re-presented" in its truth or totality and that these alleged "re-presentations" are only signs of "will to power," which is itself historically and discursively constructed, to agree with all these does not necessarily commit us to the denial of the existence of the Thing or the Event itself. The Event is not representable (i.e., it cannot be captured in its totality in any single discourse) but it does exist. Or rather, to put it in other words, that the Event is differentially representable does not prevent it from being identified, to use the language of analytic philosophers, in all possible worlds (and not necessarily as an "essence" or "content"). The Event or the Thing is not to be radically aestheticized if one wishes to have political art:

> Aesthetic distance, the very "set" towards fictionality itself, that "suspension of disbelief" which involves an equal suspension of belief, these and other characteristics of aesthetic experience as they have been theorized since Kant also operate very powerfully to turn Hitler into "Hitler," a character in a fiction film, and thus removed from the historical reality which we hope to affect. (Jameson 1992:80).

As the readers of Jameson already know, his project is to incorporate (or perhaps to reconcile) the inevitable consequences of postmodernity into Marxism. To do this he argues for the necessity of reinventing "realism"[32] (a "postmodern realism," an apparently contradiction in terms). One of the aspects of this process concerns the debate between the competing claims of an essentialist or substantialist theory of history and a differential and contextual theory of representation. My argument, following Jameson, is that these claims are not necessarily incommensurable.

The hypothetical reconstruction of the fundamental principle (i.e., the fuzzy border between fiction and reality) of the aesthetic ideology of the Islamic authorities in post-revolutionary Iran has repercussions in the works of some filmproducers, notably Abbas Kiarostami. Though Kiarostami's films have been compared at various time to those of the Italian neo-realists, particularly Vittorio de Sica, they remain uniquely Kiarostamian: amazingly simple and, at the same time, conceptually complex; poetic and lyrical and at the same time meditative and self-reflexive, they mix fiction and documentary in unique ways, often presenting fact as fiction and fiction as fact. As Kiarostami once said in an interview: "We can never get closer to the truth except through lying."

One of the major social functions of cinema in Iran is to provide social and political commentary, rather than simply entertainment. Because of censorship, Iranian filmmakers have to develop new and subtler forms of expression, which, while escaping censorship, can still be socially and politically engaged. Kiarostami's *Taste of Cherry*, in spite of its apparent simplicity, is among those films that handles the censorship, as I will argue, in a subtle way.

As *Taste of Cherry* opens, the 50-ish Mr. Badii (Homayoun Ershadi) is driving a Range Rover slowly through a Teheran morning, looking closely at men gathering on the streets for day labor. Clearly he wants to pick one of them up, although it will take 20 minutes before we find out why. "Were this not an Iranian film, one might suspect that he is a gay man cruising for a hustler. Even though this is an Iranian film, this suspicion, along with more sinister ones, remains quite evident in the reactions of the men he approaches" (Erickson 1999:52). In the next sequence Badii abandons the city for its dry and desert-like outskirts. He manages to pick up a shy, extremely nervous young Kurdish soldier (Ali Moradi) who becomes even more nervous when Badii explains what his intentions are. He is driving toward a roadside hole where he intends to commit suicide later that night by taking an overdose of sleeping pills. He wants the soldier to come back the next morning to check on his situation. If he is alive, he wants the soldier to help him out of the hole; if he is dead, he wants the soldier to bury him. For doing this, Badii offers the young soldier some amount of money. In response to this deal, the soldier suddenly bursts out of the car and runs away as fast as he can. The next person is an Afghani seminary student (Hossein Noori) whom Badii meets at a deserted construction site and is convinced (by Badii) to go for a ride with him. When the student hears Badii's request, he quotes the Koran and warns him against committing the sin of suicide. Badii drives him back to the construction site, after arguing with him for a while. His next passenger is a Turkish taxidermist (Abdolhossein Bagheri) who works at a natural history museum. Although he is against Badii's plan, he agrees to help him to carry it out. He also tries to dissuade Badii from committing suicide by telling him a personal story that describes a suicide attempt of his own, which was abandoned only after he ate mulberries and realized that life was still beautiful and had much to offer him. Nevertheless, he reluctantly agrees to help Badii.

Taste of Cherry displays an exclusive use of exteriors and a tendency to alternate between extreme close-ups of individuals and long shots of landscapes. Most of the film happens in Badii's car, conversing with his passengers in shot/reverse-shot form. During these sequences, Kiarostami shot each character separately and edited the footage together (in shot/reverse-shot form) to create the illusion of passengers sitting across from Badii. In fact, we know that it is Kiarostami himself who sits across from each actor. Kiarostami has explained in *positif* how the shots were staged: "In fact, the shooting took place without the two "actors" ever meeting. Each time a character speaks in close-ups, I was at the other side of the camera to answer him and to find ways of extracting certain emotions from him. I was the only person who spoke to the old man, the young soldier and the young seminarian, and they would doubtless be most surprised not to see me in the film!" (Mulvey 1998:26). This means that the actors in a sequence become mutually exclusive; they cannot both be present at the same time. This technique, which does not allow the actors to be present in one shot, reinforces the separation of their mentalities and their *Weltanschauungen*. It is only with the third passenger, the Turkish taxidermist, that we can have, symbolically as a result of their agreement, the images of Badii and the taxidermist in the same shot.

Deleuze's discussion of the affection-image in his *Cinema 1: The Movement-Image* can be used to illustrate the function of the close-up in *Taste of Cherry*. To begin with, the affection-image, as Deleuze maintains, is the close-up, and the close-up is the face. There are however two types of close-ups: the intensive face, associated with Eisenstein and the reflective face, associated with Griffith. The intensive face passes "from one quality to another, to emerge onto a new quality. To produce a new quality, to carry out a qualitative leap, this is what Eisenstein claims for the close-up . . ." (Deleuze 1986:89). An intensive face expresses a "pure Power" (90) which is revealed in intensive series and refers to "Desire" (90), while, on the other hand, the reflective face expresses a "pure Quality" (90) which is revealed in a reflective unity and refers to "Wonder" (90). In a reflective face the "relationship between a face and what it is thinking about is often arbitrary" (90). The affection-images in *Taste of Cherry*, as one already expects, are of a reflective, rather than intensive, type. However, the relationship between the face and its content of thought are far from being clear. The close-up of Badii's face is a tabula rasa, providing no text to be read. There are no other indications that help us fill in his blank face, as, for example, in Griffith's *Broken Blossoms*, in which we know that the young woman is thinking about her husband because we see the image of the husband immediately afterwards. Eisenstein suggested that "the close-up was not merely one type of image among others, but gave an affective reading of the whole film" (Deleuze 87). If one assumes this hypothesis to be valid in case of *Taste of Cherry*, then it is possible to read Badii's blank and expressionless face as a symptom of something else, something which is not represented/representable in film, something which constitutes, to use the Deleuzean term, the *out-of-field* of the images. Therefore, when Eisenstein says that we can infer the whole film from the close-up, "the whole" should not be interpreted as the sum total of its parts. The whole of the film implicitly refers to something beyond its limits of representation. This makes the cinematographic representation of images not a closure but an openness:

> We know the insoluble contradictions we fall into when we treat the set of all sets as a whole. It is not because the notion of the whole is devoid of sense; but it is not a set and does not have parts. It is rather that which prevents each set, however big it is, from closing in on itself, and that which forces it to extend itself into a larger set. The whole is therefore like thread which traverses sets and gives each one the possibility, which is necessarily realized, of communicating with another, to infinity. Thus the whole is the Open, and relates back to time or even to spirit rather than to content and to space. (Deleuze 1986:16)

The close-up of Badii's face is a symptom of an out-of-field which exists elsewhere: "The out-of-field testifies to a more disturbing presence, one which cannot even be said to exist, but rather to 'insist' or 'subsist,' a more radical Elsewhere, outside homogeneous space and time" (17). It is precisely the spatial closedness of the close-up of Badii's face that opens it on to time, not the time of the diegetic level of narration in the film but the time of History itself. We started with *story* and ended up with *history*.

One might be tempted to interpret Badii's face as a symptom of *ennui* (the absence of feeling in general), or, to use Thomas Aquinas's term, *acedia*. *Ennui* is a psychic condition the fundamental gesture of which is not revolt but renunciation. The diagnosis made by Freud for the condition he called "melancholia" might most fittingly apply to *ennui*: "The distinguishing mental features of melancholia are a profoundly mental dejection, abrogation of interest in the outside world, loss of the capacity to love, inhibition of all activity. . ." (Freud 1957:165). For Freud, such symptoms result from the loss of an object in which the libido has been invested. *Ennui*, a psychic condition in which all libidinal investment has been withdrawn from its attachments to objects, does not, however, imply or lead to a death-wish. The person suffering from *ennui* does not withdraw from the world but remains within it, gazing at its activities with narcotic indifference.

The description of Badii's situation in terms of *anomie* (normlessness) and anomic suicide, rather than *ennui*, seems to be more suitable. But before entering into a discussion of Durkheim's hypothesis as to the causal correlation between anomie and suicide, as well as Blanchot's remarks on the question of suicide and voluntary death, I feel the need to theoretically justify the transition from the text (or art in general) to the context (the society), or to put it differently, from superstructure to base. One of the things that struck me as an Iranian viewer of *Taste of Cherry* was the choice of as unusual a theme as suicide, which is quite unprecedented in the history of Iranian filmic representation. Assuming the social roots of art, one tends to infer that the phenomenon of suicide has become an objective issue in post-revolutionary Iran. If this is not so, then the question arises as to why bother making films about phenomena which do not even exist in a certain society, in our case post-revolutionary Iran. While assuming a general relationship between text and context (in other words, that art has something to say about the society in which it is produced), I draw on the works of Fredric Jameson for a framework to deal with the *nature* of the relationship between superstructure and base. Following Fredric Jameson in his *The Political Unconscious*, I propose the following hypothesis: the individual film as a formal structure is to be grasped as the *imaginary* resolution to a *real*, social contradiction.[33] *Taste of Cherry* is an imaginary response to the real, emerging phenomenon of suicide in post-revolutionary Iran.

In his *Suicide*, Durkheim is preoccupied with understanding the relationship between the individual and society. According to him there should be a correct balance between the individual's dependence upon society and the independence of society itself, a balance which promotes the individual's well-being. Too little or too much independence from society are both harmful. What could be a better sign of a lack of individual's well-being than those individuals should destroy themselves? Hence, what better setting for an evaluation of the relationship between individual and society than the examination of the patterns of suicide? Durkheim's study of suicide is a remarkable example, which provides the possibility of explaining the seemingly most personal actions in terms of social factors.

Durkheim distinguishes four types of suicide: anomic, fatalistic, egoistic and altruistic. Anomic and fatalistic suicide are contrasted to each other: "Anomic suicide arises when the individual is insufficiently regulated by society, and the fatalistic kind is one in which the individual is excessively regulated by social circumstances in which individuals find themselves "with futures pitilessly blocked and passions violently choked" as, for example, in the suicides of slaves or those subject to despotism" (Hughes et al 180). Durkheim's major thesis is that the rate of suicide in Protestant societies is higher than that of Catholic ones. Durkheim considers that the Catholic church produces more of "mechanical" solidarity in groupings than do the Protestant churches. In the former there is still a great deal of homogeneity of belief as well as unquestioned authority: "The Protestant churches' 'concessions' to individual judgments mean that there is no longer any consensus to serve as communal authority. However, the disproportionate inclination of Protestants to suicide is not caused by their commitment to free inquiry, but by their desire for knowledge caused by the 'loss of cohesion of religious society'" (Hughes et al 181). The Protestant church, characterized by "the loss of cohesion of religious society," produces an anomic situation, which directly, according to Durkheim, causes suicide.

It is not hard to find, in the last decade and especially after the death of Khomeini, the signs of a loss of cohesion of religious society in Iran. After the death of Khomeini, there emerged a hiatus between two groups within the political sphere, the so-called hard-liners and soft-liners. This political fragmentation and bipolarization has had far-reaching consequences in other infrastructures of the Iranian society, from micro-economy to macro-economy, from foreign affairs to domestic ones, from debates on private investments versus governmental control to cultural policies, etc. The resulting confusion is apparent not only on the legislative but also on the executive branches of the government, which means that people are confronted, on a daily basis, with this ideological conflict coming from the top. All this, as an argument goes, might be seen as a "healthy" sign of political dispute, resulting from the increasing dissolution of theocracy, leading to a more pluralistic political system. But the point remains that, as I have tried to show, these political or ideological conflicts reproduce themselves on almost every infrastructural level of society, thereby causing confusion and normlessness. Society remains the *absent cause* (Althusser) of Badii's suicide. What we see in *Taste of Cherry* is the effect of this cause, while the cause itself has been withdrawn to the out-of-field. This is Kiarostami's strategy to escape censorship: representing the effect rather than cause, which necessarily and logically draws attention to that cause itself. The *Taste of Cherry* is a dream in which its manifest content systematically diverts attention from the latent content. What is said is not the whole truth; the whole truth remains to be inferred. This inference can be drawn by looking for, not what the film says, but, what it does not/cannot say.

The landscape in *Taste of Cherry* is bleak and barren. Kiarostami shot the film in autumn to take advantage of the metaphorical significance of the season of dying. The almost "Waste Land" character of the landscape is not only an "objective correlative" (to use a term by T. S. Eliot) for Badii's inner state of mind, it is also meaningful in itself: "When the camera stands back and sweeps across the landscape it seems to translate it on to the screen as pure form, as sculpted space, but on the other hand this landscape constantly reasserts itself as a place of social meaning within which things happen, marked on to its surface by the people who live and work there" (Mulvey 26). The bleak landscape is the allegory of the society itself: The construction site is not working, a guy (who is teased by children) is picking trash, another guy (talking in the telephone-booth) is arguing about financial problems, a lack of collective solidarity implied by the spatial distance, filled by sand and barren land, between the people Badii meets, etc. In other words, the whole society, as Kiarostami sees it, is reproduced in the pale brown landscape parched by the summer heat.

The ending in *Taste of Cherry* comes as a form remarkably incongruent with the structure of the rest of the film. It reminds the spectator of the enigmatic and unconventional finales of Antonioni's film that have puzzled critics. In Antonioni's *The Eclipse*, the director surely meant the final sequence to remain ambiguous — a step in the direction of the cinema of abstraction Antonioni often advocates. Some critics see the last scene in *The Eclipse* as indicating that the final meeting of Vittoria and Piero never takes place, while others view the final sequence as an image of a dehumanized contemporary environment (Bondanella 1990:217). Similarly in *Taste of Cherry* the viewer is left, in the final sequence, with an ambiguity concerning the act of Badii's suicide, which is itself a sign of the alienated character of Badii himself.

Badii's being depicted as an alienated character (indicated for instance by his expressionless face) also resembles Antonioni's sensitivity in portraying modern alienated (sometimes neuratic) characters whose emotional lives are sterile and who seem to be out of place in their environments. Antonioni's declaration (in a statement distributed in Cannes when *L'Aventura* was first shown) that "modern man lives in a world without the moral tools necessary to match his technological skills; he is incapable of authentic relationships with his environment, his fellows, or even the objects which surround him because he carries with him a value system out of step with the times" (211) seems to be applicable to the antihero of *Taste of Cherry* too. Badii's alienation is characterized by a situation in which there are multiplicity of discourses none of which has anything common with his. Like Moretti's *Caro Diario*, *Taste of Cherry* is also the story of the multiplicity of discourses; but unlike the former film in which the main character finds some kind of truth by moving among heterogeneous discourses, in *Taste of Cherry* Badii's discourse is a discourse which rather than negating or going beyond other discourses, is the *differend* of discourse itself.

If all this seems to be merely a critique of ideology, a mere "negative hermeneutics" (Jameson), then, let me add, by way of a conclusion, a positive, utopian note to it. The utopian impulse lies not so much in the content as in the form of the film. The opening into the possibility of a utopian space is not produced by Kiarostami's "uncertainty principle" (a term used by Mulvey) in which the spectator is left with the structural impossibility of determining whether Badii in fact commits suicide or not. It is, however, produced by the very form of the ending of the film in which the spectator, after leaving Badii in the darkness of the hole, finds him/herself on another temporal level, an extra-diegetic temporality in which Homayoun Ershadi (the person playing Badii) is lighting a cigarette for Kiarostami on a spring day. This, one might argue, functions as a foregrounding of the constructedness, and thereby the contingency, of the cinematographic representation. The utopian impulse of *Taste of Cherry* lies in the thematizing of this possible temporality, which is not, however, the real time of the spectators, but, rather, a time structurally different from the diegetic time of the story. The opening into this alternative temporality is achieved as a result of a dialectical process whose means is the "kinoeye." It is dialectical because it attempts to "think another side, an outside, an external face . . . that can never be directly visible or accessible to us . . ." (Jameson 1990b:25). If the camera is the agent of this dialectics, the redemptive potentialities of the category of the aesthetic cannot be more emphasized. *Taste of Cherry* is, therefore, only a beginning of cinema.

Badii seems to find in his suicide a liberation from the oppressive and anomic societal conditions in which he finds himself. In an act of voluntary death the subject seems to regain the freedom which has been denied to him in another, i.e., societal level. For Kirilov, as discussed by Blanchot in his "Death as Possibility," voluntary death affirms his insubordination to God and his new liberty: "I recommend my death to you, voluntary death, which comes to me because I want it to . . . To eliminate oneself is the most praiseworthy of acts; it practically grants us the right to live" (96). Natural death is death in "the most contemptible conditions, a death which is not free, which does not come when it should, a coward's death. Love of life should make us wish for an altogether another death, a free and conscious death, one which is no accident and holds no surprises" (96). Nietzsche's words, as cited by Blanchot, promises the possibility of death that makes one become mortal, for "it does not suffice for him that he is mortal; he understands that he has to become mortal . . . That is his human vocation. Death, in the human perspective, is not a given, it must be achieved" (96). This voluntary death, which seems to promise a mastery of death as well as a denial of the present, is in fact, as Blanchot argues, contradictory. He who kills himself withdraws from the world and is claiming to act no more and yet this same person wishes to make death an act. This is the first contradiction. The second contradiction lies in the fact that the one who kills himself is the great affirmer, rather than denier, of the present ("I want to kill myself in an 'absolute' instant, the only one which will not pass and will not be surpassed. Death if it arrived at the time we choose, would be the apotheosis of the *instant*" 103). The third contradiction lies in mistaking one death for another, since death is somehow doubled: "there is one death which circulates in the language of possibility, of liberty, which has for its furthest horizon the freedom to die and the capacity to take mortal risks; and there is its double, which is ungraspable. It is what I cannot grasp, what is not linked to me by any relation of any sort. It is that which never comes and toward which I do not direct myself" (104). The one who commits suicide mistakes the first death for the second. By committing suicide one wants to kill oneself at a determined moment, but this "now" is, argues Blanchot, an illusion for death is never present, it remains secret, indecipherable and unrepresentable ("this essential indeterminacy — the fact that death is never a relation to a determined moment any more than it bears any determined relation to myself" 104).

We are therefore arriving at a rather revised hypothesis: while for Badii (the anti-hero) voluntary death might compensates for the loss of liberty, for Kiarostami (the director) death is a relation to that (i.e., to an excess) which will not allow itself to be charted. In *The Taste of Cherry* what we in fact witness is the impossibility of testifying to the instant of death, something that is achieved, as was explained above, through shifting the levels of narrative diegesis.

Notes

1. Sartre also argues that Heidegger's account of death "rests on an erroneous conflation of death and finitude; finitude is essentially internal to life and the grounds of

our freedom, . . . whereas death is simply an external and factual limit of my subjectivity...Since death is always beyond my subjectivity, there is no place for it in my subjectivity" (Dollimore 169). Two years before his death, Sartre reiterates his repudiation of the philosophy of death: "Death? I don't think about it. It has no place in my life, it will always be outside. One day my life will end but I don't want it to be burdened with death. I want that my death never enter my life, nor define it, that I be always a call to life." See Annie Cohen-Solal's *Sartre: A Life* (London: Heineman, 1987)

    2. See Levinas on *Autre/autre_* and *Autrui/autrui* and the distinctions between these, in *Totality and Infinity*, specifically in the section on the gift and the other.

    3. There are, therefore, at least, two understandings of death: death as *Aufhebung* and death as *différance*.

    4. In his *Paradoxes and Problems*, in "Paradox I: That All Things Kill Themselves," somehow foreshadowing Freud when the latter maintains that the goal of life is death: "To affect, yea to effect their own deaths, all living are importuned...Or how shall man be free from this, since the first man taught us this — except we cannot kill ourselves because he killed us all? Yet lest something should repair this common ruin, we kill daily our bodies with surfeits, and our minds with anguishes. Of our powers remembering kills our memory. Of affections, lusting our lust. Of virtues, giving kills liberality" (15).

    5. Benjamin in *The Arcades Project*: "A sort of productive disorder is the canon of the *mémoire involontaire*, as it is the canon of the collector . . . the *mémoire volontaire*, on the other hand, is a registry providing the object with a classificatory number behind which it disappears" (211).
The classic passage on "involuntary memory" in Proust: " . . . but since the facts which I should then have recalled would have been prompted only by the voluntary memory, the intellectual memory, and since the information which that kind of memory gives us about the past preserves nothing of the past itself...and so it is with our own past. It is a labor in vain to attempt to recapture it: all the efforts of out intellect must prove futile. The past is hidden somewhere outside of the realm, beyond the reach, of intellect, in some material object . . . which we do not suspect. And as for that object, it depends on chance whether we come upon it or not before we ourselves must die." (403)

    6. "Empty and amorphous spaces which lose their Euclidean co-ordinates, in the style of Ozu and Antonioni" (Deleuze 1997:129). Also: "dehumanized landscapes, empties spaces that might be seen as having absorbed characters and actions, retaining only a geophysical description (5). Deleuze further relates the empty space to "any-space-whatever"(5).

    7. The theorematic, for Deleuze, creates a new direction for the cinema that moves away from and abandons figures, metonymy as well as metaphor: "For example, in regard to depth of field as introduced by Renoir and Welles, it has been noted that this opened up a new direction for the cinema, no longer metaphorically or even metonymically 'figurative,' but more demanding, more constraining, in some sense theorematic" (Deleuze 173).

    8. "It is in this sense that Pasolini's deduction in *Theorem* must be understood: a problematic rather than a theorematic deduction" (175).

    9. Derrida's reference to Levinas formulations of the "invisible theater of hospitality" in which the subject is initially a host, then it becomes a hostage. See Derrida's *Of Hospitality*, 109.

    10. "To read what was never written" (Hofmannsthal) (416)

    11. In "We Travel Like All People," (in his *Unfortunately, It Was Paradise*) Mahmoud Darwish argues that there is no return but in language.

114   Toward A General Economy of Travel

12. Mahmoud Darwish conveys the same sensibility in the poem *"Who am I, without exile?"* included in his *Unfortunately, It Was Paradise*. Trans. Munir Akash and Carolyn Forché. Berkeley: U of California P, 2003.

13. cited in Cohen 1994:11

14. For a distinction between an ethics of Diaspora and an ethics of exile see Dean Franco's "Re-placing the Border in Ethnic American Literature." There Diaspora is construed to be the positive term, exile the negative. An ethics of exile is characterized by the persistence of memory with a resulting rigidification of identity. The exile is precisely the one who never forgets. This hegemony of memory in exilic experience plays a significant role in who the subject is: an exilic identity is an identity constructed away from home through the mediation of a will to memory (example: one becomes an Iranian only outside Iran.). In contrast, the diasporic experience is characterized by a weakening of memory and a dispersion and rupture of identity, a twilight of oblivion.

15. For a discussion on an elaborated process of exclusion on a daily basis see Essed (1984, 1995).

16. See Femke Halsema's (member of the Green Party in the Parliament) "Progressieve coalitie allochtonen-autochtonen nodig" (In *NRC Handelsblad*, Saturday 26 February, 2000, p. 8.) where he criticizes this position.

17. See "Paul Scheffer's "Het multiculturele drama" (NRC Handelsblad, Saturday 29, January 2000) and Peter van der Veer's "Aanpassen is geen panacee" (NRC Handelsblad, Saturday 5, February 2000)

18. In an interview with Esther Captain and Edy Seriese in NRC Handelsblat, August 14th, 1999.

19. The story of Issac has been attributed to Ismael in Islamic tradition.

20. In fact Abraham should have chosen himself as "the one who is most dear" to him. The ultimate sacrifice is self-sacrifice.

21. " . . . *the real plight of dwelling* does not lie merely in a lack of houses…The real plight of dwelling lies in this, that mortals ever search anew for the nature of dwelling, that they *must ever learn to dwell*. What if man's homelessness consisted in this, that man still does not even think of the *real* plight of dwelling as *the* plight?" (161)

22. In *Difference and Repetition* when Deleuze discusses the four paradoxes of the past: "A second paradox emerges: the paradox of coexistence. If each past is contemporaneous with the present that it was, then *all* of the past coexists with the new present in relation to which it is now past . . . In effect, when we say that it is contemporanous with the present that it *was*, we necessarily speak of a past which never was present, since it was not formed 'after'" (81-2).

23. In Joyce's *The Dead*, although the secret in the heart of Gretta is revealed, it cannot be mastered. It will keep coming back. Gabriel realizes in an epiphany that he is in fact the master of nothing. Joyce's *The Dead* brings into relationship the questions of the living dead, of the crypt, introjection and incorporation, mourning, secrecy and confession. While a discussion of the intricate relationship between these issues is beyond the scope of this chapter, I emphasize the absolute disruption and displacement that the memory of Michael Fuery produces in Gretta.

24. In the prologue we witness a curious collaboration and overlapping between the omniscient narrator and Ismael: *"We zijn met z'n tweeën. Ismael en ik. Ik ben de alwetende verteller. Ismael is de zoon van Aga Akbar die doofstom was. Hoewel ik alwetend ben, kan ik Aga Akbars notities helaas niet lezen. Ik vertel alleen het gedeelte van het verhaal totdat Ismael geboren wordt. De rest laat ik hem zelf vertellen. Maar aan het einde kom ik terug, want Ismael kan het laatste deel van zijn vaders notities niet ontcijferen* (10). [There are the two of us, Ismael and I. I am the omniscient narrator, while

Ismael is the son of Aga Akbar who was deaf. I cannot read the notes of Aga Akbar, even though I am omniscient. I will only tell that part of the story before the birth of Ismael, then he will tell us the rest of the story. But I will be back in the end because Ismael cannot decipher the last part of his father's notes]

25. "That these notes were scribbles of Agha Akbar, without meaning . . . . Ismael sat behind his desk and thought: 'How can I ever reveal the secrets of these notes? How can I let this book speak? How can I translate it into legible language?'" (104) . . . . "Because my story has to be based on the vague and unreadable thoughts of the other" (141).

26. "Nobody knew when Agha Akbar wrote in his notebook, nor what he wrote about. He had to write about things that he could not understand and were not expressible in a sign-language, about inaccessible, incomprehensible, impalpable things that held him in their grips while he remained gazing at them in all his powerlessness" (94).

27. The story of Kahaf is a story from the Koran in which a group of persecuted people seek refuge in the cave Kahaf. They fall in sleep and when they wake up they find themselves older. One of them goes to the town and tries to buy food with some coins, but he realizes that he cannot understand people's language and that his coins are not valid anymore. He returns to the cave and relates the story and they realize that they have been sleeping for three hundred years.

28. See Hans vaihinger. 1911. *The Philosophy of "As If,"* Trans. C. K. Ogden, London: Routledge, 1965.

29. See Saul Kripke, *Naming and Necessity*, Cambridge: Harvard University Press, 1980.

30. See Marie-Laure Ryan, "Fiction, Non-factuals, and the Principle of Minimal Departure," *Poetics* 9 (1980): 403-22.

31. For related discussions see the following:
Michael Loux (ed.), *The Possible and the Actual: Readings in the Metaphysics of Modality*, Ithaca: Cornell University Press, 1979.
Hilary Putnam, "Meaning and Reference," In A. P. Martinich (ed.) *The Philosophy of Language*, Oxford: Oxford University Press,1985.
Ruth Ronen, "Completing the Incompleteness of Fictional entities," In *Poetics Today* 9:3 (1988): 497-514.

32. See Jameson's "Reflections on the Brecht-Lukács Debate" in *The Ideologies of Theory*, vol. II, p. 133.

33. In his *Political Unconscious: Narrative as a Socially Symbolic Act*, Jameson proposes three concentric frameworks as an ultimate semantic precondition for a hermeneutics of cultural texts. The first framework is the political history from the perspective of which an individual cultural artifact is to be construed as a symbolic act. The second framework is society in which the object of study is transformed into "*ideologeme*, that is, the smallest unit of the essentially antagonistic collective discourses of social classes" (76). The third is that of history whose object of study id the "*ideology of form*, that is, the symbolic messages transmitted to us by the coexistence of various sign systems which are themselves traces or anticipations of modes of production" (76).

Chapter Four

Réda Bensmaïa's *The Year of Passages*: Mourning Becomes Diaspora

In the horizon of the infinite — we have left the land and have embarked. We have burned our bridges behind us — indeed, we have gone farther and destroyed the land behind us. Now, little ship, look out! Beside you is the ocean: to be sure, it does not always roar, and at times it lies spread out like silk and gold and reveries of graciousness. But hours will come when you will realize that it is infinite and that there is nothing more awesome than infinity. Oh, the poor bird that felt free and now strikes the walls of the cage! Woe, when you feel homesick for the land as if it had offered more *freedom* — and there is no longer any "land."

Nietzsche, *The Gay Science*, 181

He is the Passenger *par excellence*: that is, the prisoner of the passage. And the land he will come to is unknown — as is, once he disembarks, the land from which he comes. He has his truth and his homeland only in that fruitless expanse between two countries that cannot belong to him.

Foucault, *Madness and Civilization*, 11

In this chapter, I will read Réda Bensmaïa's *The Year of Passages* (1995) as a novel that epitomizes a general economy of travel and displacement. Both in its approach to the dilemma of memory, where any instrumental and restricted economical use of memory becomes impossible, as well as in its employment of the figure of death in terms of its spectrality (the living dead), Réda Bensmaïa's *The Year of Passages* opens itself to the outside of knowledge and representation, whereby both the subject and his experience of the foreign are reduced to ashes.

In *The Year of Passages* the event of crossing boundaries is the experience of spectrality in which neither the time of the event nor the passage itself can be represented.

Réda Bensmaïa's *The Year of Passages* (1995) is a novel of displacement in which he gives us a hilarious, ironic, and an almost self-destructive portrait of a figure moving between different continents, cultures, and idioms, without the possibility of ever being able to settle down in or belong to any of them. This aspect of the novel places it in a diasporic/exilic tradition, which will be discussed and nuanced later. The novel, furthermore, raises a series of questions about the dilemmas of practicing literature in French language in Algeria and, more generally, the postcolonial context of literary production, i.e., to write in the language of the colonizer. It also problematizes notions of identity, subjectivity, and memory in places of transition where it becomes exceedingly more difficult to determine where/what one's home is. The question is how to read this nomadic text that has no simple generic status nor any specific readership. I propose to discuss these issues by invoking figures like Gilles Deleuze, Jacques Derrida, and Jean-Louis Chrétien. I will argue that the "in-betweenness" of *The Year of Passages* is a context that allows the novel to become minor literature, trying to find a line of flight which renounces all languages of masters, as well as any determination of identity. The "in-betweeness" is not, as it were, a position among other positions, but rather a form of writing that marks the condition of the possibility of any position as such. *The Year of Passages* deterritorializes the French language in its attempt to find its own minor practice of major language from within, to find its own third world, its own desert. *The Year of Passages* in its flight from any official, national, state language and through its attempt at constructing linguistic "third world" zones by which a language can escape, becomes accented.[1] The accent being without origin, belonging to neither a home nor a host, enters, however, into a political and historical dialogue with both home and host countries, renouncing them as two forms of fascism. An accented novel, *The Year of Passages* appropriates the language of masters, of major literature, in order to dig its hole or burrow within it. Bensmaïa is writing in the language of the other and it is the only language he has: "'yes, I only have one language, yet it is not mine'" (Derrida 1996:2). This language constitutes him to the degree that he would not be himself outside it. He dwells in a language that is not his. This abiding alienation, this "structure of alienation without alienation" (25) constitutes not only the origin of his responsibility but also the property of language in general (25). This structure of alienation resists the reduction of language to the One, that is, to the hegemony of the homogeneous, the "homo-hegemony" (40). The aporia involved in digging one's intimate hole inside the French language (what Derrida calls "the degree zero-minus-one of writing" (65)) is to create an impossible, unreadable language. But that is, as Derrida argues, the condition of the possibility of events, of promised or messianic events, the promise of a still unheard-of language: "heard melodies are sweet, those unheard are sweeter." Bensmaïa's *The Year of Passages*, as an accented cultural expression, keeps memories, not of the past (empirical or phantasmatic), but of the future alive.

Before attempting any analysis of this novel, certain contextualizations, whether historical or theoretical, are in order. After a short historical background, I try to distinguish between two forms of "displaced" writing, i.e., exilic and immigrant, and suggest that Réda Bensmaïa's *The Year of Passages* does not, strictly speaking, fulfill the criteria of these two generic forms. I will proceed by a rather detailed formal analysis of the language of this text to examine to what extent it deterritorializes both the French language and the languages of conventional autobiographical, exilic narratives. In other words, in Bensmaïa's *The Year of Passages*, I would argue, exile becomes diaspora.

On Algeria

Algeria is associated, in the minds of many, with unending violence. During the 1990's, almost the only news about Algeria involved reports of massacres; more than 100,000 Algerian died in the course of the decade. One might also recall Algeria's bloody civil war in which hundreds of thousands were killed, mostly by the French colonial forces, but also as a result of regional rivalries. When these two moments of Algeria's past are put side by side, one might conclude that there is something in the culture, in the temperament of the people, that is conducive to violence. But such cultural explanations can be very misleading. After reading about the history of Algeria, one learns a great deal about the origin of violence, those aspects that are distinctly Algerian as well as those that are common to newly independent countries seeking to forge their identity in opposition to a strong colonial power. The violence would still be deplorable but at least one can understand it.

After the independence war, Algeria experiences a period of relative stability and domestic calm. Algerians were then starting to establish the preliminaries that would shape their identity as an independent people. Their leaders were however fearful that the hard-won independence might be lost as a result of internal conflicts that had been started during the revolution. The solution to this perceived fragility of a people, in the minds of its two first presidents, Ahmed Ben Bella and Hourai Boumédienne, was to assert the unity of the people by making a single party, the Front de Libération Nationale (FLN), dominant. They also lodged power in the hands of military security that claimed its legitimacy as the bearer of the legacy of the revolution. In 1989, the political system opened up and revealed the underlying diversity of the Algerian society. Dozens of new political and civic movements found their voices, and Algeria seemed to become the Arab world's first democracy. This brief moment of hope ended in January 1992 when the military intervened to end an election that would have been won by opposition Islamists of the Front Islamique du Salut (FIS). Soon after the cancellation of the election, a vicious circle of violence began, pitting Islamist radicals against government security forces. This specific Algerian situation brought up some political-theortical problems with respect to our understanding of democracy: Would the interests of democracy have been better served by letting the manifestly nondemocratic FIS assume power? How should we understand the concept of democracy if a nondemocratic regime is elected in a democratic way? For those political theorists who define democracy as the "will of the majority," this obviously causes some theoretical difficulties.

Pieds noirs[2] (literally, "blackfeet"), the Algerian French, were mostly living in cities and large towns on the eve of the Algerian War. Contrary to the popular legends, which imagined *Pieds noirs* in rural areas carefully overseeing their large land holdings, they were city dwellers mostly composed of government employees, men of law, merchants, entrepreneurs, and artisans. The Algerian French did not in any way constitute a microcosm of the French society: "Barely 3 percent of Algerian French had a standard of living above the average for the metropolis; 25 percent were more or less equal; and 27 percent had an income that was 15 to 20 percent lower, even though the cost of living in Algeria was not lower than that in France. The reason for that disparity in income lay in the economic relations between France and its principal colony. Within the framework of the 'colonial pact,' Algeria was a source of raw materials and a mere outlet for the manufactured products of the metropolis" (Stora 2001:23). Jean-Paul Sartre in his *Situations V*[3] tries to explain the situation in terms of the political economy of colonialism. Against the French colonial administration that argues that the Algerian problem is first of all economic ("a question of providing, by means of judicious reform, food for nine million people" (30)), he argues for the primacy of politics over economics, that is, the colonial system should first be shattered before any economic improvement becomes viable. The economy of French colonialism, Sartre argues, depends on a monopoly over the Algerian market by turning it into an importer of French goods. "The Algerian market" is mostly comprised of the French Algerians, the colonists, since the majority of the local Muslim population "live in intolerable poverty" (31). The question is how to make sure that the colonists possess a purchasing power: "in order to be a buyer, the colonist must be a seller. To whom will he sell? To the people of mainland France. And what can he sell without an industry? Food products and raw materials" (34). But how can the colonists produce food and raw materials if they do not have access to lands? At the beginning the slightest act of resistance was used as an excuse to confiscate indigenous lands. After all "the land must be good; it is of little importance to whom it belongs" (35). According to Sartre, "in 1850, the colonists' territory was 115,000 hectares. In 1900, it was 1,600,000; in 1950, it was 2,703,000. Today, 2,703,000 hectares belong to European owners; the French State owns 11 million in the form of 'state-owned land'; 7 million hectares have been left to the Algerians. In short, it has taken just a century to dispossess them of two-thirds of their land" (36). The lands left to the Algerians are mostly deserts, since they have been increasingly pushed to the Saharan south. To sum up: "the French State gives Arab land to the colonists in order to create for them a purchasing power which allows French industrialists to sell them their products; the colonists sell the fruits of this stolen land in the markets of France" (36). This situation leads to even more pauperization when the "concentration of land ownership leads to the mechanization of agriculture" (38). With the mechanization of agriculture, the cheap labor, mostly consisted of Algerians, is still too expensive: "you finish up taking from the natives their very right to work. All that is left for the Algerians to do, *in their own land*, at a time of great prosperity, is to die of starvation"(39). All these, according to Sartre, cannot be changed unless the political domination of French colonialism is terminated in Algeria.

The French colonial rule in Algeria had some politico-cultural aspects too. In the domain of education the colonial administration had no interest in educating the native people. The Algerian Muslims were denied the use of their own language: "Since 1830, the Arab language has been considered as a foreign language in Algeria" (41).

For Sartre, the colonist him/herself is no less a victim of the colonial domination as the Algerian natives: "Linked to the mainland by the colonial pact, he has come to market for France, in exchange for a fat profit, the goods of the colonized country. He has even created new crops [cultivation of grapes for the production of wine for which the natives were forbidden by their religion], which reflect the needs of France much more than those of the natives. He is, therefore, double and contradictory: he has his 'homeland', France, and his 'country', Algeria. In Algeria, he represents France and wants to have relations only with her. But his economic interests bring him into conflict with the political institutions of his homeland" (44).

This contradictory man, the Algerian French, betrays a "disorder of identity" [*trouble d'identité*]. Derrida recalls one aspect of this contradiction, or rather "double interdiction," in his *Monolingualism of the Other* (1998b): " . . . this *I* of whom I speak is someone to whom, as I more or less recall, access to any non-French language of Algeria (literary or dialectal Arabic, Berber, etc) was *interdicted*. But this same *I* is also someone to whom access to French was *also interdicted*, in a different, apparently roundabout, and perverted manner. In a different manner, surely, but likewise interdicted" (31).

Exile/Diaspora and the Myth of the Return

In most scholarly discussions of ethnic communities, immigrants, and aliens, and in most treatments of relationships between minorities and majorities, little if any attention has been devoted to diasporas. The absence of attention to diasporas is not surprising, for through the ages, the diaspora had a very specific meaning: the exile of the Jews from their homeland and their dispersion throughout many lands. Today, "diaspora" seems increasingly to be used as metaphoric designations for several categories of people: expatriates, expellees, political refugees, alien residents, immigrants, and ethnic and racial minorities *tout court*. Safran (1991) suggests to extend Connor's (1986) fairly broad working definition of diaspora[4] to include the following characteristics: 1) they, or their ancestors, have been dispersed from a specific original "center" to two or more "peripheral," or foreign, regions; 2) they retain a collective memory, vision or myth about their original homeland — its physical location, history, and achievements; 3) they believe that they are not- or cannot be- fully accepted by their host societies and therefore feel partially alienated; 4) they regard their ancestral homeland as their true, ideal home and as the place to which they or their descendents would, or should, eventually return; 5) they believe that they should collectively be committed to the maintenance or restoration of their original homeland; and 6) they continue to relate to that homeland in one way or another (Safran 1991:84). These characteristics might be used as criteria as well as an ideal type model to differentiate between different types of displacements: Cuban and Mexicans in the United States, Pakistanis in Britain, Maghrebis in France, Turks in Germany, Palestinian in Arab countries, blacks in North America, etc. Safran argues that only the Jewish diaspora fully conforms to this ideal type, although there are Jews who argue that with the establishment of Israel the Diaspora, in the purely theological sense, has been brought to an end. This ideal type excludes immigrants from the category of diaspora simply because immigrants barely fulfill the criteria mentioned above: they are not usually dispersed but have changed place voluntarily; the collective memory is much weaker and the process of mythologizing the original homeland is compromised by the increasing need to integrate into the host country (even though the memory is increasingly weakened, especially in later generations, it does not necessarily exempt them from being haunted by it); and, they regard the host country as the ideal home into which they try to integrate; therefore, the absence of any myth of return.

The Gypsies may, in a sense, be regarded as constituting a classic diaspora, being truly dispersed and homeless. Although there is a lack of the myth of return, and the fact that they can trace their residence in a host country through many generations, they evince the spirit of the first generation in the links they maintain with their traditional structures (Puxon 1980:142). Their situation, nevertheless, is not quite comparable to that of other diasporas: to a certain extent, their homelessness is a characteristic of their nomadic culture and the result of their refusal to be sedentarized. Moreover, diaspora consciousness is an intellectualization of an existential condition: the Gypsies have had social and economic grievances, but they have not asking themselves questions about "the Gypsy problem" in the way that the Jews have thought about a "Jewish problem," the Poles about a "Polish problem," and the Arabs about a "Palestinian problem." The Gypsies have had no myth of return because they have had no precise notion of their place of origin. All this may explain why at a world Gypsy conference in 1978 there was an emphasis on overcoming negative images of Gypsies and on ending discrimination in housing and health, but there were no references to an original homeland (Puxon 1980:5-6,13-14).

The Maghrebi and Portuguese *immigré* in France and the Turkish *Gastarbeiter* in Germany may be considered diasporas, yet their conditions differ markedly from those of the Jews and Armenians. Unlike these two latter, the Maghrebis, Portuguese, and Turks were not forcibly expelled from their countries of origin. Therefore, neither group has had the political obligation, or the moral burden, of reconstituting a lost homeland or maintaining an endangered culture. Nevertheless, a diaspora consciousness is perpetuated in both the Maghrebi and Portuguese communities. Many Maghrebis find assimilation impossible as long as France is equated with European and Christian origins and customs and as long as Islamic culture (no matter how secularized and diluted) is regarded as incompatible with it. That is why many French refer to even those Maghrebis who have forgotten most of their Arabic and who speak and write in French as "immigré de la deuxième generation" or as Algerians, and in so doing reinforce the Maghrebis' diaspora consciousness.[5]

While recently many authors, such as Tölölyan and James Clifford, have written about the history and comparative overviews of uses of the term *diaspora*, this discussion is mostly limited to the politics of African diaspora. The use of *diaspora* emerges in the 1950s with a growing interest in the Pan-African movement in particular and in black internationalism in general. It is important to recall that Pan-Africanism of both Henry Sylvester Williams and W. E. B. Du Bois arises as a discourse of internationalism whose aim was to achieve a cultural and political coordination of the interests of peoples of African descent around the world. This international Pan-Africanism was influenced by different ideologies of *return* that were so often a component of the African experience in the New World. According to Du Bois and others, if the black New World population had their origin in the fragmentation, racialized oppression, and systematic dispossession through the slave trade, then the Pan-African impulse stems from the necessity to confront or heal that legacy through racial organization itself: through ideologies of a real or symbolic return to Africa. The problematic of return consistently animated black ideologies as diverse as Garveyism (Garvey's populist and racialist version of "Back to Africa"), Negritude, and numerous black New World discourses of Ethiopianism. The African diaspora adheres to many of the elements considered to be common to the three classic diasporas (the Jewish, the Greek, and the Armenian): an origin in the scattering and uprooting of communities, a history of traumatic and forced departure, and also a sense of a real or imaginary relationship to a "homeland," mediated through the dynamics of collective memory and the politics of return.

Within the field of cultural studies, Stuart Hall, in his well-known 1980 essay "Race, Articulation, and Societies Structures in Dominance," attempts to think the relations of "difference within unity," i.e., linkage between separate societal elements within a global capitalist mode of production. The concept of articulation, in Hall's essay, offers the means to account for the cultural identity determined not through return but through difference: "not by essence or purity, but by the recognition of a necessary heterogeneity and diversity; by a conception of identity which lives with and through, not despite, difference" (Hall 1980: 235).

The turn to another explicit discourse of diaspora in cultural studies comes in 1987 in Paul Gilroy's *There Ain't No Black in the Union Jack*. In the fifth chapter, "Diaspora, Utopia and the Critique of Capitalism," which departs significantly from Hall's more Marxist vocabulary, Gilroy turns to a diasporic framework not to specify that space (as a new structure of cultural exchange) but as an alternative to the different varieties of absolutism or essentialism in racial, ethnic or national terms. In Gilroy's *Black Atlantic* (1993), the discourse of diaspora undergoes a shift. There the term "black Atlantic" usurps the space that could have been reserved for diaspora. In spite of formidable critiques (Neil Lazarus, "Is a Counterculture of Modernity a Theory of Modernity? *Diaspora* 4, Winter 1995; Laura Chrisman, "Journeying to Death: Gilroy's Black Atlantic," *Race and Class* 39, October-December 1997) it is important to remember that Gilroy himself is careful to propose black Atlantic as a heuristic term of analysis, more in order to open up a certain theoretical space than to formalize or theorize that space. The term "black Atlantic" refers, according to Gilroy, to an irreversible process that denies any possibility of return:

> First we have to fight over the concept of diaspora and to move it away from the obsession with origins, purity and invariant sameness. Very often the concept of diaspora has been used to say, 'Hooray! We can rewind the tape of history, we can get back to the original moments of our dispersal!' I'm saying something quite different. I called it Black Atlantic because I wanted to say, 'If this is a diaspora, then it is a very particular type of diaspora. It's a diaspora that can't be reversed.' (Lott 1994:56-57)

Brent H. Edwards, in his "The Uses of Diaspora," argues, quite persuasively, that there is something in the history of the use of the term "diaspora" that makes it quite different from terms like "black Atlantic" or "Pan-Africanism." A return to the intellectual history of the term is necessary because it reminds us that diaspora is introduced in large part to account for differences among African-derived population, in a way that a term like "Pan-Africanism" or "Black Atlantic" could not. He further argues that "diaspora points to difference not only internally (the way transnational black groupings are fractured by nation, class, gender, sexuality, and language) but also externally: in appropriating a term so closely associated with Jewish thought, we are forced to think not in terms of some closed or autonomous system of African dispersal but explicitly in terms of a complex past of forced migrations and racialization . . ." (64). It is therefore necessary to remember, Edwards argues, Stuart Hall's notion of diaspora as *articulated*, as a structured combination of elements "related as much through their differences as through their similarities." If a discourse of diaspora articulates difference, then one must consider the status of that difference, not just linguistic difference but, more broadly, the trace or the residue, perhaps, of what resists translation across the boundaries of language, class, gender, sexuality, religion, or the nation-state. Without claiming to formalize the difference that resists translation, Edwards proposes the notion of diaspora as *décalage*, a term used by Léopold Senghor (in his "Problématique de la Négritude" (1971). *Décalage*, although resisting translation, might nevertheless be rendered as "gap," "discrepancy," "time lag," or "interval." Edwards explains the term as follows:

> The verb *caler* means 'to prop up or wedge something' (as when one leg of a table is uneven). So *décalage* in its etymological sense refers to the removal of

such added prop or wedge. *Décalage* indicated the reestablishment of a prior unevenness or diversity; it alludes to the taking away of something that was added in the first place, something artificial . . . . (Edwards 2001:65)

By proposing a concept of diaspora as *décalage*, Edwards is trying to rethink the categories of race, gender and class, in their role of constructing identities, and argue for an originary difference:

Any articulation of diaspora in such a model would be inherently *décalé* or disjointed by a host of factors. Like a table with legs of different lengths, or a tilted bookcase, diaspora can be discursively propped up (*calé*) into an artificially 'even' or 'balanced' state of "racial" belonging. But such props, of rhetoric, strategy, or organization, are always articulations of unity or globalism, ones that can be 'mobilized' for a variety of purposes but can never be definitive: they are always prosthetic. In this sense, *décalage* is proper to the structure of a diasporic 'racial' formation, and its return . . . must be considered a necessary haunting. (Edwards 2001:66)

It seems that there is a lack of consensus in the ways scholars understand "diaspora" or "exile." I would like to propose a distinction, partly drawn from the works of the Boyarins[6] and their radical revision of diaspora, between diaspora and exile. Following the Boyarins, I would like to argue that the diaspora is precisely the condition of those who are not insisting on the preservation of memory or any return journey back home, whether mythical or historical. Diaspora is dispersion without return in which, as the Boyarins argue, the Jewish consciousness is untangled from nationalism. The Boyarins go even as far as saying that:

Indeed, we would suggest that diaspora, and not monotheism, may be the most important contribution that Judaism has to make to the world . . . Assimilating the lesson of Diaspora, namely that peoples and lands are not naturally and organically connected, could help prevent bloodshed such as that occurring in Eastern Europe today. (Boyarin and Boyarin 1993:722)

The Boyarins' idealism is a powerful and timely expression of a desire for an alternative Jewish identity, an "identity in which there are only slaves but no masters" (711). This ethics of diaspora emphasizes not the homeland (and the inter-related questions of memory and return) but the fact that many Jews feel at home (at least in culture if not in politics) living where they are. America in fact exemplifies this ethics of diaspora: America is home to many people precisely because it is diasporic. Therefore, in an ethics of diaspora, the fundamental model is that of "diaspora at home" in which one is at home and diasporic at the same time[7].

I would like to distinguish this conception of diaspora, and its emphasis on an ethics of dispersion without return (something that I associate with a general economy of displacement), from a conception of exile in which the ethical imperative emphasizes memory, return and identity (something that I associate with a restricted economy of displacement). I have already elaborated, in previous chapters, this theoretical model in which I distinguish two different typology of peregrination and displacement[8], but what I would like to show in this chapter is that Réda Bensmaïa's *The Year of Passages* exemplifies a movement from a restricted to a general economy and a transition from an ethics of exile to that of diaspora; a becoming diasporic of the exilic condition.

Immigrant Genre and Memory

Following Barbara Harlow's practice of naming literary genre by political and ideological contents rather than by formal attributes,[9] it could be argued that the contemporary literary writing in which the politics and experience of location, or rather of "dislocation," are the central narratives should be called the "Immigrant Genre." The argument for a distinct genre can be justified both thematically and pragmatically. From a pragmatic point of view, respecting the principle of differentiation, such a move lessens to some degree the burdens and constraints that contemporary criticism has placed on the category known as "postcolonial literature." In the West today, the literature that is labeled as postcolonial is that produced by authors with a "Third World" affiliation: either born, or spent the childhood or even an early education in one of the former colonies.[10] The postcolonial literature is read as being chiefly concerned with issues of nationalism and/or national allegory as well as with articulating a critique of colonialism. But since not all postcolonial literature is about the experience of displacement and homelessness, it becomes thematically viable to distinguish an "Immigrant Genre" within the general field of postcolonial literature.

The immigrant genre, like the social phenomenon from which it takes its name, is born of a history of global colonialism and is therefore a participant in decolonizing discourses. Like the distance that exile imposes on a writing subject, writers of the immigrant genre also view the present in terms of its distance from the past and future. The immigrant genre is also marked by a curiously detached reading of the experience of "homelessness" which is compensated for by an excessive use of the metaphor of luggage, both spiritual and material.

Assessing the work of immigrant writers in Canada, Jurgen Hesse has argued that the "cultural burdens" that these writers carry "will be of little or no value to them" (Hesse 1991:87). Immigrant novels themselves suggest that both travelling light as well as arriving with luggage are serviceable ways of entering the new location. Immigrants have to come to terms with the spiritual, material and even linguistic luggage they carry or inherit. Do such belongings impede or facilitate belonging? Salman Rushdie's *Shame* explores the nature of this luggage: "And what's the worst thing? It is the emptiness of one's luggage. I'm speaking of invisible suitcases, not the physical, perhaps cardboard, variety containing a few meaning-drained mementoes: we have come unstuck from more than land. We have floated upward from history, from memory, from Time" (Rushdie 1984:91). Some fictional immigrants, like Annie John, the seventeen-year old protagonist of Jamaica Kincaid's novel, determinedly leave their native lands without baggage. *Annie John* is an Antiguan *Bildungsroman*, which ends with Annie's immigration to England. On the morning of her departure from Antigua for England where she will train as a nurse, Annie resolves never to return and never to remember:

> Everything I would do that morning until I got on the ship that would take me to England I would be doing for the last time, for I had made up my mind that, come what may, the road for me now went only in one direction: away from my home, away from my mother, away from my father, away from the everlasting hot sun . . . The things I wanted to see or hear or do again now made up at least three week's worth of grocery lists. (Kincaid 1986:135)

If in immigrant literature we witness a "voluntary" repression of memory, in the literature of exile memory becomes a burden one can barely get rid of. In *After the Last Sky: Palestinian Lives*, an evocative narrative on the lives of present-day Palestinians, Edward Said writes of the ways in which Palestinians living in exile handle the baggage of memory:

> These intimate mementos of a past irrevocably lost circulate among us, like the genealogies and fables of a wandering singer of tales. Photographs, dresses, objects severed from their original locale, the rituals of speech and customs: much reproduced, enlarged, thematized, embroidered, and passed around, they are strands in the webs of affiliations we Palestinians use to tie ourselves to our identity and to each other.

> Sometimes these objects, heavy with memory — albums, rosary beads, shawls, little boxes — seem to me like encumbrances. We carry them about, hang them up on every new set of walls we shelter in, reflect lovingly on them. Then we do not notice the bitterness, but it continues and grows nonetheless. Nor do we acknowledge the frozen immobility of our attitudes. In the end the past owns us.

> (Said 1986:14)

The vicious injustice of exile that coats the narrative here is missing in the immigrant novel. The immigrant genre is often marked by detached and unsentimental reading of the experience of "homelessness," which has (as in the case of *Annie John*) often been read as indicative of the apolitical stance adopted by immigrants.[11]

Therefore, to sum up, I would like to argue that Réda Bensmaïa's *The Year of Passages* is neither a work of immigrant literature (a total celebration of the host country, detached reading of the experience of homelessness and uprooting, etc) nor an example of the literature of exile (the persistence of memory, the feeling of loss, the trauma of absence, etc); it is rather diasporic (the experience of homelessness without nostalgia for a lost home, the experience of being haunted by the past but not being able to return).

The Year of Passages: Exile Becomes Diaspora

The narrator in Réda Bensmaïa's *The Year of Passages* wishes to shake off the legacy of French canonical writers whose writings he considers to be clinical, whether in a psychoanalytic sense of relieving the patience of his/her neurosis or in a medical sense of curing the latter of his/her illness. What stands over the French "clinical" literature is the writings of Franz Fanon or Louis-Ferdinand Céline who is France's "infamous little literary secret" (7). The French colonial administration promoted reading of certain French canonical texts such as Sartre, Gide, Camus, and Proust and not others: "You've been verbalized, Francophoneyed! C'mon, fess up, fess up to mommy France, my little baby boy! Write her your great love letter! Tell mommy how much you've suffered! Tell her what makes you grieve! Tell her where it hurts! Say Sartre, Gide, Camus, Proust, or you'll be cuffed! Say Freud, Marx, Lenin, Jean-Jaurès in French, or you'll funk! Freud, Marx, but not Fanon, you dumb idiot!" (5). As for Céline, "hell no! no way, José! Louis-Ferdinand Céline, no! Too delicate! . . . Even we don't know how to handle it yet!" (6-7). Céline, argues the narrator, makes one nervous, while those French canonical writers "transform literature into cultural anesthesia" (7). Tom Conley in his afterword to *The Year of Passages* argues that Bensmaïa's text accords with some of the precepts of Deleuze with regards to a minor literature. According to Deleuze, a minor literature refuses to seek identity through a dialectical relation with a dominant culture. That is to say, in a Nietzschean way, it is active rather than reactive. A minor literature also "emits *other* languages within its own idiom" (Conley 1995:144). According to Conley, Bensmaïa animates at least two "other" languages: those of Céline and Artaud.

> In order to mobilize and animate the novel Bensmaïa finds two of his "other" voices in the tempo of Louis-Ferdinand Céline and in the glyphic, explosively self-contained, but also self-eradicating form of Antonin Artaud's poetry. Céline, the writer who crowns his sentences with exclamation points, uses punctuation and spacing to yield a music of fear, desperation, irony, comic helplessness, and wit. For Bensmaïa Céline's style and rhythm are not merely vehicles of ideology, but energies that can be used for effractive *operations*, creative praxes, that shred every kind of received belief. Artaud...is used to project...photographic shots, that turn the representation of speech into something that might be called a "becoming-image," an indeterminate . . . picture of a writing self getting lost in the blitz of the passage of time.   (Conley 1995:144-45)

Neither the narrator's simple rejection of the ideology of the canonical francophone literature, nor the fact that the novel is written by an ethnic minority within French culture necessarily turns it into a minor literature. It was in their study of Kafka that Deleuze and Guattari first mapped out what they called "a minor literature." Although they initially defined it as a kind of work constructed by minorities within a major literature (e.g. the German-Czech-Jew Kafka within German literature, the Black-American within American literature, etc), a definition of "minor literature" is not necessarily exhausted under this condition. The project of "becoming minor" (the unraveling of hegemonic structures of identity) and the machinery of "minorization" are open, at least theoretically, to everyone and not limited to ethnic, whether possible or actualized, minorities. In other words, being a minority is not a sufficient condition; one should "become minor."[12] Another aspect of the concept of "minor literature" is the work that is produced not just within a major literature but more specifically within a major author. The minorization of a major author would consist in reading him/her in spite of him/herself. Although a major author acts as a molar agency, in every subject position there is a molar and a molecular side. The point is to elaborate the molecular aspects of a work of a major author and allow them to proliferate, without necessarily engaging in doing violence to the text. No "criticism" would be necessary since nothing fails; the point is to see how/when a major author is "useful" for a minor purpose. That is why Deleuze does not see any point in criticizing an author to the extent that his ideal becomes ." . . to write nothing which might cause him sadness, or if he is dead, which would make him weep in his grave."

The narrator in *The Year of Passages* finds himself, as an exiled ex-colonial subject, within a confounded situation of a double impossibility: on the one hand, he does not belong to Algeria because he is a fierce critic of it; on the other hand, as an exile in a foreign country, he finds himself irrelevant: a living dead, not a ghost but a zombie, deprived of its power to haunt as a ghost. He is not entangled in a double bind between the memories of home and belonging, on the one hand, and the exigencies of forgetting and reinvention required of a life in a foreign land on the other. He is not an immigrant subscribing to a "both/and" logic ("both this and that"). He is rather an exile whose options are between a desert and a cemetery, caught between two deaths, while opposing both, "neither/nor." Therefore he does not characterize the conventional exile who is still engaged with his/her past and cherishes memory.

Algeria is a place where writing is a misdemeanor,[13] where thought stagnates and succumbs to doctrines ("Algeria is stagnation!" (101), " . . . enough Algeria to destroy all thinking!" (89), "My son, you defend yourself from doctrines and doctrinaires!" (102)), and where his *Deal Letters* is called satanic. He criticizes the colonial and postcolonial subjects as much as he criticizes the colonizers (Naipaul). The subaltern, for him, writes like a courtesan ("they hated it, but they were still doing it!"): "It's because of your vanity! Your overblown vanity as a writer and the pride you take in being a *subaltern*! Former teachers and generals are the ones who created subalterns, the noncoms, the underlings, the flunky servants, the corporals, the courtesans! It's high time that a subaltern stopped writing like a courtesan! What, ex-colonial *Vanity*! *Arrogance* of a subaltern! Arabic *pride*! It all stinks, Macha! Neocolonialism will have to pass!" (100). For Bensmaïa (or his narrator with whom he can be identified) as for his fellow-Maghrebian, Abdelkebir Khatibi, the process of decolonization involves a double critique, of both the colonizer and the colonized. Abdelkebir Khatibi, the Moroccan writer and theorist, argues for the necessity of the production of a "plural" Maghreb freed from unitary, theological notions of national and cultural identity. For Khatibi, the attempt to pluralize the Maghreb is synonymous with decolonization. The process of decolonization, according to Khatibi, requires a double critique of Arab-Islamic institutions and culture on the one hand, and of the colonizing, imperial, and therefore universalizing, dynamics of Western culture and metaphysics on the other. The process of decolonization, in other words, requires a neither /nor logic: an identification with neither (the norms and values of) the outside, the colonial, the oppressor, nor (the norms and values of) the inside, the colonized, the oppressed. This logic involves a rejection of the Hegelian binarism, which Nietzsche characterizes, in his *On the Genealogy of Morals*, as represented by a man of *ressentiment* where the latter pictures his enemy as evil so that he himself appears as the "good one." The strong man, according to Nietzsche, loves his enemy, "For he desires his enemy for himself as his mark of distinction; he can endure no other enemy than one in whom there is nothing to despise and *very much* to honor!" In contrast to this, Nietzsche pictures the enemy as the man of *ressentiment* conceives him: "he has conceived the 'evil enemy,' '*the Evil One*,' and this in fact is his basic concept, from which he then evolves, as an afterthought and pendant, a 'good one' — himself!" (39) What Nietzsche is basically saying here is that, to put it bluntly, the sheer fact that I am hurt neither makes my enemy an "evil" one nor makes me, by definition, "good." There is a sense in which both Khatibi and Bensmaïa try to find a third route. Khatibi in his *Maghreb pluriel* argues for: "neither reason nor unreason as the West has thought them in its totality, but a subversion that is, in a sense, double, and that, giving itself the power of word and action, sets to work in an intractable difference. To decolonize ourselves and each other would be another name of this other-thought" (Woodhull xi).

Re-placing Language: Abrogation and Appropriation

This third route passes, however, inevitably through language. The crucial function of language as a medium of power demands that postcolonial writing defines itself by seizing the language of the center and re-placing it in a discourse fully adapted to the exigencies of the colonized place. There are two distinct and logical processes by which it does this. The first, the abrogation or denial of the privilege of the language of the colonizer, involves a rejection of the metropolitan power over the means of communication. The second is the appropriation and reconstitution of the language of the center, the process of capturing and remolding the language to new usages.

Abrogation is a refusal of the categories of the imperial culture, its aesthetic, its illusory standard of normative or "correct" usage, and its assumption of a traditional and fixed meaning "inscribed" in the words. It is characteristic of the radicality of early phases of decolonization, but without the process of appropriation the moment of abrogation would end in a reversal of the assumptions of privilege, the "normal," and "correct" inscription. Appropriation, on the other hand, is the process by which the language of "masters" is "taken hostage" and is made to bear the burden of testifying to one's own cultural experiences, or, as Raja Rao puts it, "to convey in a language that is not one's own the spirit that is one's own" (Rao 1938:vii). Language is adopted as a tool and utilized in various ways to express widely differing cultural experiences of crisis of identity, loss, etc. The postcolonial literature is therefore written out of the tension between the abrogation of a received language, which speaks from a center, and the act of appropriation which brings it under the influence of a vernacular tongue or perception. Since through language a "world" can be textually constructed (rather than being a representation of the world), it is a powerful means of constructing difference, separation, and absence from the metropolitan norms.

One of the most well-known examples of linguistic appropriation is the Creole continuum in the Caribbean[14]. The postcolonial writers throughout the Caribbean employ highly developed strategies of code-switching and vernacular transcription, which, at the same time, abrogates the Standard English as well as appropriates it for local discourses: "The theory of the Creole continuum, undermining, as it does, the static models of language formation, overturns 'concentric' notions of language which regard 'Standard' English as a 'core'. Creole need no longer be seen as a peripheral variation of English. Those rules which develop as approximation of English rules are by no means random or unprincipled, and the concept of what actually constitutes 'English' consequently opens itself to the possibility of radical transformation" (Ashcroft 2002:46). This strategy is what underlines the deliberate Creole re-structuring undertaken by the populist politico-religious Rastafarian movement of Jamaica: "The Rastafarians attempt to 'deconstruct' what they see as the power structures of English grammar, structures in themselves metonymic of the hegemonic controls exercised by the British on Black peoples throughout Caribbean and African history — controls no less present today, though they may take different forms. While the language remains as it is, however, there is no hope of genuine 'freedom', and consequently the Rastafarians have adopted various strategies by which language might be 'liberated' from within" (47). Although the basis of Rasta speech is still Jamaican Creole, it is deliberately altered in a number of ways: the first person singular is usually expressed by the pronoun "me." The turning of the subject into an object is used in contexts where the author wishes to conjure the subservient attitude into which Blacks were forced. The Rasta speech, however, utilizes the personal pronoun "I" to represent the singularity of the individual: "The pronoun 'I' has a special importance to Rastas and is expressly opposed to the servile 'me'. Whether in the singular ('I') or the plural ('I and I' or briefly: 'I-n-I') or the reflexive ('I-sel', 'I-n-I self') the use of this pronoun identifies the Rasta as an individual . . . Even the possessive 'my' and the objective 'me' are replaced by 'I'" (Owens 1976:65-66).

A similar strategy is used in Réda Bensmaïa's *The Year of Passages* with respect to the proper name of the narrator of the novel, Mourad. In exile, his proper name has been burned to ashes; it does not refer to a singular existence, if it ever did. The burning to ashes of proper names is not an absolute death and disappearance; it is rather transformed and reborn every time it is used, turning any identity into a multiplicity and a becoming:

> If you swoon in your name of Joachim
>
> Be not afraid

For names are no more than wisps of smoke. Adventures, happy voyages, Joachim, your name was too good for me after all,

Phoenix,

Phoenix abolished in ashes

Or Fenimore   <Fais no more! Be done with things!>

Destined to respond to this name Mrad X

Is worth being written Rmaed (Ashes)

                        And Μουραδ   (33)

The function of exile is in fact that of a writer: to burn everything. "For writers above all want to be born of the ashes of their mental disorder, they want to tell the story of their afterlife, they first of all want to turn everything into ashes, they want to kill, they want to die, to die over and over again . . . . And what is literature without this descent into the assholes of hell?" (38). To write, which is always writing in exile, is to get rid of one's proper name: "to write in order to be unrecognizable, to write in order to be rid of one's name, of one's face, and of one's memory, a memory without name . . . " (52).

The name of the narrator in *The Year of Passages*, who is an Algerian exile first in Paris then in Minnesota, is every time pronounced differently to the extent that it becomes in fact difficult to know his real name[15]. In a conversation with his new neighbors, (those who care to talk to him, not the Lendstroms who since he moved to the dead-end street "haven't yet even said hello to me! They probably think that with the way I look I won't be around here for long. *Why bother, dear? These foreigners! They come and go like mosquitoes!*" (82)), his name is each time pronounced in different ways; even where he comes from or what he does undergo transfigurations: identity under erasure. Yakoff and "his significant other," Vava, and "his better half," Valentina, who live at the entry of the dead end, are among the people who care to talk to him, perhaps partly because Yakoff himself is a refugee from the Soviet Union, who is a surgeon specialized in genital prostheses and sex-change apparatus. Yakoff's wife trying to figure out the narrator's name and origin:

Rmad Bensmaïa, Madam.

Monsewer Bensmaïer . . .

Bensmaïa, Madam, Bensmaïa, A, I, A . . .

Oh yes, Bensmaya, I see, you must originally be of a German descent? . . .

Algerian, <algorithmic>, not German . . . (83)

But Mr. Benslama . . . I never forget it, for you see, you're the first Nigerian that I have ever met . . . (84)

Dear Monsieur Radar (85) Monsieur Ramed (90) . . . Mister Redmer (96) . . . Mister Armada (96) . . . .

In fact, in the whole novel, names, whether common or proper, are subjected to a range of possible permutations, associations, or connotations (Jean-Paul Tartre 7, Gidea, gidiocity 55, passmort 24, Washington-DCeased 105, history of fifisophy 108, cacade*mies*118, Fir$t World! 15) or contain other words different from their formal meaning (in Francophony there is Franco! 87; in immatriculation there is also 'cul' and 'trickle' 16; in immatriculated there is the word trick, says Aely, and the words mac and immaculate 13;). The process of naming is, first of all, an impossible thing to do, but once it is in place, it becomes, as it were, a machine, which needs to be taken apart and re-assembled:

> List of <formal> difficulties: (1) *proper* names: what name can be given to the enervating red color of the flower of the Bougainvilleas of Blinda in springtime? A *rogue* red such as Francisco suggests . . ., or *blidique* red, <*bleeding Red*>? What name can be given to the odors that waft from the toilets of Tabarin? *Arabic Foehn* or *Fun odiférant*? Etc. (*prudently, I began by naming things all over again, giving them the renown they merited*) (*I will return to this: for this is surely a machine that has to be assembled and taken apart*) . . . . (97)

The process of re-naming involves a foregrounding of the metonymic relationships as contrasted to metaphoric ones that have always been privileged in the Western civilization. Conventionally, metaphor has always been preferred to other rhetorical devices for its power of revealing unexpected truth. The importance of the metaphor/ metonymy distinction was first suggested by Roman Jakobson in his article "Two Types of Language and Two Types of Aphasic disturbances" (Jakobson and Hall 1956:78). Paul de Man summarizes the preference for metaphor over metonymy by aligning analogy with necessity and contiguity with chance: the inference of identity and totality that is constitutive of metaphor is lacking in the purely relational metonymic contact (de Man 1979:14). The importance of the metaphor/metonymy distinction to postcolonial texts is also raised by Homi Bhabha. His point is that the perception of the figures of the text as metaphors imposes a universalist reading because metaphor makes no concessions to the cultural specificity of the text. For Bhabha it is preferable to read the tropes of the text as metonymy, which symptomizes the text, reading through its features the social, cultural, and political forces that traverse it (Bhabha 1984:14). Nominal transformations, in *The Year of Passages*, are more often than not ironic: they not only give the text a critico-political tone, but also expose it to the possibility of re-writing certain conventional values according to the exigencies of certain particular standpoints, something that inscribes difference in the text. The use of untranslated words has also the important function of inscribing difference through metonymy. In fact they are a specific form of metonymic figure, the synecdoche, through which is conveyed a sense of cultural distinctness as well as the necessity of active engagement with the horizon of the culture in which those terms have meaning. Australian writer Randolph Stow's novel *Visitants*, set in Papua New Guinea, uses Biga-Kiriwini words throughout the English text. The use here of untranslated words is a clear signifier of the fact that the language that actually informs the novel is an/Other language. *The Year of Passages* goes even further. The reader comes across, more often than not, untranslated, strange, foreign words, but, rather than having another meaning in another language, they are, are devoid of any determinate meaning; they are "non-sense."

The Year of Passages subjects the language (original French as well as, to a great extent, the English translation) to a stammering not only on the lexical level but also in its totality, the whole language itself. Deleuze, in his "He Stuttered," points out three possibilities of marking voice modulations in novels. The first two are either to do it, or else to say it without doing it. While this corresponds to the conventional distinction between "showing" and "telling," both of which occur on the diegetic level, the third possibility presents itself as being performative, no longer affecting preexisting words but the whole language itself. The stuttering *of* language, rather than stuttering *in* it, is "an affective and intensive language," which has nothing to do with the affection of the speaker, or his/her speech (23). Everything depends, argues Deleuze, on the way language is thought: "if we extract it like a homogeneous system in equilibrium, or near equilibrium, and we define it by means of terms and relations, it is evident that the disequilibriums and variations can only affect speech. But if the system appears to be in perpetual disequilibriums, if the system bifurcates — and has terms each one of which traverses a zone of continuous variation — language itself will begin to vibrate and to stutter, and will not be confused with speech, which always assumes only one variable position among others and follows only one direction" (24). One can understand this in terms of Jakobson's attempt at marking the distinctiveness of the poetic language, where, in the latter's famous formulation, "the poetic function projects the principle of equivalence from the axis of selection into the axis of combination" (Jefferson and Robey 1991:56).[16] This is in fact what Deleuze is rather explicitly arguing: that our understanding of language should be "poeticized,"[17] and this, as it were, constitutes the challenge of responding to "*the outside* of language," or as Blanchot puts it, responding to the impossible, the unknown, which engage us in "a denunciation of all dialectical systems, of ontology, and even of nearly all Western philosophies, at least those that subordinate justice to truth or only take as being just a reciprocity of relations" (Blanchot 1993:58). The outside of language is not simply the result of a reterritorialization in language (to replace one speech with another), but a new language, which is not external to the language system but marks its "asyntactic limit" (28). The event of this "foreign language within language" (28) not only imposes upon us the ethical imperative of hospitality to the other, the outside, the foreign (none of them in any sense external or anthropological), but also constitutes the very raison d'être of all true speech: "There is language because there is nothing in 'common' between those who express themselves: a separation that is presupposed, not surmounted, but confirmed, in all true speech. If we had nothing *new* to say to one another, if through discourse there did not come to me something foreign, something capable of instructing me, there would be no question of speaking. This is why man — or so one may suppose — would lose both his visage and his language in a world where nothing would reign but the future of dialectical accomplishment, the law of the same" (Blanchot 1993: 55).

"Creative stuttering," "a ramified variation of the language system," and "a syntax in the process of becoming," give birth to a foreign language within language (an invention of a minor use of the major language), which undermine any determination of identity. *The Year of Passages* makes the French language stutter, stammer, and cry; it is not written in French.[18] Conley, in his afterword to *The Year of Passages* argues that:

> The overall effect is one of a continuous self-questioning and fragmentation. Many of the effects are obtained through a polyglot register. The text is written in several languages at once, which often translates into one idiom what it hears in another. Puns abound. The French of the original is stippled with English, Arabic, German and Latin. The narrator has the childish trait of writers — like a Maria Tsvetaeva — who listen and look to language for its multiple, confusing, wondrously generative, nonmimetic traits that expand and explode from within its own confines. The narrator is thus always *rewriting* what he hears (an inner voice, Aely, constantly informs him of anagrams that flicker on the surface of the words he sees and hears). His consciousness, a clownlike personification of one of his many alter egos, always intervenes between brackets or arrows to mock the serious tenor that pervades discourses that are being heard. (145)

If stuttering in Péguy "fits language so well that it leaves the words intact," or in Roussel "it does not affect particles or complete terms, but it affects propositions . . . according to a proliferating system of parentheses" (27), in Bensmaïa it operates through a variety of ways on a macro level (the micro already discussed): by conflating various discourses, a conflation that throws each discourse into a state of disequilibrium, and by a conception of language as a machine of assembly. The appropriation of language in *The Year of Passages* is not geared toward any determinate use (replacement of one meaning with another), it is to make language and meaning tremble, so that, out of this trembling, the machine of language is made to produce an event. Before talking about the event and the machine, it is necessary to analyze the way in which *The Year of Passages* denies the primacy of memory, since without the disruption of memory, there will not be any event.

What Bensmaïa says of the Algerian film-maker Assia Djebar, and her *La Nouba des Femmes du Mont Chenoua*, can also be said of his own novel: that the relationship to time, in *The Year of Passages*, is subject to a disjunctive movement: "time is out of joint!" Time has become dislocated and fragmented; it is broken into discontinuous moments or snapshots. Indeed, rather than exploring the psychology of a character, *The Year of Passages* functions first of all as a "geodetic" survey of diasporic places, not only in the geographical sense but also in the rhetorical sense of home, memory and identity. This is an absolutely indispensable detour that must be taken if we are to avoid seeking a single meaning or construct a uni-directional temporality. *The Year of Passages* does not present a simple diasporic autobiography or an exilic personal history, but, one might say, a disporic topography; it is a matter of making a topography, a map of a continent as yet undiscovered, at the same time as inventing a new "chronotope": that of disporic time(s).

The new chronotope of disporic autobiography does not assume, as *The Year of Passages* repeatedly tries to show, the possibility of any appropriation of the past time into a coherent memory or narrative; it rather prepares itself for the "labor of anamnesis" or recollection without memory, in which memory, in its spectral structure, happens as an event. To further develop this notion, I would like to invoke Jean-Louis Chrétien and his *The Unforgettable and the Unhoped For* (*L'inoubliable et L'inespéré*, 1991). Chrétien's *The Unforgettable* starts with a fundamental question: "Is there an initial forgetting? Can thought turn toward a radical forgetting that would not presuppose memory and would not consist in interrupting it by adding to or suspending one or another of its powers?" (1) This question, which has serious ramifications for our understanding of historiography, futurity, and so forth, can be crucial for postcolonial theory and the idea of re-writing history. For Chrétien, this radical, initial forgetting should be an "absolute immemorial" that has nothing to do with memory: "If there is an initial forgetting, what it would make emerge must be an absolute immemorial: not a past that, having been present and thus already open and destined to memory, would afterward become inaccessible in memory or for memory, but a past that is initially past and originally lost: a past that is, in advance and essentially, in withdrawal from all future memory, a past that, simultaneous to its own passage and slipping away, is always already past, always already disappeared, and exists only as having disappeared" (2).[19] This "forgotten past" is not a matter of simple forgetting, since after all and after Heidegger, forgetting, to be true, should always be double, i.e., the forgetting of forgetting, otherwise it is still of the order of memory, a mode of remembering that permits us to rediscover what was forgotten. In other words, this forgotten past is radically inaccessible and unrepresentable, a "loss that one cannot even retain as loss, and loss where nothing is lacking and which does not hollow out anything in us that we might wish to fill" (2). One can easily see how this idea is contrary to many works of postcolonial historiography in their attempt to re-write "the" history of colonialism by replacing one "presence" with another.

Chrétien subjects Plato's theory of anamnesis, or recollection, to a novel reading to develop his point. According to him, the possibility, itself aporetic, of a forgotten past has already been thought by Plato but was reduced by subsequent philosophers. For Plato, especially in *Meno*, the *Phaedo*, and the *Phaedrus*, our soul, before incarnation in human form, had already contemplated the Truth and Ideas that are lost or forgotten at birth. This immemorial knowledge is later characterized as *a priori* by Leibniz or as *Er-innerung*, according to the manner that Hegel understands this word: inwardization, movement toward self, gathering of thought and memory of the universal. For Plato, Chrétien argues, this forgetting "expels not only a past, but an *other past*, a past other than any past where I am already human" (11). This past, this "other" past, always already forgotten, is what makes one human. The institution of our humanity thus lies together with the institution of forgetting.[20] The immemorial (as "what is so ancient that it leaves no memory") is what we lived before being human, and in order to finally become human: "what in us overcomes the human and exceeds it is what alone renders us human" (12). Chrétien further argues that, according to Plato, the immemorial of a knowledge that "one must recapture by uprooting forgetting is what gives us the future; it is what opens a future where rediscovering is not repeating, and where the second time of recollection does not at all reproduce the first, antenatal time" (12). This passage sets recollection up against memory: "recollection does not lead to an exercise of memory, but an exercise of anticipation" (13).[21] It is not in any way a matter of becoming able to remember what it is that took place in the past, nor of what we ourselves were in an anterior state. Socrates himself, man of recollection, frequently presents himself as having a bad memory or its power of retention.[22] "The way of recollection, just like the way of love, begins with emptiness and dispossession, and not with the accumulation of rediscovered or re-conquered memories" (14).[23]

The immemorial has the spectral structure of the event: it arrives unannounced, has a double structure,[24] and belongs to language.[25] In *The Year of Passages* the event of the immemorial, as it happens in language, is the Sentence: "Sentences have no conscience. No one can underestimate what a body of sentences can do. For sentences love solitude, they love silence, and we persist in wanting to make them talk . . . . At any moment a sentence can be torn apart from its silence and thrust into your brain. And the resonance of that very sentence is what no one can ever predict. Nothing tells of its coming, nothing. It comes unannounced . . . . The sentence that has a love of ashes. The sentence that turns you into ashes. Nothing . . . . A sentence without sunshine that reduces literature to ashes. An immemorial sentence that renders memory impossible" (25).

The sentences in *The Year of Passages* are not mimetic, i.e., re-presenting any determinate state of affairs; they are rather events celebrating the coming into being of language itself. Their mission is neither to reproduce, by means of memory, any form of identity that things might have possessed, nor to retrieve the truth of what has been repressed. They are rather performative indications of the power of language to bring about an event and to open a path towards a future, which is not simply a foreseeable repetition of the same. Bensmaïa gives us *The Year of Passages* as, on the one hand, a textual machine[26] that functions beyond the intentionality of the subject[27] and, on the other hand, as an event that responds to the unknowability and anonymity of the immemorial (the "beyond memory of the immemorial"[28]). I would like to invoke Derrida's "Typewriter Ribbon: Limited Ink (2) ('within such limits')" to throw some light on not only the relationship between the machine ("word processing") and the event ("expression" without subjectivity), but also the possibility of the impossibility of thinking them together at the same time. Derrida reminds us of an apparent antinomy between the concepts of the event and that of the machine, for if by "machine" we understand something inorganic, an indifferent automaton, that operates by means of technicity, repetition and calculability and is independent from the subject, then it is in sharp contrast to the event, which is supposed to be organic, incalculably singular, and marked by performativity (Derrida 2001:279-336). To think these two together, one assumes, would result in a "monstrous" figure. If we think of syntax and grammar (or language in general) as machine, then the (apparent) aporia involved in thinking the event and the machine in accord with each other can be formulated as follows: how can I say "I," and refer to the singularity of my being, in language, which is universal? How can I express a particular being in a universal medium? This is already a Hegelian problem, which he tries to solve by subsuming the singularity under the universality of the concept in language.[29] Against this common assumption, Derrida argues for the possibility of an event happening precisely through and by the machine. As he tries to show, in a detailed analysis of Rousseau's confession of guilt and his "excuses" in *Confessions*, it is precisely language as machine that "overturns the machination" (292) and produces an unforeseeable event. Language as machine is different from other machines of mechanical reproduction; every time that it produces a text, it is a singular event, a unique intersection of different forces, idioms, deliberations, and styles. It is, apropos of de Man, the materiality of language, a "machinistic materiality without materialism" (281), that produces the event, "an event, the only and the first possible event, because im-possible. That is why I venture to say that this thinking could belong only to the future — and even that it makes the future possible" (278). From the standpoint of the subject, this language-machine can only be experienced as castration and decapitation, since "writing always includes the moment of dispossession in favor of the arbitrary power of the play of the signifier" (357). The narrator in *The Year of Passages* is caught among different machines that produce the events of his life,[30] as a writer and an exile, beyond his control. In such a machinery, there is no need of the self; it should be burned to ashes, buried, and dissolved.[31]

The protagonist of *The Year of Passages*, as an Algerian in exile, is in fact, to allude to Agamben's discussion of it, a *Muselmann*,[32] the living dead in the Auschwitz of America. He is the mark of the threshold between life and death as well as between the human and the inhuman (a monstrous biological machine). In him one is confronted with the fundamental aporia of testimony: all he can testify to is the impossibility of testimony, a "true" witness who cannot bear witness to the disaster overcoming him; his passage is ultimately unrepresentable.

As an intellectual in exile, his language and the historical context of his relevance have been expropriated. Adorno, in his *Minima Moralia*, describes this exilic displacement as follows:

> Every intellectual in emigration is, without exception, mutilated, and does well to acknowledge it to himself, if he wishes to avoid being cruelly apprised of it behind the tightly-closed doors of his self-esteem. He lives in an environment that must remain incomprehensible to him . . . his language has been expropriated, and the historical dimension that nourished his knowledge, sapped . . . all emphases are wrong, perspectives disrupted. Private life asserts itself unduly, hectically, vampire-like, trying convulsively, because it really no longer exists, to prove it is alive. (Adorno 2002:33)

To sum up, the protagonist of *The Year of Passages* is caught between two forms of fascism, two exiles, two deaths: A desert and a cemetery. On the one hand, the desert of Algeria, the dormitory of thought, where thought is under house (*Oikus*) arrest: "enough Algeria to destroy all thinking!" (89) and whose ghost keeps haunting the protagonist. On the other hand, the Swan Cemetery, the cemetery of Minneapolis, where he is buried alive, turned into a zombie. He is given a cemetery to bury his thoughts, either simply because they are not relevant anymore, or because they are assimilated, domesticated (93), or institutionalized[33]. This is what Adorno calls the reification of life that manifests itself both in the consumer society of late capitalist era, as well as in an exilic situation: "The past life of émigrés is, as we know, annulled. Earlier it was the warrant of arrest, today it is intellectual experience, that is declared non-transferable and un-naturalizable. Anything that is not reified, cannot be counted and measured, ceases to exist" (Adorno 46). There is no exit but to dig a hole for himself[34], a hole in language. This hole, as a line of flight, serves not to save himself (he is already dead) but is in fact a promise of a future to come, the only *Principe der Hofnung*. This future whose advent is promised by this new language is first and foremost textual: the domains of the political and the aesthetic are so interwoven in *The Year of Passages* that, while one haunting the other, freedom from political coercion is predicated on the freedom from aesthetic coercion.

Notes

1. I borrow this term from Hamid Naficy's *An Accented Cinema: Exilic and Diasporic Filmmaking* (2001), where he analyzes marginal filmic productions by filmmakers whose liminal subjectivities and interstitial locations mark their difference: "By and large, they operate independently, outside the studio system or the mainstream film industries, using interstitial and collective modes of production that critique those entities. As a result, they are presumed to be more prone to the tensions of marginality and difference. While they share these characteristics, the very existence of the tensions and differences helps prevent accented filmmakers from becoming a homogeneous group or a film movement. And while their films encode tensions and differences, they are not neatly resolved by familiar narrative and generic schemas — hence their grouping under accented style . . . . Their similarities stem principally from what the filmmakers have in

common: liminal subjectivity and interstitial location in society and the film industry" (10).

2. There are different versions of the exact origin of this term. Some say it may have been invented by the Arabs, surprised to see soldiers landing in 1830 with black boots on their feet. Others suggest it was the color of the feet of wine growers in Algeria, tramping grapes to make wine. Whatever the explanation, the French of Algeria did not encounter that characterization until they arrived in the metropolis in 1962. see Benjamin Stora, *Algeria 1830-2000: A Short History*, (p.8) for a history of French minorities in Algeria and their relation to Muslim population.

3. Sartre's *Situations V* was first published in French in 1964. The English translation of this classic work on colonialism was first published in 2001. *Colonialism and Neocolonialism*, as the English title goes, is a passionate critique of French policies in Algeria in the 1950s and 1960s. It had an important impact on the conduct of the Algerian war itself. It is also famous for its controversial call, similar to Fanon's position, for the use of violence in achieving political ends.

4. Walker Connor in his "The Impact of Homelands Upon Diasporas" proposes diaspora as "that segment of a people living outside the homeland" (16). See Connor in Gabriel Sheffer (ed.) *Modern Diaspora in International Politics*.

5. *Year of passages*, in a style full of puns and reminiscent of Céline: "They treat you like dogs! You say Amenokal! Before and after, no matter! Dogs in the shit! Nigger trash! Ratons! Khorotos! Beurs! Robbeurs! Railers! Bicos! Assholes! Stinkers! Arabs! Rilers! Rattlers! Only Rrrr's remain! There's only growls! There's only growling arabs! Grrarabs up for grabs! We can help them if they want! Arabuggers! Arababblers! Arabums! Aracrybabies! Arabrats! Slobbereres! Muzzling Muslims! Moslemouseshit!]

6. See Jonathan and Daniel Boyarin's "Diaspora: Generation and the Ground of Jewish Identity." *Critical Inquiry* 9 (Summer 1993): 693-725. Also their *Powers of Diaspora: Two Essays on the Relevance of Jewish Culture*. Minneapolis: University of Minnesota Press, 2002.

7. The idea of "diaspora at home" is very close to what Bharati Mukherjee discusses under the "immigrant experience." In her article, "Two Ways of Belonging to America," Mukherjee tells the story of her and her sister's integration into American culture. Both sisters, Mira and Bharati, have lived in the United States for some thirty-five years, but they find themselves on different sides of the current debate over the status of immigrants. Bharati is an American citizen and Mira an alien resident. Bharati married an American of Canadian parentage. By choosing a husband who was not her father's selection, she believes she was opting for "fluidity, self-invention, blue jeans and T-shirts, and renouncing 3,000 years (at least) of caste-observant, 'pure culture' marriage in the Mukherjee family" (Kumar 2004:272). Mira married an Indian student and after thirty-five years as a legal immigrant in America, "she clings passionately to her Indian citizenship and hopes to go home to India when she retires' (271). To Bharati, her sister, Mira, is an expatriate, professionally generous and creative, socially courteous and gracious, and that's as far as her Americanization can go. She is here to maintain an identity, not to transform it" (273). As for Bharati, she considers herself married to America: "America Spoke to me . . . I embraced the demotion from expatriate aristocrat to immigrant nobody, surrendering those thousands of years of 'pure culture', the saris, the delightfully accented English. She retained them all. Which of us is the freak?" (273). Mukherjee concludes her essay with a distinction between an exile and an immigrant: "The price that the immigrant willingly pays, and that the exile avoids, is the trauma of self-transformation" (274).

8. In earlier chapters I drew a distinction between two types of travel in general, the mimetic and non-mimetic (along with their restricted and general economies) to which the distinction between an ethics of exile and an ethics of diaspora can be shown to respectively correspond. Within this context, I further distinguished between two different ways of understanding and relating to memory, which I tentatively call "memory as standing reserve" and "memory as event" and are to be understood within an economic (restricted and general) context of displacement.

9. See Barbara Harlow, "The Theoretical-Historical Context," in *Resistance Literature* (New York: Methuen, 1987) in which she builds on the theory put forward in 1981 by Ngugi Wa Thiongo which divided literature into that of oppression and that of the struggle for liberation, thus challenging the conventional practice of distinguishing between literary texts on the basis of form.

10. There is a recent debate on the politics of postcolonial studies in which the "Third World" Westernized intellectuals are contrasted with others who live in Africa or other ex-colonies. Kwame Anthony Appiah puts this distinction as follows:

> Postcoloniality is the condition of what we might ungenerously call a comprador intellegentsia: a relatively small, Western-style, Western trained group of writers and thinkers, who mediate the trade in cultural commodities of world capitalism at the periphery. In the West they are know through the Africa they offer; their compatriots know them both through the West they present to Africa and through an Africa they have invented for the world, for each other, and for Africa. (Appiah 1996:62)

Arif Dirlik formulates the case against "postcolonialism" most vehemently: he argues that David Harvey and Fredric Jameson have established an interrelation between postmodernism and late capitalism that can now be extended to postcolonialism. According to Dirlik "postcolonialism" is a "child of postmodernism" and both postmodernists and postcolonialists celebrate and mystify the workings of global capitalism (Dirlik 1994: 340-42).

11. Perhaps the best way to access the political critique of cultural colonialism in Annie John is to read it alongside Kincaid's *A Small Place*. In this anti-travel guide to Antigua, Kincaid exposes the unseen cultural violence in a place like Antigua where outright racism is seen by genteel colonials as a severe case of "bad manners."

12. For the distinction between these two ways of understanding minority see Paul Patton, *Deleuze and the Political*, where he argues that the difference between these two ways is the difference between qualitative and quantitative multiplicities. A quantitative minority is directed at the "installation of new constants or the attainment of majority status" (48), while the qualitative minority is a becoming-minority of everyone (including the bearers of minority status), a becoming-different or divergence from the majority (47-8).

13. "they have caught another Algerian writer in misdemeanor of writing, on our territory, you see dear emissary of liberties, in our country writing is a misdemeanor, we amputate the hands of burglars and petty thieves and it clearly follows that the tongue will be cut out and the writing hand — left or right — will be cut off, according to public opinion, of those who transgress this taboo! That's our way of showing that we are the last human beings who really take literature seriously! Do you understand? It makes writers responsible for their actions! Before they start scribbling they'd better reflect twice on what they're doing!" (95)

14. See for further discussion Ashcroft, et al.'s *The Empire Writes Back*, 43.

15. The renaming ritual is a common theme of many immigrant autobiographies. In Eva Hoffman's *Lost in Translation*, a teacher renames Ewa, Eva, and her sister Alina, Elaine. Referring to "this careless Baptism," Hoffman states:

> The twist in our names takes them a tiny distance from us — but it's a gap into which the infinite hobgoblin of abstraction enters. Our Polish names didn't refer to us; they were as surely us as our eyes and hands. These new appellations, which we ourselves can't yet pronounce, are not us. They are identification tags, disembodied sounds pointing to objects that happen to be my sister and myself. We walk to our seats, into a roomful of unknown faces, with names that make us strangers to ourselves. (59)

16. The distinction between the axis of selection and that of combination corresponds to Saussure's distinction between associative (paradigmatic) and syntagmatic relationships, between relationships of absence and presence in language. Reformulating Saussure, Jakobson has pointed out that every linguistic message is the product of a double process: (1) the act of selection among items not present in the message but associated in the language system or *langue*, and (2) the combination of the items selected into a sequence. While the relationship between items present in the sequence is one of contiguity, the relationship between those not present is similarity or equivalence. For Deleuze, the transference of the principle of equivalence from one axis to another subjects the language to "two stutterings." In " He Stuttered," he argues: "language is subject to a double process of choices to be made and sequences to be established: disjunctions or selection of similars; connection or sequel of combinables. As long as language is considered as a system in a state of equilibrium, disjunctions will necessarily be exclusive (we do not say "passion," "ration," "nation" all at once, we must choose) and connections progressive" (26). For a further discussion of the importance of linguistics to literature see Jakobson's "Closing Statement" in the third volume of his *Selected Writings*. See also Jefferson and Robey's *Modern Literary Theory*, second chapter.

17. In his "He Stuttered: "language merges with speech only in the case of a very special speech, a poetic speech realizing all the power of bifurcation and variation, of heterogenesis and modulation that characterize language" . . . "We discover at this point the principle of a poetic understanding of language itself . . . " (24-25).

18. Deleuze says, in his "He Stuttered," of Lawrence's Seven Pillars of Wisdom: "What better compliment is there than the one of a critic saying of *Seven Pillars of Wisdom* that it is not written in English. Lawrence made English stumble in order to draw out of it the melodies and the visions of Arabia" (25). It is written neither in the language of the other, Arabic, nor in the other *of* language, which amounts to silence. It is, rather, written in the language of the other in language (LOL).

19. One can see a similar notion in the following passage by Derrida in which he gives the name of *Chora* to the radical unrepresentability of a forgotten past: "*Chora* is nothing (no being, nothing present), but not the Nothing which in the anxiety of *Dasein* would still open the question of being. This Greek noun says in our memory that which is not reappropriable, even by our memory, even by our 'Greek' memory; it says the immemoriality of a desert in the desert of which it is neither a threshold nor a mourning (Derrida 1998: 21).

20. Bernard Stiegler, in his *Technics and Time, 1: The Faults of Epimetheus*, discusses the role of forgetting in constituting humanity from the perspective of the Greek mythology and the two ideas of *promētheia* and *ēpimētheia*. According to the

Greek mythology, Epimetheus, charged with allotting suitable powers to each kind of mortal creatures, left the human race (non-aloga) unprovided for. Prometheus came to inspect the work and found the other animals well off, but man naked and unarmed. He therefore, in order to recompense for this forgetfulness, stole from Hephaestus and Athena the gift of skill in the arts, together with fire, and bestowed them on man. Therefore, at the origin there is a double fault: Epimetheus's forgetting and Prometheus's theft. There is "nothing at the origin but the fault, a fault that is nothing but the de-fault of origin or the origin as de-fault" (188).

21. See Stiegler's discussion of *Elpis* (196-199) as anticipation, as the relation to the indeterminate, that is the anticipation of the future, and as such, "the essential phenomenon of time" and of human mortality, his being-toward-death: "This being-toward-death, ecstasies, being-outside-oneself, in expectation, hope or fear, configures a particular mode of being of mortals among themselves, a being together that does not come into existence before Epimetheus's act of forgetting" (198).

22. In *Protagoras*: "And I said, Protagoras, I have a wretched memory, and when any one makes a long speech to me I never remember . . . so now, having such a bad memory, I will ask you to cut your answers shorter (sec.334). In *Meno*: "I have not a good memory, Meno, and therefore I cannot now tell what I thought of him at the time (sec.71).

23. T.S.Eliot in his "East Coker" points to a similar notion. One needs to notice that what Eliot has in mind is a dialectical circle (starting from possession, moving toward dispossession only to recuperate it for the subject), which is far from what Chrétien is arguing for. For Chrétien, what is recollected has never a determinate content; it is rather what makes thought and future possible: the opening and the gift of the future, which will never become phenomenal. This recollection is not of a past that can be present or represented, it rather comes back to us from the future (Schlegel's figure of the historian as a prophet facing backwards).

24. One the one hand, there is the moment of actualization of the event, and, on the other hand, there is that part of the event, which cannot realize its accomplishments, and can be called its counter-actualization. Deleuze, in his *The Logic of Sense*, puts it as follows: " With every event, there is indeed the present moment of its actualization, the moment in which the event is embodied in a state of affairs, an individual, or a person, the moment we designate by saying 'here, the moment has come.' . . . But on the other hand, there is the future and the past of the event considered in itself, sidestepping each present, being free of the limitations of a state of affairs…forming what might be called the counter-actualization (151).

25. Deleuze in *The Logic of Sense*: "Nevertheless, the event does belong to language, and haunts it so much that it does not exist outside of the propositions which express it" (181). "What renders language possible is the event insofar as the event is confused neither with the proposition which expresses it, nor with the state of the one who pronounces it, nor with the state of affairs denoted by the proposition" (182). "The Verb is the univocity of language, in the form of an undetermined infinitive, without person, without present, without any diversity of voice" (185).

26. Conley in his afterword to *The Year of Passages* calls the latter a novel-machine. He argues that if the traditional machine of writing takes the form of pen and ink ("as long as I have enough ink and paper, " Montaigne wrote at the beginning of his essay on vanity, "I can travel forever and endlessly") and modern writers such as Burroughs "let the typewriter become the machine that takes over their affective lives" (146), or "for Godard and his followers the camera becomes an autonomous writing instrument" (146), for Bensmaïa the "electronic machine, a Macintosh Power Book 140"

(146) patterns *The Year of Passages* and takes over any subjective intentionality to either produce meaning or reproduce experience. " Both in proper names and in the syntax the reader will note abrupt shifts signaled by "plain text," "italic," "bold," or other commands set in 12-point Chicago type along the top of the Microsoft menu. These ruptures of thought, action, and deliberation that turn between expression and word processing bring us back to the kernel of the creation, to an object-self that is *outside* of the writer's psyche or consciousness" (146).

27. For a characterization of a machinic operation the reader comes across passages like this: "While he meditates and takes his breaks, I aim my cursor at the *save* key and don't stop. The Automaton wakes up *illico* and begins to record the debate, it swallows the debacle . . . the Automaton goes into the sleep mode, *zerrrrrrrrrr*! You might think it's swooning, a *mental collapse*! The conversation takes a bad turn, he doesn't feel concerned anymore, the obscurity *shuts him up*...The Automaton is always on the sleep mode, but in fact it'd sleeping with only one eye closed . . . for him it's *pure automatism* . . . . (112-113).

28. For a discussion of ghosts in relation to immemoriality (and immemorial community, the community of death, or the community of ghosts) see Ross's Clarkson's "Jack Spicer's Ghosts and the Immemorial Community," in which he analyzes the poetry of Spicer (A Bay Area poet in the 1950s and 1960s) in terms of the effect of spectrality. Inspired by Jean-Luc Nancy's critique of "communion" as against "community," in *The Inoperative Community*, Clarkson argues for an understanding of poetry and poetic community in terms of a relationship to the ghosts, to immemorial others who are beyond memory. For Clarkson, "Spicer's experience of the immemorial retains the singularity of all those who are beyond memory. These past beings are anonymous, but the reality of their past is no less real because we can't see their faces; we may not know who they were, but we know *that* they were" (209).

29. Derrida, in his "Typewriter Ribbon," formulates this apparent aporia as follows: " . . . the singularity and the generality of every "I." Nothing is in fact more irreducibly singular that "I" and yet nothing is more universal, anonymous, and substitutable" (326).

30. From the war machine to the machinery of nation-building in post-independence Algeria, to the machines of capitalist institutions, all contribute to his expatriation against his own will, to his sense of inability to do anything about bloodshed and terror that goes virtually unnoticed in the world, and even the fact that his book, *Dead Letters*, is burned without even being read: "There is nothing satanic about my *Dead Letters*! . . . Satan is the body and soul and spirit and sex of people who don't know how to read!" (100).

31. ". . . she asked me what I did with my *Self*, and I'll write her back to explain to her that in order to extirpate it from my nervous system I had to be rid of my *fat Self soup*, . . . I had to get dissolved" (130-131); "I will reduce my identity to ashes, but I'm ready; it will make me almost unrecognizable, even to my own eyes . . ." (127); "Let me explain: you've got to begin by being dead, you've first got to die . . ." (122).

32. *Der Muselmann*, literally "the Muslim," is a term used in Auschwitz to designate a prisoner who was giving up or was given up by his comrades, no longer had room in his consciousness for any feeling or intellect or moral judgments. He was a staggering corpse, a living dead, reduced to his physical functions. The expression was common especially in Auschwitz: In Majdanek the living dead were called "donkeys"; in Dachau they were "cretins," in Stutthof "cripples," in Mauthausen "swimmers," in Neuengamme "camels," in Buchenwald "tired sheiks," and in the women's camp at Ravensbrück Muselweiber (female Mulims) (Agamben 2002:44).

33. ." . . behind the wall where we are all *buried alive*, but today I know that Minneapolis-U.S.A. is the great cemetery of the modern living dead, I know that Charlottesville-U.S.A. is the great dormitory of moderns in exile, I know that Washington-DC*eased* is the great mortuary of the modern living dead, and for that reason I have been sent here, they sent me here to bury me alive, in Minneapolis, Minnehaha, *the river that goes haha! The river that laughs at death! The city that commits Harakiri! No rectifications!*" (105).

34. Becoming invisible is what allies him with all the underground figures, from Dostoyevsky's *Notes from Underground* to Ellison's *The Invisible Man*.

Chapter Five

Conclusion

The Political Economy of Displacement

In this concluding chapter I would like to explore some of the consequences that might be drawn from a discourse on the general economy of travel and displacement. I would like to discuss these consequences in political as well as ethical terms. One of the political consequences to be drawn has to do with the notion of (national) boundaries and borderlines. It is not simply a matter of saying that at a designated geographical point lies the boundary. Boundaries are neither natural nor substantial. It is not geographical lines that decide boundaries, but, rather, geographical lines are assigned to space on the basis of complex discourses of difference. For instance, the simple evaluation of familiarity/unfamiliarity might serve as the practical logic of difference, in which the borderline will be inscribed at the limit of one's own horizon of familiarity. At the same time, as I have tried to show, boundaries are untenable because there is always an originary contamination[1] and an openness to the outside that is not always acknowledged. We saw in immigrant autobiographies and especially in Jasmine's discourse of migration a tendency towards a domestication of the hauntological forces of the past that culminated in a reified memory. On the other hand, Kader Abdolah's *Spijkerschrift*, Kiarostami's *The Taste of Cherry*, and Réda Bensmaïa's *The Year of Passages*, all in their own way, addressed the unrepresentability of these hauntological forces. In *Spijkerschrift*, the question of witnessing the exteriority of the outside is presented in terms of a textual inheritance from the past whose meaning is not destined for any particular audience and is open to reception and interpretation while keeping its secrets. In *The Taste of Cherry*, while the boundary between life and death is deconstructed by cinematographic means, the figure of death comes to stand for that which cannot be represented. And then in the final chapter, *The Year of Passages* proposes a novel, and rather pessimistic, reading of the hauntological situation. Derrida has argued that the forces of the outside and the ghosts of the past are constantly undermining the present of the subject while, at the same time, promising the arrival of future. *The Year of Passages*, however, poses the hauntological question in a different way: what if the ghosts are becoming irrelevant because they have lost their context of responsibility and emergency? How should one imagine the hauntological structure in cross-cultural domains? Can one be haunted by a ghost from another culture? In *The Year of Passages* the protagonist is being haunted by the specters of the past but instead of promising a future to come, the ghosts of the past become ineffective simply because in the New World they are not relevant anymore; it is the ghosts themselves, as well as their time, that are out of joint. To put this differently, in *The Year of Passages* the protagonist, rather than being haunted by the ghosts of the past, is himself becoming a ghost, a living-dead. To say that the subject is haunted by ghost is a pre-deconstructive statement. The subject, if there is any, is not simply haunted by ghosts; it is rather a ghost itself. I argued that this is one of the fundamental characteristics of the diasporic condition, that is, the becoming ghost of the subject (i.e., the becoming guest of the host). From the stand point of the subject, this is an experience of political castration or decapitation that renders the former docile; a docility that is ontological rather than psychological.

The formation of national boundaries rarely acknowledges the mixed economy of its origin and is, in fact, haunted by the other who is supposed to be outside the walls of the city[2]. The penetrability of borders also affects the identity of individuals residing within those borders. The supposed homogenous identities of individuals need to be rethought in the light of the openness of their space of dwelling to an outside. Identities open to alterity do not belong to a universal whole (e.g., the discourse of nationalism) but rather appear as singularities; it is what Agamben calls "whatever":

> Whatever is the figure of pure singularity. Whatever singularity has no identity, it is not determinate with respect to a concept, but neither is it simply indeterminate; rather it is determined only through its relation to an idea, that is, to the totality of its possibilities . . . . It belongs to a whole, but without this belonging's being able to be represented by a real condition: Belonging, being—such, is here only the relation to an empty and indeterminate totality . . . . But a singularity plus an empty space can only be pure exteriority . . . . Whatever, in this sense, is the event of the outside. (Agamben 1998:67)

Therefore, in a discourse of displacement aware of the forces of a general economy, identities are less essentialistic as well as less nationalistic (which is to say less fascistic), and in their non-belonging to a determinate space, they are open to pure exteriority, which is always already inscribed within the interiority. The emergence of this new diasporic subjectivity opens a space to pose the question of justice in terms of the heterogeneity and untranslatability of the regimes of phrases that Lyotard talks about in his *The Differend*. After everything is said and done, justice amounts to no more than an ethical imperative to respect the specter of the irreducible difference.

The Ethics of Displacement

Another consequence of a general economy of travel and displacement for the production of what I called the diasporic subjectivity, is the emergence of the ethical imperative of travel as a mode of encounter with difference that leads to the performative enactment of "becoming other." The quest into the labyrinthine mystery of travel, and the increasing awareness of the fact that despite moving so much and so far in space, travelers of the traditional kind, that is, the mimetic, dialectical and sedentary,[3] do not seem to have traveled at all, inexorably leads one to an ethical exploration that culminates in a forgetting of the same, a hospitality to difference and bearing witness to its alterity.

The restricted economy of travel, as a machine of representation and production of knowledge that can be assimilated and subsumed under a mimetic discourse, remains blind to the forces of the outside that nevertheless defines it. The enclosure and self-sufficiency that a restricted economy brings about are based on the premise that there should be a separation between the inside and the outside. In *Madness and Civilization* (1961), Foucault shows how the emerging culture of enlightenment, of which the founding of the Hôpital Général in Paris in 1656 stands both as a symbolic and technical expression, produced a new kind of spatial boundary that is premised on the separation of the inside and the outside: the result is "a new homeland for madness" (46). The wall of the asylum will create a rigid boundary between the world of the normals (reasonable, sane, non-criminals, non-delinquent) and the excluded (unreasonable, insane, criminal, delinquent). Thus the homelands of the same and the other will be cut off by unsurpassable boundaries. The figure of the *same*, the inhabitant of the homeland of the sane, will frequent, like Conrad's sedentary traveler, the spaces of the other only to return back home, after having exercised the power of the *same* to the *same*; his movement is a pseudo-movement. This scenario of internal difference within post-enlightenment Europe, through analogy and displacement, is duplicated in its cross-cultural relationships with other spaces within traditional travel discourses. The homeland of the others, beyond the boundary of Europe, would come to mirror the "homeland of madness" within. Similarly, like the functionaries of the self-same rationality (doctors and prison guards), the travelers from Europe would frequent the homelands of the other, either on a mission to represent, or to conquer or govern, and return to the fold of the *same* without ever having risked traveling. On the other hand, the madman, condemned never to return and never to arrive, is, for Foucault, not only the condition of the possibility of reason but also "the Passenger *par excellence*":

> It is for the other world that the madman sets sail in his fools' boat; it is from the other world that he comes when he disembarks. The madman's voyage is at once

a rigorous division and an absolute Passage .... His exclusion must enclose him; if he cannot and must not have another *prison* than the *threshold* itself, he is kept at the point of passage. He is put in the interior of the exterior, and inversely ... The madman is delivered to the river with its thousand arms, the sea with its thousand roads, to the great uncertainty external to everything. He is a prisoner in the midst of what is the freest, the openest of routes: bound fast at the infinite crossroads. He is the Passenger *par excellence*: that is, the prisoner of the passage. And the land he will come to is unknown — as is, once he disembarks, the land from which he comes. He has his truth and his homeland only in that fruitless expanse between two countries that cannot belong to him. (Foucault 1988:11)

In the preface to his *The Order of Things*, Foucault offers an image of this other space from which true passengers disembark and at which they arrive. This space, which he calls *heterotopia*, is the opposite of the panopticon and the carceral space. The panopticon space, as the readers of *Discipline and Punish* readily recognize, is not a space of travel and passage; it is rather a taxonomic grid of knowledge and space that produces the docile soul of the "normal" subject who, in the final analysis, knows only itself. *Heterotopia* is another space, a fold of the outside, which offers perilous voyages beyond the threshold of the self/same. *Heterotopia* is the affirmative space of which Zarathustra spoke to himself on the way to his "last summit" where "summit and abyss — they are now united in one!" The journey towards this last summit requires that the individual go beyond herself and erase all paths behind her in recognizing that there will be no return:

> You are treading your path of greatness: now it must call up all your courage that there is no longer a path behind you!...And when all footholds disappear, you must know how to climb upon your own head: how could you climb upward otherwise?...In order to see much one must learn to look away from oneself — every mountain climber needs this hardness ... Zarathustra was a friend to all who take long journeys and do not want to live without danger. (Nietzsche 1969:173-76)

Zarathustra, who "wanted to leave the Blissful Islands" (173), in his journey to the last summit is absolutely aware of the necessity of forgetting the familiarity of what lies behind him and embracing something different that, more often than not, appears fearful in its monstrosity: "Ah, you fond fool, Zarathustra, too eager to trust! But that is what you have always been: you have always approached trustfully all that is fearful. You have always wanted to caress every monster. A touch of warm breath, a little soft fur on its paw — and at once you have been ready to love and entice it" (175).

What Foucault has done is to show how in bringing inside the asylum the outside exteriority, the Western discursive practices have produces an otherness, i.e., a relative rather than an absolute otherness, within the totality in which the self/same operates. This produced other (or the othered-other) is never a difference in kind, but rather a conceptual differentiation set in motion by "reason," through different mechanism of representation,[4] for the subject's own identity and self-realization. The restricted and general economy of travel can also be characterized in relation to alterity: A restricted economy of travel produces difference as gain, cultural capital, body of knowledge, etc., while a general economy of travel tries to go beyond the mediated difference and the closed circuit of totality by bearing witness, and by being hospitable, to a pure difference with which one can have no relation.[5]

Understanding the general economy of travel and peregrination in terms of the ethical imperative of an openness to alterity has significant consequences for one's notion of travel. One of the paradoxical inferences that one can draw is that in order to travel, in its ethical sense, it is not necessary for the subject to move in space.[6] One can become a traveler, often through a performative act, by becoming hospitable to the other. Movement in space is not a necessary condition of the experience of the foreign. In other words, the essence of peregrination is not itself peregrinatory.[7] This is the "immobile voyage" of which Deleuze and Guattari speak when analyzing the animal essence in Kafka's stories. They argue that becoming-animal is a way out, a line of escape that constitutes "an absolute deterritorialization of the man in opposition to the merely relative deterritorialization that the man causes to himself by shifting, by traveling" (Deleuze and Guattari, Kafka 35). What is important to recognize about the becoming-animal (becoming-other) as an absolute voyage is that there is nothing transcendental about it: one does not go elsewhere but is carried along by the immanent speed of self-differentiating forces.[8] The immobile voyage in which a general economy of travel manifests itself has no beginning nor any end; it is a circulation in the middle[9], dwelling in the multiplicities of the in-betweens and a hospitality to the other, the event, chance, encounter, and, above all, the ghost who, while disrupting the temporality of travel, does not belong to any territory and is homeless in its coming and going. The middle is a more "just" space of travel in which all claims of origin and destination have been relinquished and an opposition between the inside and the outside is abandoned. The protagonist of *The Year of Passages* learns to live precisely in this middle ground. The middle is a sea without shores whose beautiful monstrosity is celebrated by Nietzsche.[10] The middle is a topos proffering a horizon for becoming other, which is neither a question of mimicry nor a literal embodiment. It is neither simply a metaphor nor is it totally unreal: it is a process of self-transformation in the proximity of the other. In the proximity, which is at the same time infinite distance, to the other, the self-presence of the "I," the immobile being in the present who masters and represents, loses its ground. The middle is where/when ghosts travel.

Notes

1. Derrida (on different occasions such as "The Law of the Genre," "Living On, Border Lines," and *The Truth in Painting*) has shown that the borderline or boundary marking the separation of the inside and outside is an essential part of the metaphysical

thinking. In *The Truth in Painting* Derrida focuses on Kant's distinction between the Greek terms *ergon* or "work" and *parergon*, or "outside the work," in order to show that the frame belongs to neither the *ergon* nor the *parergon*. The inside of the work (its essential originality and integrity) is in fact given to it by the work of the frame. The *ergon* is produced by the frame because to be constituted as a work in itself the *ergon* must be set off against a background, and that is what the frame does. In "The Law of Genre" Derrida argues, through a detailed discussion of two imaginary statements: "genres are not to be mixed" and "I will not mix genres," that the law establishing the boundaries of genres in fact opens it to contamination (Derrida calls this process "re-marking").

2. Amos Oz's "Khamsin" is the story of this hauntological structure where the phantom of the other, in its monstrosity, slips through the walls of the city and causes trembling: "The inner circle, the circle of lights, keeps guard over our houses and over us, against the accumulated menace outside. But it is an ineffective wall, it cannot keep out the smells of the foe and his voices. At night the voices and the smells touch our skin like tooth and claw" (Oz 1983: 10). In Oz's "Nomad and Viper" the enclosed inside of the kibbutz is haunted not by the nocturnal cry of the allegorical figures of jackals but by the voices of the nomads. Not only the nomad's voices penetrate the fence of the kibbutz, but their bodies also intrude into the inside, constantly creating real or imaginary danger. Guela, still without a man in her life, is a dutiful daughter of the inside. One day, at the edge of the kibbutz, she comes across an intruder from the desert. This chance meeting at the border zone was an encounter that could traverse the line and make Guela into a traveler. Yet, burdened by the memories drummed into her of the horror of the outside, she is only capable of a paranoid gesture. Yet, the force of the encounter affects her later when recollected in tranquility. Away from the border zone and back in the sanctum of the inside, the real drama of that event unfolds. Guela, incapable of hospitality (like Janine in Camus's "The Adulterous Woman"), presents us with the last image of the nomad in its starkest otherness: the nomad suddenly stops speaking Hebrew and lapses into Arabic. More disturbingly, animal that he is in his otherness, the nomad becomes one with his goats as he disappears amidst their "dark, terrified, quivering mass" (34).

3. Syed Manzurul Islam, in his *The Ethics of Travel: from Marco Polo to Kafka* (1996), distinguishes between the sedentary traveler, who settles for a representational practice that scarcely registers an encounter with and hospitality to the other, and the nomadic one who in his/her encounter with difference and alterity "fractures both a boundary and an apparatus of representation" (vii). According to Islam, only the nomadic travel deserves the name "travel."

4. The hypothesis that the othered-other is a mediated difference within the plane of representation can further be elucidated by reference to the four principles that Gilles Deleuze proposes in *Difference and Repetition*: " There are four principal aspects to 'reason' in so far as it is the medium of representation: identity, in the form of the undetermined concept; analogy, in the relation between ultimate determinable concepts; opposition, in the relation between determinations within concepts; resemblance, in the determined object of the concept itself. These forms are like the four heads or the four shackles of mediation. Difference is mediated to the extent that it is subjected to the fourfold root of identity, opposition, analogy and resemblance" (29).

5. Levinas insists that the ethical response to the other cannot be formulated in a cognitive or propositional language. If I make the other reveal itself by representing it, I would be betraying its otherness. All one can do is to say *Me Voici*, here I am, as a witness of the Infinite, but a witness that does not thematize what it bears witness to, a witness that is commanded to responsibility, in a language of hospitality, without asking any questions (Levinas 1981: 146).

6. Italo Calvino, in *Invisible Cities*, makes a very similar point. Kublai Khan, the master of the semiotic game, soon discovers that Marco Polo's journeys are anything but passages through space. Calvino writes: "Kublai Khan had noticed that Marco Polo's passage involved not a journey but a change of elements (36). For Calvino, travel becomes a semiotic game in which the traveler enacts his passage from point to point in discourse, therefore she does not need to undertake arduous journeys in "real" space.

7. Compare to Heidegger's argument, in his "The Question Concerning Technology," that the essence of technology is not itself technological.

8. The self-differentiating forces (the movement of self-difference) that cause one to be different from oneself is what Heraclitus talks about in the following passage: "Men do not know how that which is drawn in different directions harmonises with itself. The harmonious structure of the world depends upon opposite tension like that of the bow and the lyre."

9. Deleuze and Guattari in *A Thousand Plateaus*: "Making a clean slate, starting or beginning again from ground zero, seeking a beginning or foundation — all imply a false conception of voyage and movement (a conception that is methodical, pedagogical, initiatory, symbolic...). But Kleist, Lenz, and Büchner have another way of traveling and moving: proceeding from the middle, through the middle, coming and going rather than starting and finishing. American literature, and already English literature, manifest this rhizomatic direction to an even greater extent; they know how to move between things, establish a logic of the AND, overthrow ontology, do away with foundations, nullify endings and beginnings" (25).

10. Nietzsche in *The Gay Science*: "*At the sea* — I would not build a house for myself, and I count it part of my good fortune that I do not own a house. But if I had to, then I should build it as some of the Romans did — right into the sea. I should not mind sharing a few secrets with this beautiful monster" (214).

Bibliography

Abdolah, Kader. *Spijkerschrift*. Breda: De Geus, 2000.
Aciman, Andre. *False Papers: Essays on Exile and Memory*. New York: Farrar, Strauss and Giroux, 2000.
———. *Out of Egypt: A Memoir*. New York: Riverhead, 1994.
Adorno, Theodor. *Minima Moralia: Reflections from Damaged Life*. Trans. E. F. N. Jephcott. New York: Verso, 2002.
Agamben, Giorgio. *The Coming Community*. Trans. Michael Hardt. Minneapolis: U of Minnesota P, 1998.
———. *Language and Death: The Place of Negativity*. Trans. Karen E. Pinkus with Michael Hardt. Minneapolis: U of Minnesota P, 1991.
———. *Potentialities: Collected Essays in Philosophy*. Trans. Daniel Heller-Roazen. Stanford: Stanford UP, 1999.
———. *Remnants of Auschwitz: The Witness and the Archive*. Trans. Daniel Heller-Roazen. New York: Zone Books, 2002.
———. *Stanzas: Word and Phantasm in Western Culture*. Trans. Ronald L. Martinez. Minneapolis: U of Minnesota P, 1993.
Alhadeff, Gini. *The Sun at Midday: Tales of a Mediterranean Family*. New York: Pantheon, 1997.
Antin, Mary. *The Promised Land*. Boston: Houghton Mifflin, 1912.
Anzaldua, Gloria. *Borderlands/La Frontera: The New Mestiza*. San Francisco: Spinsters/Aunt Lute, 1987.
Appadurai, Arjun (ed.). *The Social Life of Things: Commodities in Cultural Perspective*. Cambridge: Cambridge UP, 1986.
Appiah, K. A. "Is the Post in Postmodernism the Post in Postcolonialism?" In *Contemporary Postcolonial Theory: A Reader*. Ed. by P. Mongia. London: Arnold, 1996.
Ashcroft, Bill, Gareth Griffiths and Helen Tiffin. *The Empire Writes Back: Theory and Practice in Post-Colonial Literature*. London: Routledge. 2002 [1989].
Attar, Farid Al-Din. "The Conference of the Birds (Manteq Al-Tayr)." Trans. Afkham Darbandi and Dick Davis. *The World of Literature*. Ed. Westling et al, Upper Saddle River: Prentice Hall, 1999.
Baranczak, Stanislaw. *Breathing Under Water and Other East European Essays*. Cambridge: Harvard UP, 1990.
Barth, Fredrik (ed.) *Ethnic Groups and Boundaries: The Social Organization of Cultural Difference*. Boston: Little Brown, 1969.
Barthes, Roland. *Empire of Signs*. Trans. Richard Howard. New York: Hill and Wang, 2000.
Baudrillard, Jean. *America*. Trans. Chris Turner. London: Verso, 1988.
Behdad, Ali. "Nationalism and Immigration in the United States." *Diaspora* 6.2 (1997): 155-179.
Benjamin, Walter. *The Arcades Project*. Trans. Howard Eiland and Kewin McLaughlin. Cambridge: The Belknap of Harvard U P, 2004.
———. *Illuminations*. Ed. Hannah Arendt. Trans. Harry Zohn. New York: Schocken Books, 1968.
Bensmaïa, Réda. *The Year of Passages*. Trans. Tom Conley. Minneapolis: U of Minnesota P, 1995.
———. "La Nouba des Femmes du Mont Chenoua: Introduction to the Cinematic Fragment." *World Literature Today* 70.4 (Fall 1996): 65-81.

Berman, Antoine. *The Experience of the Foreign: Culture and Translation in Romantic Germany*. Trans. S. Heyvaert. New York: State U of New York P, 1992.
Bhabha, Homi. "Representation and the Colonial Text: A Critical Explorations of Some Forms of Mimeticism." *The Theory of Reading*. Ed. Frank Gloversmith. Brighton: Harvester, 1984.
———. "Locations of Culture," Introduction to *The Location of Culture*. New York: Routledge, 1994.
Blanchot, Maurice. *The Infinite Conversation*. Trans. Susan Hanson. Minneapolis: U of Minnesota P, 1993.
Blanchot, Maurice. "Death as Possibility." *The Space of Literature*. Trans. Ann Amock. Lincoln: The U of Nebraska P, 1982.
———. "Rilke and Death's Demand." *The Space of Literature*. Trans. Ann Amock. Lincoln: The U of Nebraska P, 1982.
Blanchot, Maurice. "Literature and the Right to Death." *The Gaze of Orpheus*. Trans. Lydia Davis. New York: Station Hill Press, 1981.
Boelhower, William. "The Making of Ethnic Autobiography in the United States." *American Autobiography: Retrospect and Prospect*. Ed. Paul John Eakin. Madison: U of Wisconsin P, 1991.
———. "The Necessary Ruse: Immigrant Autobiography and the Sovereign American Self." *Amerikastudien* 35.3 (1990): 297-319.
———. *Immigrant Autobiography in the United States: Four Versions of the Italian American Self*. Verona: Essedue Edizioni, 1982.
———. "The Brave New World of Immigrant Autobiography." *MELUS* 9.2 (1982): 5-23.
Bondanella, Peter. *Italian Cinema: From Neorealism to the Present*. New York: Continuum, 1990.
Bourdieu, Pierre. *Distinction: A Social Critique of the Judgment of Taste*. Trans. Richard Nice. Cambridge: Harvard UP, 1984.
Bowen, Elizabeth. *The Hotel*. London: Penguin, [1927] 1987.
Boyarin, Daniel, and Jonathan Boyarin. "Dispora: Generation and the Ground of Jewish Identity." *Critical Inquiry* 9 (Summer 1993): 693-725.
Browdy de Hernandez, Jennifer. "The Plural Self: The Politicization of Memory and Form in Three American Ethnic Autobiographies." *Memory and Cultural Politics: New Approaches to American Ethnic Literatures*. Ed. Amritjit Singh, Joseph T. Skerrett, Jr., and Robert E. Hogan. Boston: Northeastern UP, 1996.
Brown, Royal S., "Hiroshima mon amour," Cineaste 29.1 (Winter 2003).
Brydon, Diana. "Re-Writing the Tempest." *World Literature Written in English*. 23.1 (1984): 75-88.
Butler, Judith. *The Psychic Life of Power: Theories in Subjection*. Stanford: Stanford U P, 1997.
Byron, George Gordon, Lord. *Letters and Journals*. Ed. by Leslie A. Marchand. 13 vols. London: John Murray, 1973-94.
———. *The Complete Poetical Works*. Ed. by Jerome J. McGann. 7 vols. Oxford: Oxford University Press, 1980-92.
Calvino, Italo. *The Invisible Cities*. Trans. William Weaver. New York and London: Harcourt Brace & Company, 1974.
Carter, Paul. *The Road to Botany Bay: An Exploration of Landscape and History*. New York: Alfred A. Knopf, 1988.
Carter-Sanborn, Kristin. "`We Murder Who We Were': Jasmine and the Violence of Identity." *American Literature* 66.3 (1994): 573-93.

Cerquiglini-Toulet, Jacqueline. *The Color of Melancholy: The uses of Books in the Fourteenth Century*. Trans. Lydia G. Cochrane. Baltimore: The Johns Hopkins U P, 1997.
Chard, Chloe. *Pleasure and Guilt on the Grand Tour: Travel Writing and Imaginative Geography 1600-1830*. Manchester: Manchester U P, 1999.
Chrétien, Jean-Louis. *The Unforgettable and the Unhoped For*. Trans. Jeffrey Bloechl. New York: Fordham U P, 2002 [1991].
Clarkson, Ross. "Jack Spicer's Ghosts and the Immemorial Community," *Mosaic* 34.4 (December 2001), 199-211.
Cliff, Michelle. *No Telephone to Heaven*. New York: A Plum Book, 1996.
Clifford, James. "Introduction: Partial Truths," *Writing Culture: The Poetics and Politics of Ethnography*. Eds. James Clifford and George E. Marcus. Berkeley: U of California P, 1986.
Cohen, Anthony. *Self Consciousness: An Alternative Anthropology of Identity*. London: Routledge, 1994.
Cohen-Solal, Annie. *Sartre: A Life*. London: Heineman, 1987.
Conley, Tom. "Afterword: A Novel Machine." *The Year of Passages*. Minneapolis: U of Minnesota P, 1995
Dallmayr, Fred. *Life World, Modernity and Critique*. Cambridge: Polity Press, 1991.
Darwish, Mahmoud. *Unfortunately, It Was Paradise*. Trans. Munir Akash and Carolyn Forché. Berkeley: U of California P, 2003.
———. *Memory for Forgetfulness: August, Beirut, 1982*. Trans. Ibrahim Muhawi. Berkeley: U of California P, 1995.
Dayal, Samir. "Creating, Preserving, Destroying: Violence in Bharati Mukherjee's Jasmine." *Bharati Mukherjee: Critical Perspectives*. Ed. Emmanuel S. Nelson. New York: Garland, 1993.
de Certeau, Michel. *The Practice of Everyday Life*. Trans. Steven F. Rendall. Berkeley: U of California P, 1984.
———. *The Mystic Fable*. Trans. Michael B. Smith. Chicago: U of Chicago P, 1992.
Delbo, Charlotte. *Auschwitz and After*. Trans. Rosette C. Lamont. New Haven and London: Yale U P, 1995.
Deleuze, Gilles. *Cinema 1: The Movement-Image*. Trans. Hugh Tomlinson and Barbara Habberjam. Minneapolis: U of Minnesota P, 1986.
———. *Cinema 2: The Time Image*. Hugh Tomlinson and Robert Galeta. Minneapolis: U of Minnesota P, 1997.
———. *Difference and Repetition*. Trans. Paul Patton. New York: Columbia U P, 1994 (b).
———. "He Stuttered." *Gilles Deleuze and the Theater of Philosophy*. Ed. Constantin Boundas and Dorothea Olkowski. New York: Routledge, 1994 (a).
———. *The Logic of Sense*. Trans. Mark Lester. New York: Columbia U P, 1990.
Deleuze, Gilles and Félix Guattari. *Kafka: Toward a Minor Literature*. Trans. Dana Polan. Minneapolis: U of Minnesota P, 1986.
———. *A Thousand Plateaus: Capitalism and Schizophrenia*. Trans. Brian Massumi. Minneapolis: U of Minnesota P, 1994.
de Man, Paul. *Allegories of Reading*. New Haven: CT: Yale U P, 1979.
Derrida, Jacques. "Fors: The Anglish Words of Nicholas Abraham and Maria Torok." Trans. Barbara Johnson. *The Wolf Man's Magic Word: A Cryptonomy*. Nicholas Abraham and Maria Torok. Trans. Richard Rand. Minneapolis: U of Minnesota P, 1986 (a).
———. "The Pit and the Pyramid." *Margins of Philosophy*. Trans. Alan Bass. Chicago: The U of Chicago P, 1986 (b).

———. "différance." *Margins of Philosophy*. Trans. Alan Bass. Chicago: The U of Chicago P, 1986 (c).
———. *The Gift of Death*. Trans. David Wills. Chicago: The U of Chicago P, 1995.
———. "The Law of the Genre," Trans. Avital Ronell, *Glyph* 7 (1980): 202-29.
———. *Memoires: For Paul de Man*. Trans. Cecile Lindsay, et al. New York: Columbia U P, 1989.
———. "Economimesis," The Derrida Reader: Writing Performances. Ed. Julian Wolfreys. Lincoln: U of Nebraska P, 1998 (a).
———. *Monolingualism of the Other or the Prosthesis of Origin*. Trans. Patrick Mensah. Stanford: Stanford U P, 1998 (b).
———.*The Other Heading: Reflections on Today's Europe*. Trans. Pascale-Anne Brault and Michael B. Naas. Indianapolis: Indiana U P, 1992.
———. "'Le Parjure,' Perhaps: Storytelling and Lying ('abrupt breaches of syntax')." *Acts of Narrative*. Ed. Carol Jacob and Henry Sussman. Stanford: Stanford U P, 2003.
———. *Specters of Marx: The State of the Debt, the Work of Mourning, and the New International*. Trans. Peggy Kamuf. New York: Routledge, 1994.
———. *The Truth in Painting*. Trans. Geoff Bennington and Ian McLeod. Chicago: U of Chicago P, 1987.
———. "Typewriter Ribbon: Limited Ink (2) ("within such limits")." *Material Events: Paul de Man and the Afterlife of Theory*. Ed. Tom Cohen, et al. Minneapolis: U of Minnesota P, 2001.
Derrida, Jacques and Anne Dufourmantelle. *Of Hospitality*. Trans. Rachel Bowlby. Stanford: Stanford U P, 2000.
Derrida, Jacques and Gianni Vattimo (eds.) *Religion*. Stanford: Stanford U P, 1998 (c).
Dirlik, A. "The Postcolonial Aura: Third World Criticism in the Age of Global Capitalism." *Critical Inquiry* 20.2 (Winter 1994): 328-346.
Dollimore, Jonathan. *Death, Desire and Loss in Western Culture*. New York: Routledge, 1998.
Donne, John. Ed. Carey, John. Oxford: Oxford U P, 1990.
Dostoyevsky, Fyodor. *Notes from the Underground*. Trans. Serge shishkoff. *The World of Literature*. Ed. Westling et al. New Jersey: Prentice Hall, 1999.
Durkheim, Emile. *Suicide: A Study in Sociology*. London: Routledge, 1951.

Duyvendak, Jan Willen. "Inleiding: Fear of a Queer Planet?" *De verzuiling van de homobeweging*. Ed. J. W. Duyvendak. Amsterdam: SUA, 1994.
Eaton, Charlotte. *Rome in the Nineteenth Century*. 3 vols. London, 1820.
Edwards, Brent Hayes. "The Uses of Diaspora," *Social Text* 19.1 (Spring 2001): 45-74.
Eliot, T. S. "East Coker." *T. S. Eliot: Collected Poems: 1909-1962*. London: Faber & Faber, 1974.
Epstein, A. L. *Ethos and Identity: Three Studies in Ethnicity*. London: Tavistock, 1978.
Erickson, Steve. "Taste of Cherry." *Film Quarterly* 52.3 (Spring 1999): 52-5.
Essed, Philomena. "Gender, Migration and Cross-Ethnic Coalition Building." *Crossfires: Nationalism, Racism and Gender in Europe*. Ed. H. Lutz, A. Phoenix and N. Yuval-Davis .London: Pluto Press, 1995.
———. "Contradictory Positions, Ambivalent Perceptions: A Case Study of a Black Woman Entrepreneur." *Shifting Identities, Shifting Racisms: A Feminism and Psychology Reader*. Ed. K. K. Bhavnani and A. Phoenix. London: Sage, 1994.
———. *Alledaags racisme* (Everyday Racism). Baarn/Den Haag: Ambo/VOVIB, 1984.
Fanon, Frantz. *Black Skin, White Masks*. Trans. Charles Lam Markmann. New York: Pluto, 1986.

Favell, Adrian. *Philosophies of Integration: Immigration and the Idea of Citizenship in France and Britain*. New York: St. Martin's Press, 1998.
Fischer, Michael M. J. "Ethnicity and Postmodern Arts of Memory." *Writing Culture: The Poetics and Politics of Ethnography*. Ed. J. Clifford and G. E. Marcus. Berkeley: U of California P, 1986.
Fischer-Rosenthal, Wolfram. "The Problem with Identity: Biography as Solution to Some (post) Modern Dilemmas." *Comenius* 3 (1995): 250-266.
Foucault, Michel. *Madness and Civilization: A History of Insanity in the Age of Reason*. Trans. Richard Howard. New York: Vintage Books, 1988.
Franco, Dean. "Re-Placing the Border in Ethnic American Literature." *Cultural Critique* 50 (Winter 2002): 104-134.
Franklin, Benjamin. *The Autobiography of Benjamin Franklin*. Berkeley: U of California P, 1949.
Freud, Sigmund. "A Disturbance of Memory on the Acropolis," [1936] *Sigmund Freud: Collected Papers*. Ed. By James Strachey, Vol. V. New York: Basic Books, 1959, 302-313.
———. "Mourning and Melancholia." *The Standard Edition*, Volume XIV (1914-1916). London: The Hogarth Press, 1957.
Friedman, Jonathan. "Global Crises, the Struggle for Cultural Identity and Intellectual Porkbarreling: Cosmopolitans versus Locals, Ethnics and Nationals in an Era of De-hegemonization." *Debating Cutlural Hybridity: Multicultural Identities and the Politics of Anti-Racism*. Ed. Pnina Werbner and Tariq Madood. London: Zed Books, 1997.
———. *Cultural Identity and Global Process*. London: Sage, 1994.
Ghorashi, Halleh. *Ways to Survive, Battles to Win: Iranian Women Exiles in the Netherlands and the US*. Unpublished Ph.D Dissertation. Nijmegen, 2001.
Giddens, Anthony. *Modernity and Self-Identity: Self and Society in the Late Modern Age*. Cambridge: Polity Press, 1991.
Gray, Robert. *Letters during the Course of a Tour through Germany, Switzerland and Italy, in the Years 1791 and 1792, with Reflections on the Manners, Literature, and Religion of Those Countries*. London, 1794.
Grewal, Inderpal. "Autobiographic Subjects and Diasporic Locations: Meatless Days and Borderlands." *Scattered Hegemonies: Postmodernityand Transnational Feminist Practices*. Ed. Inderpal Grewal and Caren Kaplan. Minneapolis: U of Minnesota P, 1994.
Hall, Stuart. "Cultural Identity and Diaspora." *Identity, Community, Culture, Difference*. Ed. Jonathan Rutherford. London: Lawrence and Wishart, 1990.
Hammermeister, Kai. "Heimat in Heidegger and Gadamer." *Philosophy and Literature* 24 (2000): 312-326.
Hargreaves, Alec G. *Immigration, 'Race' and Ethnicity in Contemporary France*. London and New York: Routledge, 1995.
Hazlitt, William. "On Going a Journey." [1822] *The Essays of William Hazlitt: A Selection*. London: Macdonald, 1949.
Heidegger, Martin. *Being and Time*. Trans. Joan Stambaugh. New York: State U of New York P, 1996a.
———. *Hölderlin's Hymn "The Ister."* Trans. William McNeill and Julia Davis. Bloomington: Indiana U P, 1996b.
———. "Building Dwelling Thinking." [1954]. *Poetry, Language, Thought*. Trans. Albert Hofstadter. New York: Harper and Row Publishers, 1971.
Heraclitus. *Fragments: The Collected Wisdom of Heraclitus*. Trans. Brooks Haxton. New York: Viking Penguin, 2001.

Hesse, Jurgen Joachim. "Speaking with Voices of Change: Immigrant Writers and Canadian Literature." *The Journal of Ethnic Studies* 19.1 (Spring 1991): 45-67.
Hoffman, Eva. *Lost in Translation: A Life in a New Language*. Harmondsworth: Penguin, 1990.
hooks, bell. "Choosing the Margin as a Space of Radical Openness." *Yearning: Race, Gender and Cultural Politics*. Boston: South End, 1990.
Horowitz, Gregg M. *Sustaining Loss: Art and Mournful Life*. Stanford: Stanford U P, 2001.
Horst, Han van der. *The Low Sky: Understanding the Dutch*. Schiedam/Den Haag: Scriptum Books/Nuffic, 1996.
Hughes, John A. *Understanding Classical Sociology: Marx, Weber, Durkheim*. London: Sage Publications, 1996.
Islam, Seyed Manzural. *The Ethics of Travel: From Marco Polo to Kafka*. Manchester: Manchester U P, 1996.
Israel, Nico. *Outlandish: Writing between Exile and Diaspora*. Stanford: Stanford U P, 2000.
Jakobson, Roman. "Closing Statement." *Selected Writings*. The Hague, 1981.
Jakobson, Roman and Morris Hall. *Fundamentals of Language*. S-Gravenhave: Mouton, 1956.
Jameson, Fredric. *Late Marxism: Adorno, or, the Persistence of the Dialectic*. London: Verso, 1990a.
———. "Modernism and Imperialism." *Nationalism, Colonialism, and Literature*. Ed. Terry Eagleton, Fredric Jameson, and Edward Said. Minneapolis: U of Minnesota P, 1990b.
———. *The Political Unconscious: Narrative as a Socially Symbolic Act*. Ithaca: Cornell U P, 1981.
———. "Reflections on the Brech-Lukács Debate." In Fredric Jameson, Ideologies of Theory. Vol. II. Minneapolis: U of Minnesota P, 1988.
———. *Signatures of the Visible*. New York: Routledge, 1992.
Jefferson, Ann, and David Robey (eds.) *Modern Literary Theory: A Comparative Introduction*. London: B. T. Batsford Ltd, 1991.
Jenkins, Richard. *Social Identity*. London: Routledge, 1996.
Kincaid, Jamaica. *Annie John*. New York: Plume Press [Penguin], 1986.
———. *A Small Place*. New York: Plume Press, 1987.
Kowalewski, Michael (ed.) *Temperamental Journeys: Essays on the Modern Literature of Travel*. Athens: The U of Georgia P, 1992.
Kripke, Saul. *Naming and Necessity*. Cambridge: Harvard U P, 1980.
Kristeva, Julia. "A New Type of Intellectual: The Dissident." *The Kristeva Reader*. Ed. Toril Moi. London: Blackwell, 1986.
———. *Black Sun: Depression and Melancholia*. Trans. Leon S. Roudiez. New York: Columbia U P, 1989.
Kulisher, Eugene M. *Europe on the Move: War and Population Changes, 1917-47*. New York: Colombia U P, 1948.
Lacoue-Labarthe, Philippe. *Typography: Mimesis, Philosophy, Politics*. Trans. Christopher Fynsk. Stanford: Stanford U P, 1998.
Leacock, Stephen. *My Discovery of the West*. Toronto: Thomas Allen, 1937.
Levinas, Emmanuel. *Otherwise than Being or Beyond Essence*. Trans. A. Lingis. The Hague: Martinus Nijhoff, 1981.
Lévi-Strauss, Claude. *Tristes Tropiques*. Trans. John and Doreen Weightman. New York: The Modern Library, 1997.
Lott, Tommy. "Black Cultural Politics: An Interview with Paul Gilroy," *Found Object* 4 (Fall 1994): 56-57

Loux, Michael (ed.). *The Possible and the Actual: Readings in the Metaphysics of Modality*. Ithaca: Cornell U P, 1979.
Lyotard, Jean-François. "Domus and the Megalopolis," *The Inhuman: Reflections on Time*. Trans. Geoffrey Bennington and Rachel Bowlby. Stanford: Stanford U P, 1991.
———. "Oikos," *Political Writings*. Trans. Bill Readings and Kevin Paul. Minneapolis: U of Minnesota P, 1993.
Macherey, Pierre. *A Theory of Literary Production*. Trans. G. Wall. London: Routledge, 1978.
Malabou, Catherine, and Jacques Derrida. *Counterpath: Traveling with Jacques Derrida*. Trans. David Wills. Stanford: Stanford U P, 2004.
Malkki, Liisa. "Refugees and Exile: From 'Refugee Studies' to the National Order of Things." *Annual Reviews Anthropology* 24 (1995): 495-523.
Matthiessen, Francis Otto. *From the Heart of Europe*. New York: Oxford U P, 1948.
Montesquieu, Charles Louis. *The Spirit of Laws*. Trans. and edited by Anne M. Cohler, Basia Carolyn Miller, and Harold Samuel Stone. Cambridge: Cambridge U P, 1989.
Mörchen, Hermann. *Adorno und Heidegger: Untersuchung einer philosophischen Kommunicationsverwigerung*. Stuttgart: Klett-Cotta, 1981.
Mukherjee, Bharati. *Jasmine*. New York: Grove Press, 1989.
Mulvey, Laura. "Kiarostami's Uncertainty Principle." *Sight and Sound* 8:6 (June 1998): 24-7.
Naficy, Hamid. *An Accented Cinema: Exilic and Diasporic Filmmaking*. Princeton: Princeton U P, 2001.
———. *The Making of Exile Cultures: Iranian Television in Los Angeles*. Minneapolis: U of Minnesota P, 1993.
Ngugi, Wa Thiong'o. *Homecoming: Essays on African and Caribbean Literature, Culture and Politics*. New York: Lawrence Hill and Company, 1973.
Nietzsche, Friedrich. *The Gay Science*. Trans. Walter Kaufmann. New York: Vintage Books, 1974.
———. *Thus Spoke Zarathustra*. Trans. R. J. Hollingdale. Harmondsworth: Penguin Books, 1969.
Owens, Joseph. *Dread: The Rastafarians of Jamaica*. London: Heinemann, 1976.
Oz, Amos. "Khamsin." *Where the Jackals Howl*. Trans. Nicholas de Lange and Phillip Simpson. London: Flamingo, 1983.
———. "Nomad and Viper." *Where the Jackals Howl*. Trans. Nicholas de Lange and Phillip Simpson. London: Flamingo, 1983.
Pasolini, Pier Paolo. *Heretical Empiricism*. Trans. Ben Lawton and Louise K. Barnett. Bloomington: Indiana U P, 1988.
———. *Pasolini on Pasolini: Interviews with Oswald Stack*. Bloomington: Indiana U P, 1969.
Patton, Paul. *Deleuze and the Political*. London: Routledge, 2000.
Pfeil, Fred. "No Basta Teorizar: In-Difference to Solidarity in Contemporary Fiction, Theory, and Practice." *Scattered Hegemonies: Postmodernity and Transnational Feminist Practices*. Ed. Inderpal Grewal and Caren Kaplan. Minneapolis: U of Minnesota P, 1994.
Pratt, Mary Louise. *Imperial Eyes: Travel-Writing and Transculturation*. London: Routledge, 1992.
Putnam, Hilary. "Meaning and Reference." *The Philosophy of Language*. Ed. A. P. Martinich. Oxford: Oxford U P, 1985.
Puxon, Gratton. *Roma: Europe's Gypsies*. London: Minority Rights Group, 1980.

Raban, Jonathan. "The Journey and the Book." *For Love and Money: Writing, Reading, Travelling 1969-1987*. London: Collins Harvill, 1987.
Rao, Raja. *Kanthapura*. New York: New Directions, 1938.
Redford, Bruce. *Venice and the Grand Tour*. New Haven and London: Yale U P, 1996.
Ricciardi, Alessia. *The Ends of Mourning: Psychoanalysis, Literature, Film*. Stanford: Stanford U P, 2003.
Rodriguez, Richard. *Hunger of Memory: The Education of Richard Rodriguez*. New York: Bantam, 1988.
Rogers, Samuel. *Italy: A Poem*. London, [1822] 1830.
Ronen, Ruth. "Completing the Incompleteness of Fictional Entities." *Poetics Today* 9.3 (1988): 497-514.
Rooy, Piet De. "Farewell to Pillarization." *The Netherlands Journal of Social Sciences*, 33.1 (1997):27-41.
Rumi, Jalaludin. *Mathnavi*. Translated and edited by Reynold Nicholson. Cambridge: Cambridge U P, 1925-40.
Rushdie, Salman. *Imaginary Homelands: Essays and Criticisms 1981-1991*. London: Granta Books, 1992.
———. *Shame*. New York: Random House, 1984.
Ryan, Marie-Laure. "Fiction, Non-Factuals, and the Principle of Minimal Departure." *Poetics* 9 (1980): 403-22.
Safran, William. "Diasporas in Modern Societies: Myths of Homeland and Return." *Diaspora* 1.1 (Spring 1991): 83-99.
Said, Edward. *After the Last Sky: Palestinian Lives*. New York: Pantheon Books, 1986.
Sartre, Jean-Paul. *Colonialism and Neocolonialism*. Trans. Azzedine Haddour. London: Routledge, 2001.
Sayre, Robert F. "Autobiography and the Making of America." *Autobiography: Essays Theoretical and Critica*l. Ed. James Olney. Princeton: Princeton UP, 1980.
Schivelbusch, Wolfgang. *The Railway Journey: The Industrialization of Time and Space in the nineteenth Century*. Berkeley: U of California P, 1986.
Schorer, Mark. "Moll Flanders." *Daniel Defoe: A Collection of Critical Essays*. Ed. Max Byrd. New Jersey: Prentice-Hall Inc, 1976.
Shami, Seteney. "Feminine Identity and Ethnic Identity: the Circassians in Jordan." *Who is Afraid of Femininity? Questions of Identity*. Ed. M. Brügmann, S. Heebing, D. Long and M. Michielsens. Amsterdam and Atlanta: Rodpoi, 1993.
Sheffer, Gabriel. (ed.) *Modern Diasporas in International Politics*. New York: St. Martin's, 1986.
Shelley, Mary. *Journals 1814-1844*. Ed. Paula R. Feldman and Diana Scott-Kilvert. Two vols. Oxford: Oxford U P, 1987.
Silverman, Maxim. *Deconstructing the Nation: Immigration, Racism and Citizenship in Modern France*. London and New York: Routledge, 1992.
Sollors, Werner. *Beyond Ethnicity: Consent and Descent in American Culture*. New York: Oxford UP, 1986.
———. "Nine Suggestions for Historians of American Ethnic Literature." *MELUS* 11 (1984): 95-96.
Somers, Margaret, and Gloria Gibson. "Reclaiming the epistemological Other: Narrative and the Social Constitution of Identity." *Social Theory and the Politics of Identity*. Ed. Craig Calhoun. Oxford: Blackwell, 1994.
Spivak, Gayatri C. and Sneja Gunew. "Questions of Multiculturalism." *The Cultural Studies Reader*. Ed. Simon During. London: Routledge, 1994.
Spurr, David. *The Rhetoric of Empire: Colonial Discourse in Journalism, Travel Writing and Imperial Administration*. Durham: Duke U P, 1993.
Steiner, George. "Our Homeland, the Text." *Salmagundi* 66 (winter/Spring 1985).

Stiegler, Bernard. *Technics and Time, 1: The Faults of Epimetheus*. Trans. Richard Beardsworth and George Collins. Stanford: Stanford U P, 1998.
Stora, Benjamin. *Algeria 1830-2000: A Short History*. Trans. Jane Marie Todd. Ithaca: Cornell U P, 2001.
Sweet, Freddy. *The Film Narratives of Alain Resnais*. Ann Arbor: UMI Research Press, 1981.
Theroux, Paul. "Stranger on a Train: The Pleasure of Railways." *Sunrise with Seamonsters: Travel and Discoveries, 1964-1984*. Boston: Houghton Mifflin, 1985.
Todorov, Tzvetan. "The Uses and Abuses of Memory." Trans. Lucy Golsan. *What Happens to History: The Renewal of Ethics in Contemporary Thought*. Ed. Howard Marchitello. New York: Routledge, 2001.
Vaihinger, Hans. *The Philosophy of "As If."* Trans. C. K. Ogden. London: Routledge, 1965.
Van den Abbeele, George. *Travel as Mataphor: From Montaigne to Rousseau*. Minneapolis: U of Minnesota P, 1992.
Veer, Peter van der. "Introduction: The Diasporic Imagination." *Nation and Migration: The Politics of Space in the South Asian Diaspora*. Ed. van der Veer. Philadelphia: U of Pennsylvania P, 1995.
Walcott, Derek. "The Caribbean: Culture or Mimicry?" *Journal of Interamerican Studies and World Affairs* 16.1 (1974): 3-13.
Wald, Alan. "Theorizing Cultural Difference: A Critique of the `Ethnicity School.'" *MELUS* 14.2 (1987): 21-33.
Waldinger, Roger and Mehdi Bozorgmehr (eds.). *Ethnic Los Angeles*. New York: Russel Sage Foundation, 1996.
Warminski, Andrzei. "Monstrous History: Heidegger Reading Hölderlin." *The Solid Letter: Readings of Friedrich Hölderlin*. Ed. Aris Fioretos. Stanford: Stanford U P, 1999.
Waugh, Evelyn. *Labels: A Mediterranean Journal*. Harmondsworth: Penguin, [1930] 1985.
Wekker, Gloria. "'After the Last Sky, Where do the Birds Fly?' What Can European Women Learn from Anti-Racist Struggles in the United States?" *Crossfires: Nationalism, Racism and Gender in Europe*. Ed. H. Lutz, A. Phoenix and N. Yuval-Davis. London: Pluto Press, 1995.
Willems Wim, Annemarie Cottaar and Daniel van Aken. "Indische Nederlanders: van marginale group tot succesvolle migranten?" *Van Ooast naar West: Racisme als mondiaal verschijnsel* [From East to West: Racism as a Global Phenomenon]. Ed. D. van Arkel, et al. Baarm: Ambo, 1991.
Wong, Cynthia Sau-ling. "Immigrant Autobiography: Some Questions of Definition and Approach." *American Autobiography: Retrospect and Prospect*. Ed. Paul John Eakin. Madison: U of Wisconsin P, 1991.
Woodhull, Winifred. *Transfiguration of the Maghreb: Feminism, Decolonization, and Literatures*. Minneapolis: U of Minnesota P, 1993.
Young, Mary E. *Mules and Dragons: Popular Culture Images in the Selected Writings of African-American and Chinese-American Women Writers*. Westport: Greenwood, 1993.
Zaborowska, Magdalena. *How We Found America: Reading Gender through East European Immigrant Narratives*. Chapel Hill: U of North Carolina P, 1995.

Author Bio

Afshin Hafizi is Professor of Liberal Arts at the Savannah College of Art and Design (SCAD) where he teaches courses in English, World Literature, History of Literary Criticism, and the Cinema of the Middle East and North Africa. He has studied English Language and Literature at Kerman University, Iran; Comparative Literature and Literary Theory (*Algemene Literatuurwetenschap*) at the University of Utrecht, The Netherlands; International Affairs at The Florida State University (FSU) and English at the University of Florida (UF). He has also been a Marion L. Brittain Post-Doctoral Fellow in Technical Writing/Communication at the Georgia Institute of Technology, Atlanta. He has been teaching at the University of Florida, Santa Fe Community College, City College, Georgia Perimeter College, Kennesaw State University, Georgia Institute of Technology, South University Online, and Strayer University Online.